Endorsements for *My Giddy Aunt*

Around the story of these key characters, Connolly weaves an intricate and original account of an important era in Australian cultural history. We meet not only her particular subjects but also learn about the people they worked for and with and the people they set out to entertain.

ANN CURTHOYS

This book had me at 'professional ladywhistler' – a wonderful true story about some fabulous funny women.

KAZ COOKE

Sharon Connolly

A former documentary filmmaker, television producer and chief executive of Film Australia, Sharon Connolly has been involved in making many landmark history programs since her first film, *Red Matildas*. In her first book, *My Giddy Aunt*, she once more writes some remarkable yet uncelebrated women back into the stories of Australia.

Sharon Connolly

My Giddy Aunt

and her sister comedians

UPSWELL

First published in Australia in 2022
by Upswell Publishing
Perth, Western Australia
upswellpublishing.com

ISBN: 978-0-6452479-8-5

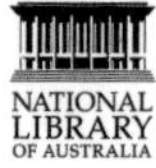

A catalogue record for this book is available from the National Library of Australia

Cover design by Chil3, Fremantle
Cover image: *Gladys Shaw*, Cinesound Productions: 'Casting Book': ca. 1935, National Film and Sound Archive, Title No: 1461422
Typeset in Foundry Origin by Lasertype
Printed by McPherson's Printing Group

Author's Note

This book contains offensively racist terms, including words that were wrong in the past, and are disgraceful today. In recounting this history, I in no way sanction the use of such language, then or now.

In memory of my father, Keith Connolly,
and my brother, Steve Connolly.

Contents

Foreword

This is a wonderful book. Sharon Connolly has had a brilliant career as a filmmaker, and now she comes up with this stunning and original work of family, cultural, and social history. What a good start this is for Upswell Publishing.

My Giddy Aunt has several layers, all of them fascinating. The main story concerns the women vaudevillians in Connolly's family background. Her great-grandmother, Mary Agnes Connolly, was a vaudevillian and burlesque artist who sang, acted, and played the piano. She began performing in the 1890s; after marrying Edward Connolly and bearing two sons, she left her husband and sons for another man, with whom she travelled and performed for years and with whom she had three children, Gladys, Keith, and Gerald. Gladys, Sharon Connolly's great aunt, was an expert *siffleur* (whistler), singer, dancer, comic actor, and, in later years saxophone player and even cowgirl whip-handler, who performed with various troupes in Australia and New Zealand. Some of the time she teamed up with her brother Keith, and sometimes with other performers, such as Lynette and her Six Redheads, a band of women who played saxophones, trumpet, trombone, piano, banjo and drums. Keith often played the straight man in comedy duos, and married Elsie, a girl from Perth, a connection that draws a considerable amount of the family action to Western Australia. Elsie Connolly, our author's grandmother, was a singer, dancer, and all-round performer, known especially for singing light-hearted happy songs.

The tale of these women and the popular theatre and entertainment industry they worked in for many decades is meticulously constructed, bringing together tiny details from newspapers, photographs, theatre programmes, and advertisements. This is not easily gathered material, for Mary Agnes, Gladys, and Elsie left few if any letters, diaries, or other written work to help the historian and biographer reconstruct their lives. They were immensely mobile and the account in this book of their travels on tour and seeking work dazzles us with so many moves to so many places. In such lives, there was little place for keeping letters, though thankfully they did keep photographs, for it is from these that Connolly begins her search. Connolly's experience as a documentary filmmaker serves her well, drawing out an absorbing and meaningful story from visual fragments.

It must have been a tough self-imposed assignment, this one, for the lives of such women would not have been easy to reconstruct. They were extraordinarily mobile not only in the physical sense but also in terms of their public identities – there are many name changes, both personal and professional. Even the name Connolly tells a complicated story. When Mary Agnes married, she became Mrs Connolly, but by the time she gave Gladys, Keith, and Gerald the surname Connolly she had long since left her husband and the children's father was, in fact, a man who called himself Gerald Shaw but whose real name was Harry Morewood Thomson. There are so many name changes that it's truly a wonder that we can keep up with who's who, but Connolly skilfully enables us to do so.

Around the story of these key characters, Connolly weaves an intricate and original account of an important era in Australian cultural history. We meet not only her particular subjects but also learn about the people they worked for and with and the people they set out to entertain. Her story begins in the era of minstrel shows and other forms of popular theatre in the 1890s and continues into the new century and through the arrival of jazz, silent movies, radio, and sound movies in the first half of the twentieth century. Along the way we meet the enormously successful comedy duo, Stiffy and Mo, some intriguing male impersonators, the wildfire spread of jazz in the mid-1920s, and the struggles of live performers during the 1930s, the war years, and afterwards. We learn about the wider society as well – such as women voting for the first time and the ways in which divorce and family law affected their lives. Through the story of grandfather Keith's experience of the First World War, we learn about the ordeal of the trenches, the horror of the fighting, and the conflicts over conscription for military service. After a decade of recovery and innovation in the 1920s, we see the effects of the Great Depression of 1929, with its unemployment, swagmen, and despair. Connolly provides an especially striking discussion of Australian culture's lack of interest in older women, leading Mary Agnes, Gladys, and Elsie to play girls

> for as long as they could, lying about their ages and acting youthfully on stage. Then, mortified by middle age, they were redundant. The shame of it not only magnified their frailties but also robbed them of belief in themselves and their achievements. Lacking that confidence, Grandma Elsie couldn't tell her grandchildren proud and satisfied stories about her rainbow days.

There are several sub-themes that drew my attention as a feminist historian interested in Australia's cultural, social, and political history. One is a theme of mental health and illness – how the women in this story experienced mental illness and how society dealt with it. In 1886, Mary Gertrude, mother of Mary Agnes, was reported to hear voices, talk to imaginary spirits, and suffer from melancholia. She was admitted to Gladesville Hospital for the Insane at the age of 46 and lived in similar institutions for 43 years, that is, for the rest of her life. In the mid-1950s, both the daughter and daughter-in-law of Mary Agnes would be treated for mental illness. Gladys spent twelve months in Morrisett Hospital, north of Sydney, for alcoholism, while Elsie, suffering from anxiety and obsessive-compulsive disorder, was subjected at the age of 47 to a leucotomy, also known as a lobotomy. Connolly writes of all this in spare clear prose, but her anger at the treatment and incarceration of women is palpable.

Another, difficult, theme is that of the racism endemic in Australian society in this period, which sometimes influenced the songs and skits Mary Agnes, Gladys, and Elsie performed. There is a remarkable discussion of the 'coon songs' of the late 19th and early 20th centuries, songs that caricatured African Americans while at the same time 'setting toes tapping with their syncopated and complex rhythms'. In a thoughtful conclusion, Connolly reflects on the 'racism, anti-Semitism and sexism of so much that was vaudeville', a racism she notices and condemns while also allowing space for her remarkable story of female audacity and tenacity.

A third sub-theme, or perhaps it is, after all, the main theme, is a tribute to Australian cultural endeavour. There is discussion of the troubled history of the Australian film industry, which flourished for a while in the 1920s and then was gradually squeezed out for around five decades by government policies which favoured international distributors and exhibitors. While Connolly shows how Australian vaudeville performers loved to learn the latest from overseas touring groups, she also celebrates their local innovations, such as the 'revusical', a revue with a loose connecting plot, and local adaptations of international dance and music crazes. As she says towards the end of this remarkable book, 'My inheritance was a powerful idea, handed down through my father to his children, that Australians could create their own art and entertainment. From childhood I knew that art – high or low – did not have to be imported.'

It gives me great pleasure, then, to recommend this book to devotees of art and culture, high or low, lovers of stories about women, and fans of family history and memoir. It's all here, always intersecting with wider histories, of Australia and the world beyond.

Ann Curthoys
Sydney, 2021

Prelude

My father was only four, so the story goes, when the great comedian Mo persuaded him to turn a bowl of porridge upside-down on his head. It was a trick that would change his life, for it made his mother Elsie decide to give her son a better home. Until then young Keith had lived with his vaudevillian parents in theatrical boarding houses shared with fellow artists. Sometimes, when his parents were on tour, he stayed with family friends in Sydney. But following the porridge incident his mother sent him across the continent to Perth, where he would be raised by his maternal grandparents.

I knew my father's mother as 'Grandma Elsie'. To me, this title suggested that she was a less authentic grandparent than the one we called just plain 'Grandma'. That was my mother's mother and she was certainly more present in the lives of her grandchildren. But neither grandmother was close. Both lived in Perth, thousands of miles from Melbourne, where I was brought up, along with two brothers and a sister. In leafy middle-class East Malvern we rarely saw any of our grandparents.

The last time I did see Grandma Elsie, she was in her eighties and living out her lonely final years in a retirement village in suburban Perth. On a business trip to the west I spent a few hours there. I took a gift, a book about the history of Australian theatre. When it came back to me after her death I saw that it contained nothing about Elsie and precious little about her colleagues and the kind of popular theatre in which they worked. I wished then that I'd simply taken flowers.

I don't know whether Grandma Elsie minded that her history had more or less disappeared. At her funeral Dad spoke about his mother's years on the stage and in radio drama, years in which he said she'd 'earned her own living in an exacting and sometimes cruel profession'. Yet he thought she would rather be remembered for this early work than for the later part of her life. I strained to hear his frail voice as he spoke – too far from the microphone. Dad was her only child and though they'd not been close, he found proud things to say about his mother.

After the funeral, Dad returned from Perth with a shabby black case stuffed full with papers and photographs. Weeks later my siblings and I gathered at our parents' home for Christmas and, once the feasting was done, my brother Steve and I opened Grandma Elsie's archive. We found precious few conventional family images among the many photographs it contained – just one wedding and one birthday party. Old portraits filled a leather-bound album, but Dad had no idea whose faces they showed. The shallow case, once used to house a musical instrument – perhaps a zither – mostly contained theatrical contracts, yellowed newspaper clippings and publicity shots.

The more animated images all seemed to have been captured in the 1920s. Groups of young people smiled for the camera at railway stations, laughed and cavorted on beaches. In parks they made human pyramids; on the stage they made a merry band – whooping it up in the roaring tempo of their times.

The number and faces of the band's members varied from photograph to photograph. One showed eight performers – six of them men in shiny dinner suits playing an array of instruments: saxophone, banjo, clarinet, drums, trumpet and trombone. The horns and the musicians' attention pointed to a seventh man who danced above them at the rear, leering at the camera. We recognised him as our grandfather, another Keith, known to us only from a handful of Mum and Dad's wedding

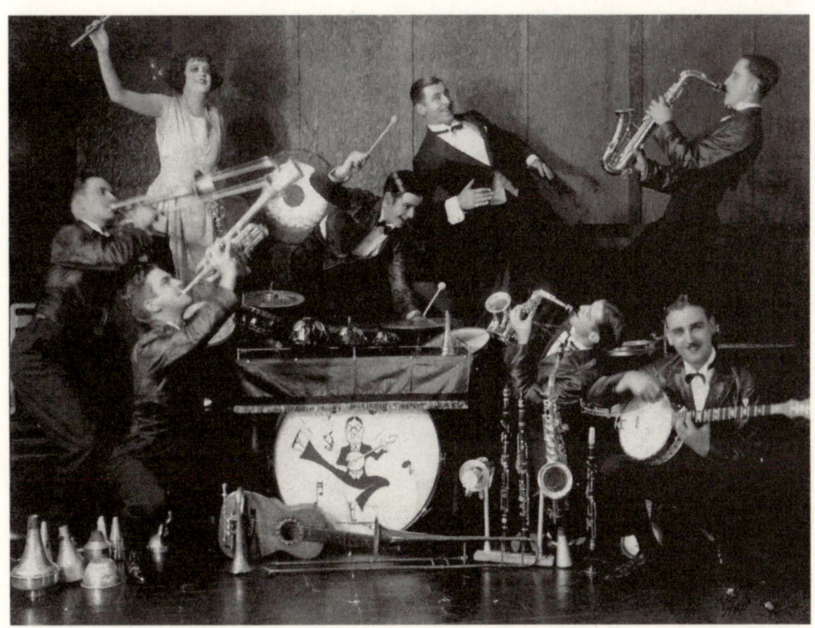

Whooping it up in 1926

photographs. Dad identified his Uncle Gerry on percussion, and in the top left hand corner he pointed out his Aunt Gladys, holding aloft a small mallet for a gong suspended on the wall behind her. The only woman in the picture and the only performer not dressed in black, Gladys was luminous and gleeful.

In another image she is one of three women among a ten-member ensemble. Drumsticks at the ready, Gladys takes centre stage, appearing to direct the music. Downstage, in spectacles and short skirt, a second woman dances the Charleston. The third, with a flourish of her bare arms, drew my eye to the top left of the picture. It was a young Grandma Elsie.

'I want what they're having', said Steve.

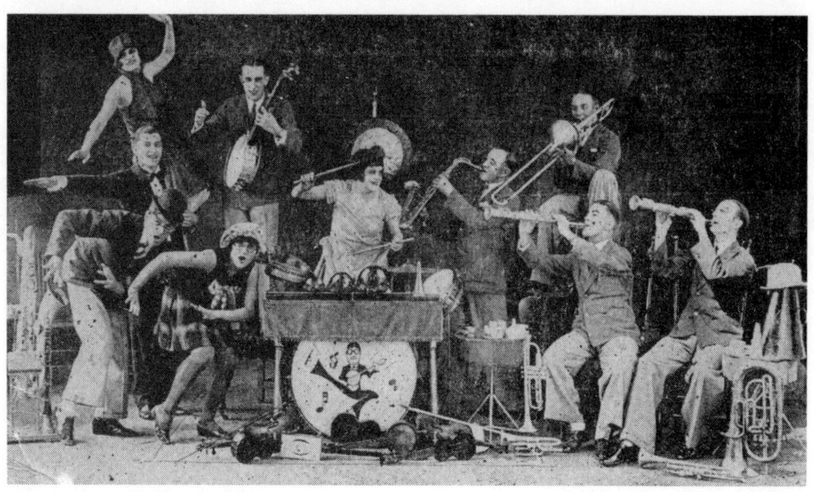

Whooping it up in 1927, Gladys (centre), Elsie (top left)

At my father's funeral I didn't tell the story about Mo and the bowl of porridge, though I mentioned Dad's habit of quoting from films starring George Wallace, another great Australian comedian who, Dad told us, was his godfather. It was a rare piece of information about his early family life. My father seldom spoke about his parents, though he had remarkable recall of less personal details – of cricket matches, football games and, most of all, lines from movies. Films were never far from his mind. He earned his living writing about them.

Until then I'd earned mine in the making of them. After my first documentary, a film inspired by my maternal grandmother's life as a Communist, I went on to work in documentary and drama, for production companies, funding agencies and television networks. But as the internet began reshaping film and television my career began to deflate. Amid the turbulence I thought of Gladys and Elsie. I wanted to know more about how they survived the arrival of new media – of cinema, talkies and radio. Faintly I hoped their stories might rescue me.

Elsie and her sister-in-law Gladys lived in remarkable times. The machinery, forms and fashions of popular entertainment changed dramatically in the twentieth century and both women were inspired and buffeted by the upheavals. They had unusually long stage careers, in years when the earliest sound recordings were made and cinema was born – silent, black and white. They listened to its first words. And themselves spoke and sang some of the earliest heard on radio.

When I opened Grandma Elsie's case of souvenirs again it was Gladys who shone brightest from its tattered velvet interior. In photographs she wore an almost maniacal grin and a mop of dark unruly hair. She was small and often draped affectionately around her brothers and fellow performers, or they around her. She looked much more than a support act.

At first her story proved elusive. There were relatively few photographs of Gladys in the old zither case, which contained remnants of several collections of memorabilia saved by Grandma Elsie after the deaths of various family members. But for a time those photographs were the only clues I had. Gladys left little else behind – no children, no diaries, no letters.

Hers was not the kind of private and settled domestic life of most Australian women of her generation. She had neither the habit of diary-keeping nor an enduring home in which to collect the letters and keepsakes of a lifetime. She was something of a nomad who lived, unusually for a woman of her era, in the public gaze.

Gladys and her colleagues worked in times when print proliferated across the land, when almost every town and settlement had its own press. Now available online, their publications became the territory I searched for signs of my great aunt. It would be newspaper and magazine accounts that eventually illuminated what I gleaned from Grandma Elsie's case. In them Gladys was often described as a 'soubrette' and a 'siffleur'. I had to check the dictionary. The first meant she typically played characters who were girlish, mischievous, coquettish and gossipy. A siffleur, I learned, was a whistler.

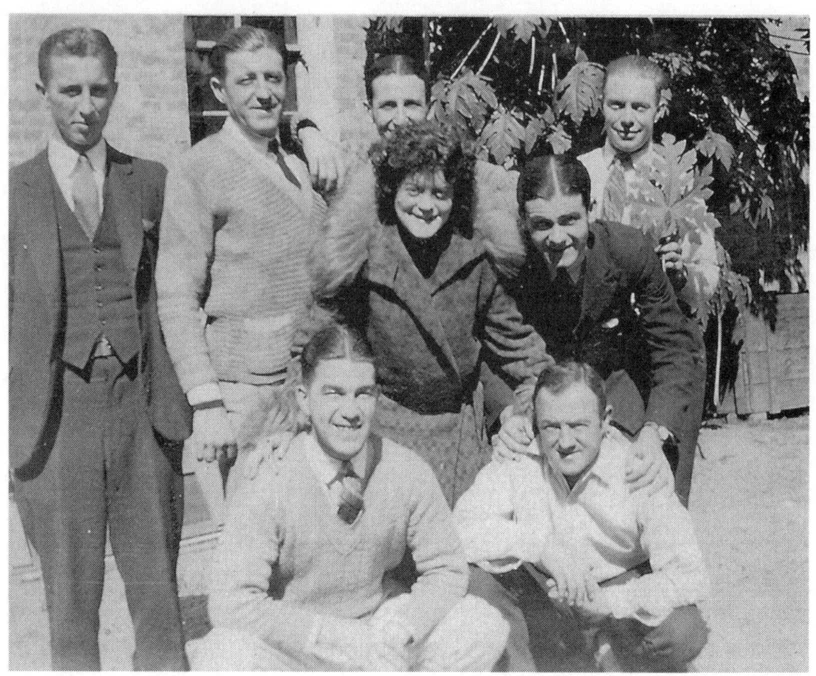

More than a support act – Gladys and the Syncopating Jesters, 1926

Her mother, Mary Agnes, was easier to summon up. There were birth certificates for her five children as well as photographs, hospital records and the evidence of divorce. I found a handful of letters, one containing a rare mention of Gladys, her only daughter: 'her name is Muriel Gladys Warrington and she was born almost on the stage. I will bring her up to it as she shows signs of being remarkably intelligent'. And so the tale grew to embrace Mary Agnes too.

Grandma Elsie's zither case had led me to the stories of two generations of female entertainers. Elsie and her sister-in-law Gladys, and before them Mary Agnes, were among hundreds of women who took to the stages of Australia in the late nineteenth and early twentieth centuries. This sisterhood of jesters entertained a new nation in days of minstrel shows, vaudeville, war and hardship.

They were also times in which 'new women' campaigned for and won the right to vote, and challenged conventional ideas about how they should behave. Among them were female entertainers. Often 'unladylike', they danced without inhibition, played instruments thought unseemly for women and music deemed to be sinful. Comediennes acted the fool, the vamp and women of all kinds. They even played men.

Most had lives not at all like those I'd imagined for earlier generations of Australian women. Regardless of the demands of family they travelled relentlessly, appearing everywhere from the smallest mining settlements to our biggest bustling cities. They were astonishingly mobile even before railways and aeroplanes connected the continent, taking steamships from one side of the country to the other and often to New Zealand. Some left Australia forever to make names for themselves in South Africa, Britain and the United States.

The business of popular theatre and the working arrangements of entertainers were complex and changeable. Individuals, duos, ensembles and whole companies signed on to play seasons and circuits, in grand theatres, town halls and under marquees. Their engagements were fleeting in small places, often longer in towns and cities. Despite competition between performers a strong sense of community grew from their years of travelling, performing and living with one another. Artists shared tricks of the trade, made friends and enemies, and had lovers, spouses and children who themselves took to the stage.

The cast was huge, with thousands of theatrical workers roaming the country in the late nineteenth and early twentieth centuries. My great-grandmother Mary Agnes, my great-aunt Gladys and my Grandma Elsie play principal roles in this tale, but there are many others without whom it can't be told. They include some of my male relatives, and artists like George Wallace, Mo and Stiffy – men who became legends. Female entertainers who were no less remarkable, but whose names are less well known, are also among the players. Why I had heard so little of them – especially those to whom I was related – was a mystery only solved by following some extraordinary stories to their very ends.

1
The Wages of Sin

Mary Agnes Connolly was a woman of many names. At the age of twenty-eight she called herself 'Claire Delmar' to appear with Dan Tracey's Vaudeville and Minstrel Company at the Sydney School of Arts on the evening of Saturday 6 February 1892.

Hard times did little to deter an unusually large crowd from attending the entertainment that night. Despite a run on the banks and a large demonstration of the unemployed in the preceding week, there were so many people vying to be in the audience that some were turned away at the door. On the following Monday the *Sydney Morning Herald* attributed the size of the crowd to the programming of two new male artistes, and to a mandoline player, Señor Manuel Lopez. But it also noted that Claire Delmar, making her first appearance, was a 'burlesque actress, with a pleasing voice'.[1]

This was not to say that she performed a striptease act – a later American understanding of burlesque. In the late nineteenth century, especially in Britain and its colonies, burlesque performers appeared in theatres and music halls, offering musical sketches peppered with political and social satire. Sometimes they parodied more serious operatic and dramatic works.

Claire Delmar – with its echoes of French and Spanish words about light and sea – was not an unusual choice of stage name. There were probably some Claire Delmars before Mary Agnes used the alias, and there were certainly some who came after. A North American Claire appeared, uncredited, to dance with Rudolf Valentino in *The Four Horsemen of the Apocalypse* and with Al Jolson in *The Jazz Singer*, the first talking picture.

But long before that, even before silent movies flickered into existence, Sydney's Claire Delmar posed for a photograph in front of a studio backdrop hand-painted with vaguely Grecian columns and cordylines. Draped in a voluminous shift, arms bare and hair falling over one shoulder, she holds flowers to her breast and gazes into the distance.

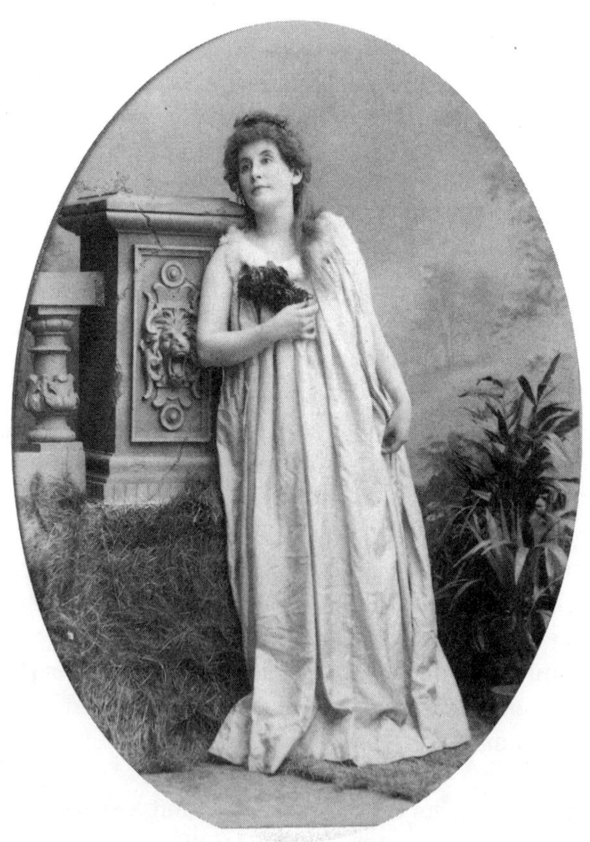

'Claire Delmar', ca. 1892

It's one of the more incongruous images among those to emerge from the old zither case. A wistful expression suggests the lovelorn, yet its wearer doesn't cut a tragic figure. She is no tubercular victim. Nor does she appear ethereal, nor divine. She is womanly, more Mother Earth than light of the sea. Claire Delmar wasn't quite the right name for Mary Agnes's stage persona.

Born in 1864, Mary Agnes was the first of two daughters produced by Mary Gertrude and John Warrington. She grew up in Sydney, surrounded by her mother's large, prosperous and well-established family.

Her mother, Mary Gertrude, expected to inherit five North Sydney properties from her timber-merchant father, who had bequeathed them to his youngest child 'for her own sole and separate use free from the debts control or interference of any husband whom she may marry'. Mary Gertrude would not control the properties until her mother was also dead, but her father's wording, in a will made before married women had property rights, put her inheritance beyond the reach of any future husband.

That husband would be John Frederick Warrington, youngest son of a renowned English stained-glass artist, William. With two brothers ahead of him and the family firm in decline, John had left England for New South Wales in 1861. In the colony he swiftly found work as a clerk[2] and two years after his arrival made a promising marriage to Mary Gertrude Boyd, yet to inherit the properties her father had left her. The couple had two daughters – Mary Agnes and Maud – and lived close to Mary Gertrude's family on Sydney's lower north shore. John became a partner in a firm of law stationers, crossing the harbour each day to work in the city. Mary Agnes and her sister Maud were aged seventeen and fifteen when their mother, Mary Gertrude, finally came into her inheritance. The young women could look forward to a comfortable life.

Mary Agnes and her mother established a dressmaking business at one of Mary Gertrude's properties in Mount Street, North Sydney. John Warrington didn't entirely approve. He wanted to employ a manager who might have kept his wife and daughter at a respectable distance from the world of work.[3] Yet mother and daughter carried on, acquiring a Wertheim sewing machine and advertising for apprentices and other staff.[4] Mary Agnes also began promoting herself as a teacher of music and theory. Even before coming of age, she was keen to make a more independent life for herself. She had the accomplishments expected of a young lady and, possibly encouraged by her mother, wasn't about to settle for a purely private, domestic nor dependent existence.

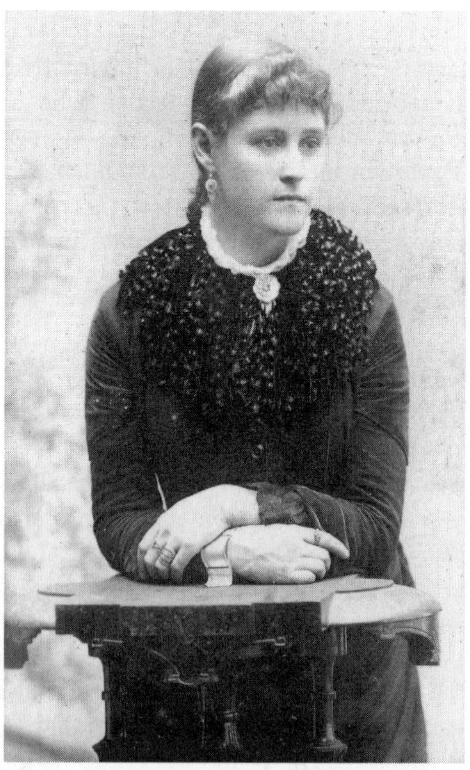

Mary Agnes aged about 18, ca. 1882

Two years after establishing their dressmaking business, her mother fell ill. Mary Gertrude began to hear voices and to suffer 'melancholia'. At first her daughters looked after her. Then her husband moved his family from the home they'd known all their lives and the properties in which they worked, across the harbour to Smith Street in busy Balmain, near the Bald Rock Hotel. He advertised for a servant for this small household.

If she was disturbed by moving from the relative quiet of the north shore to crowded, clanging Balmain, Mary Gertrude was in no position to object. After eighteen months her condition hadn't improved and she was still experiencing auditory hallucinations and depression.

In May 1886 her husband requested that she be admitted to Gladesville Hospital for the Insane. He said she was occasionally violent, talked to imaginary spirits and was very restless at night. Forty-six years old when admitted, she was, recorded the hospital, 'looking older than her given age':

> Her height is 5 feet 3 inches. She has grey hair, hazel eyes, a small face, a straight but slightly turned up nose, upper incisor teeth absent, a large mouth and a clear complexion. All her systems as far as can be ascertained are normal. It is probable however that her mental illness is due really to the climacteric period.[5]

The mental illness said to have been brought on by her menopause, or possibly by shock at the sudden death of a friend,[6] would see her hospitalised for the next forty-three years.

John Warrington took his daughters to Grafton, 400 miles away from their mother in Sydney. He found a temporary post with the Lands Department and, only three months after committing his wife to Gladesville Hospital, paid a deposit for a 50-acre selection of land. Maybe he hoped for a fresh start. Mary Agnes may have thought he acted with unseemly haste.

She and her sister Maud had ideas of their own and would not be kept from city life for long. In 1887 both returned to Sydney where, a few days before her twenty-first birthday, Maud married a publican named John Connolly. By the end of the same year twenty-three-year-old Mary Agnes had married his brother, Edward, who was usually known as Ted.

Although she described herself as a music teacher on her marriage certificate, Mary Agnes was soon otherwise occupied as the mother of two boys, Reginald and Leslie. When the demands of husband, family and home allowed, Mary Agnes visited her mother at Gladesville and later at Callan Park Hospital for the Insane.

Transferred there in 1891 when she was fifty-two, Mary Gertrude was described as 'a stout old woman with grey hair, brown eyes and a round full face.' Hospital records noted that 'she hears people talking and they say many things: she sometimes hears her husband speaking and at times other people.'[7]

John Warrington paid £3 5s each month for his wife's upkeep in hospital and continued working for the Lands Department in regional towns. Mary Agnes was not fond of him, nor of the sister she nicknamed 'Lady Maud'. In a letter to her husband she wrote that Maud was 'like the old man, likes to talk about what she has done for people'.[8] What her father had done for her mother was to consign her to an asylum. His oldest daughter may have had her suspicions about his motives.

Leaving her boys with a housekeeper, Mary Agnes rode the ferries across glistening Sydney Harbour and up the Parramatta River to see her mother. Set in rolling landscaped gardens on the shores of Iron Cove, Callan Park Hospital for the Insane was designed as a tranquil, therapeutic environment. Yet in her years at both Gladesville and Callan Park, Mary Gertrude's condition changed little. She continued imagining 'a bad spirit constantly tearing at her right breast'.[9] She kept one hand in her dress and refused to plait her hair on her right side. The records say that she never lay down.

For Mary Agnes, Callan Park must have been one of Sydney's more desolate places. When she rode the ferry home after visiting her distressed mother, even the harbour might have lost its shine.

Mary Agnes and her husband Ted lived with their boys in beachside Manly. Ted was a draper with Anthony Hordern and Sons, the largest retailer in the colonies. He called Mary Agnes 'Bunny' and was not enthusiastic about his wife's growing interest in a theatrical career. Indeed, he said that she pursued it 'contrary to his express will'.[10] But pursue it she did.

These were times in which women might dare to dream of more public lives – on the stage, in politics, or in publishing. In Sydney young, middle-class women like Mary Agnes might have read about female authors and singers as well as suffragettes in the pages of the *Dawn, A Journal for Australian Women*. Edited by Louisa Lawson – writer, editor and mother of the more famous poet Henry – it published domestic advice, a children's page and short fiction, alongside commentary on political and legal issues of the day. Louisa argued for women's right to vote, and for divorce law reform. Though New South Wales divorce law advanced considerably in the 1890s, it would be 1934 before women won equal custody rights to the children of marriages ending in divorce.

The 'woman movement' of the 1880s and 1890s was the first phase of Australian feminism and was concerned to reform liquor laws and raise the age of consent. These causes, like that of divorce law reform, required women to have political power if change was to be achieved, and so they fuelled a campaign for suffrage. In South Australia, a Women's Suffrage League was formed in 1888. In 1891, 30 000 women in the colony of Victoria demanded the right to vote in the 'Monster Petition'. Made of paper pasted on fabric and rolled on a cardboard spool, it took three hours to unroll. In the same year, Louisa Lawson helped to found the Womanhood Suffrage League of

New South Wales. Two years later some New Zealand women became first in the world to achieve the vote, followed closely – in 1894 – by their South Australian sisters.

Still, Lawson described the lives of many young women of the day as a 'dreary round of monotony':

> ...in suburban places and small country towns...a dull stagnation of living prevails and no one makes the effort to strike free of its shackles and get away from its enervating effects.[11]

In Manly, Mary Agnes had her own ideas about escaping the tedium, though it would require great determination to see them through. Blessed with a fine singing voice, she hoped her talents would qualify her for roles in the musical burlesques popular at the time.

The theatre had long offered women opportunities for more public lives, less constrained by Victorian ideas that required respectable women to confine themselves to the private sphere. 'The microcosm of the theatre', says journalist and biographer Claire Tomalin, writing of England in the first half of the nineteenth century, differed in almost every respect from the social world surrounding it.

> An actress could, for instance, command payment equal to that of a man, or better. She could make her own working contracts. Her horizons, instead of being limited to a domestic circle, were as wide as the English speaking theatre. She could, and frequently did, flout the prevailing sexual rules.[12]

Mary Agnes had heard of such women, even in Australia. Woolloomooloo-born soprano and actress Nellie Stewart was a famous star of light opera and operetta who'd been on the stage since her childhood. Born into a theatrical family, by the time Stewart reached her twenties she had a reputation for both her performances and for her unconventional domestic arrangements. She and theatrical entrepreneur George Musgrove had a long-term partnership on and offstage, despite both having been married to others. Yet Nellie continued to be feted at home and in London for her work in pantomime and comic opera.

The world's most famous actress, Frenchwoman Sarah Bernhardt, was notorious for her scandalous private life. But it hadn't impeded her progress to financial and career success. By the late nineteenth century, Bernhardt was in demand all over the world. In 1891 she left San Francisco as a blonde and arrived a brunette on Australian shores – the *Pall Mall Gazette* suggesting the colour change helped relieve the dreariness of the voyage.[13]

Mary Agnes followed Bernhardt's progress in Sydney newspapers gushing with welcome:

TO SARAH BERNHARDT
Oh, golden-tongued daughter of Thespis,
Her highest high priestess of Art –
Australia smiles at thy advent,
And greets thee with welcoming heart.[14]

Bernhardt was given a town hall reception at which the Marseillaise was played in her honour. A photography enthusiast, she was photographed at Sydney's fashionable Falk Studios, in the character of Marguerite Gautier in *La Dame aux Camelias.*

For two months Bernhardt thrilled audiences in Melbourne, Adelaide and Sydney, in roles including *La Dame aux Camelias, La Tosca, Jeanne D'Arc* and *Cleopatra*. Offstage she played lover to a twenty-five-year-old visiting Frenchman, Adrien Loir.[15]

When Bernhardt departed, her lover remained in New South Wales, along with a theatrical company reeling from the expense of her tour, and more than a few women inspired less by the doomed heroines she portrayed than by Bernhardt's personal independence.

Mary Agnes's influences may have included another theatrical phenomenon as notorious as the 'divine Sarah'. In 1890, the same year

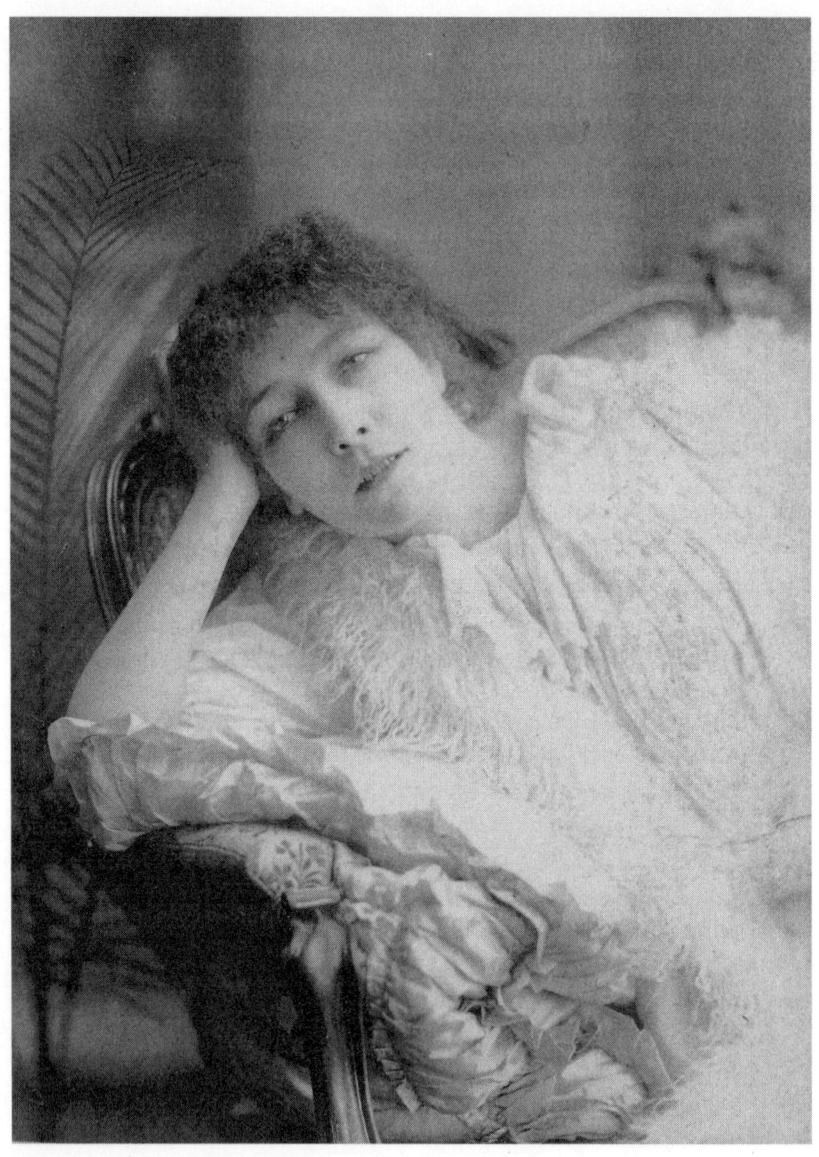

Sarah Bernhardt, Sydney, 1891

in which Mary Agnes gave birth to her second son, Leslie, *A Doll's House* came to Sydney. Whether or not Mary Agnes was able to attend a performance of Ibsen's infamous play, she could hardly have missed the controversy and discussion it provoked. When Janet Achurch and her husband Charles Carrington played Nora Helmer and her spouse Torvath, Sydney newspapers published many thousands of words inspired by the drama; reviews and letters of condemnation and congratulation.

The *Sydney Morning Herald* was appalled by the 'booing, and yelling and catcalling' with which the play was greeted when first performed at Sydney's Criterion Theatre. Despite deploring this 'unchivalrous' and 'unmanly' reception, the reviewer went on to say of the character of Nora:

> What possible interest, what vestige of sympathy can exist for a vain, frivolous creature who, having been married for eight years, and having borne her husband three children, takes offence at the upbraiding by her husband for a crime which she has committed, abandons husband and children, and goes forth alone, no one knows wither, and, possibly, no one cares. It is not natural. Such a person may exist in real life, but she would be a rare exception. The stage should portray the types of character, not its exceptions, but more than this, it should be true to life. This Nora Helmer is not true to life. Like the so-called drama in which she appears, she lacks that one touch of nature without which no drama can live. She is as unreal, as unnatural, as she is giddy, hollow, and cold.[16]

In response many words were submitted, but perhaps those from the pen of one 'Rose de Boheme' (the pen name of poet and critic Agnes Rose-Soley) were strongest:

> 'To thy own self be true', Old Polonius has been quoted times out of number in advice to young men, but Nora Helmer is the first person of my acquaintance who has applied his saw to young women. The latter have it persistently dinned into their ears that they must be true to their proper sphere; to husband, child, family

> circle, and social tradition. But it required a prophet from the land of the Viking to proclaim the new gospel of a higher duty which necessarily precedes and includes those others – the wife and mother's duty to herself...[17]

With the examples of Nellie Stewart, Sarah Bernhardt and Nora Helmer before her, Mary Agnes persisted with her dream of a life in music and theatre. It was a vision that had become as necessary to her as Ted, her children and her home. She was not deterred by her husband's objections – perhaps she feared that abandoning her theatrical dreams might cause her, like her mother, to lose her mind.

She won two small roles for her alter-ego Claire Delmar in a Newcastle production of *The Two Orphans*, a melodrama set during the French Revolution. 'As Julie and also the Countess de Liniere, Miss Claire Delmar was excellent, her rendition of the song 'See How It Sparkles', being very well received by the audience.'[18]

Also appearing in *The Two Orphans* was an Adelaide Cushman. A Newcastle newspaper reported that 'this young lady has only recently accepted the stage as a profession, and she has done remarkably well during the short time she has been on the boards.'[19]

Despite a seven-year gap in their ages, Mary Agnes and Adelaide Cushman became friends, encouraging and emboldening one another as they took to the stage, regardless of their husbands' disapproval. They exchanged publicity shots; Mary Agnes as Claire Delmar, photographed in Newcastle's Elite Studio, and Adelaide, pictured at Falk Studios in Sydney. There she posed as La Dame aux Camelias, just like Sarah Bernhardt, for an image that found its way into Mary Agnes's photo album and, long after, into Grandma Elsie's zither case.

Detroit-born Adelaide was the daughter of a judge whose family included the great and famously lesbian tragic actress Charlotte Cushman. Charlotte's performances in female and male parts, including those of Hamlet and Romeo, were acclaimed in the first half of the nineteenth century.

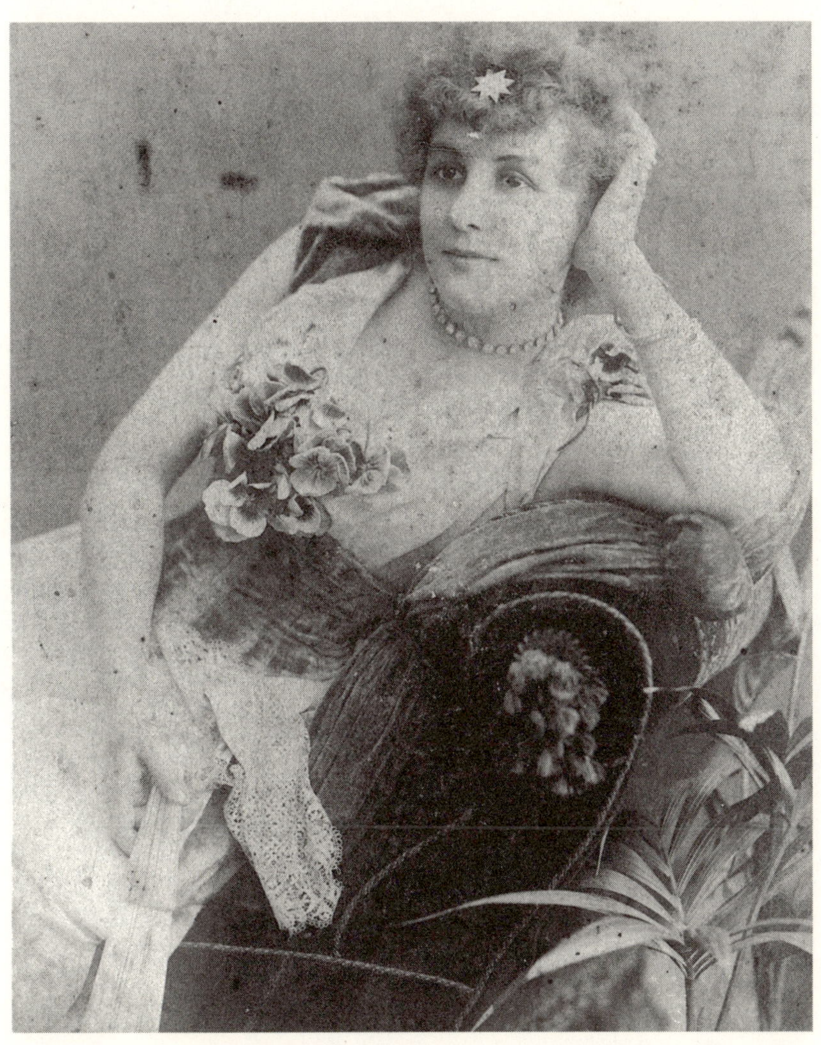

Adelaide Cushman in a popular pose, ca.1892

Charlotte died a dozen years before her seventeen-year-old kinswoman Adelaide married a wealthy Boston businessman named Kenneth Skinner and travelled to the colonies that would soon become Australia.[20] Adelaide took to the stage, carving out the beginnings of a reputation in Tasmania, Victoria, Queensland and New South Wales, where she was praised for her work.

In 1891 she appeared in *The Wages of Sin*, a melodramatic morality tale, and was described by the *Maitland Mercury* as a young woman with a 'bright future, as she is intelligent, has a first class presence and, for the nonce loses her everyday surroundings.'[21]

Adelaide Cushman returned to the United States without her husband in 1892, only a few months after appearing with Mary Agnes in *The Two Orphans*. One Sydney newspaper reported her drowned en route to San Francisco, but some weeks later corrected its facts when it learned Adelaide was in London. She went on to enjoy considerable praise in New York and Philadelphia and joined the Castle Square Theatre Company in Boston.

She married for a second time, to Broadway heart-throb Edward J Morgan. Their union was brief and unhappy. During divorce proceedings Adelaide, said to have possessed 'dramatic fire to a wonderful degree',[22] assaulted Edward in a New York street.

A few years later illness forced her from the stage and she died in Connecticut in 1904, aged only thirty-three.

Mary Agnes's sons, Reg and Leslie, were aged three and two when their mother appeared under her stage name 'Claire Delmar' in *The Two Orphans*, and a few weeks later at the Sydney School of Arts. A housekeeper cared for her children when she moved on to a Newcastle production of the nautical drama *Insured at Lloyds*, and then to perform with Caroline Keightley in Goulburn and Cootamundra in March 1892. Mrs Keightley produced and played herself in *Bail Up*, the story of her own dramatic horse ride to save her policeman husband's life.[23]

Mary Agnes's theatrical career was launched in precarious times. In the early 1890s boom years were followed by collapses in property prices and bank failures. The world of theatre was not immune. Weakened by poor management, Sydney theatres like the Alhambra Music Hall and companies run by the likes of clog-dancing comedian and entrepreneur Dan Tracey were struggling. His policy of engaging local artists met with new competition in the form of a former partner, Harry Rickards. An artist turned theatrical mogul, Rickards was intent on expanding his Tivoli operation. He recruited performers from abroad, entertainers who would appear alongside locals but garner more publicity and larger audiences.

Dan Tracey's company soon ceased to exist, and so did Mary Agnes's engagements in Sydney. Her friend Adelaide Cushman having departed, Mary Agnes had few others to encourage her further pursuit of a stage career. She wasn't like Adelaide: beautiful, young, and well connected. And she was no Sarah Bernhardt, despite her French-sounding stage name.

In 1894 she again left town, telling her husband Ted that she would play to audiences on the south coast. On 18 December, the *Sydney Morning Herald* carried an advertisement for a pianist and a skirt dancer, both wanted to play small parts with 'The Claire Delmar Concert and Comedy Company'. A popular spectacle in the music halls of the 1890s, skirt dancers worked long, layered costumes to form swirling, illuminated, billows of fabric. Practitioners of this slightly risqué art were invited to apply to the company's business manager at Tony's Hotel, Kiama.

Mary Agnes had found a new supporter. Twenty-one years of age, Gerald Shaw was a painter of scenery, handbills and posters, who had worked for touring dramatic companies. He may have met thirty-year-old Mary Agnes when she had her photograph taken before a backdrop he painted. Or perhaps the pair became acquainted when both worked in theatres around Newcastle. Whatever the circumstances of their introduction, Gerald made quite an impression on Mary Agnes. He became her 'business manager'. Though nothing came of their attempts to create a performing troupe in Claire Delmar's name, at Tony's Hotel in Kiama they formed a new company of another kind. It's unclear whether Mary Agnes left her husband and young sons for the stage or for Gerald Shaw, or both. It made little difference to her reputation. Lacking the celebrity that might have diffused the whiff of scandal, Mary Agnes would now be regarded by respectable Sydney as a woman who had deserted husband and family and, in doing so, forfeited her right to mother her boys.

She returned briefly to Manly, where Ted asked her to remain at home to look after the children. Mary Agnes refused his request. She didn't tell him about Gerald Shaw, but said that she was going to 'follow up her profession', though she wouldn't say where. She asked Ted for money to travel, a request that he refused.[24] Mary Agnes didn't see her husband or her boys again before leaving Sydney.

She did make one other visit – to Callan Park Hospital for the Insane. She wrote that on this occasion she found her mother to be 'very well considering all things. Her memory is getting much better and she is not quite so stout. If ever she does get better poor thing she will make some of them sit up. I guess poor thing if she were right I should never want for a few pounds.'[25]

Not only had Mary Gertrude lost her mind, she'd also lost control of her assets. Despite Thomas Boyd's careful will and though her daughter had need of money, Mary Gertrude's properties and the income they earned were now controlled by the Master in Lunacy, an officer appointed under New South Wales law to manage the estates of people considered insane. The Master protected their property, but also had the power to dispose of assets in order to meet the costs of their care.

Mary Agnes was forced to borrow travel funds from her housekeeper, Mrs Nicholls, who cared for her sons in their mother's absence. On 13 February 1895 she wrote a parting note to Ted:

> I am leaving this afternoon by the Tasmania for New Zealand. I thought you might have written to the GPO Sydney but I did not receive any answer to the letter I wrote you. If you care to write you can send to GPO Auckland…I hope we have a good passage across for I don't feel very grand now and the sea is pretty rough near New Zealand. With best love for you and kisses for the boys. I remain affectionately, Bunny.[26]

But she wasn't his Bunny any longer. Six weeks pregnant when she boarded the SS *Tasmania*, Mary Agnes would become 'Mrs Shaw', discarding the name Connolly and taking that of a man who became her next partner, in life and on the stage.

2
The Wrong Man

Gerald Shaw was only twenty-one when he ran away to New Zealand with thirty-year-old Mary Agnes. In an early photograph, the props intended to convey the gravitas he lacked couldn't conceal his youth. A bowler hat, cape and cane were not an especially effective costume, though his offstage disguise was arguably more successful.

Gerald's real name was Harry Morewood Thomson. Born in Little River, Victoria, in 1873, he was the ninth of ten children born to Charles and Fanny Thomson. Scottish Charles worked as an inspector on the New York to Albany rail line and in the USA married Fanny, a serving girl from Manchester. The Thomsons and two small daughters arrived in Australia in 1858, during Victoria's gold rush. Charles became an inspector on the new Melbourne and Geelong rail line, then nearing completion. He and Fanny had two more girls and six sons.

Harry, youngest but one of this large brood, grew up not far from the colony's famous goldfields, filled with fortune-seekers and entertainers who came in their wake. Many years later, perhaps inspired by a childhood spent around gold diggers of various kinds, Harry himself would become known as the 'musical mineralogist'.

Why Harry changed his name remains a mystery, but he did so well before he left Australia with Mary Agnes. Two years earlier Gerald Shaw was advertised as the advance representative for Lyle's Dramatic Company, in towns of the Riverina and Northern Rivers

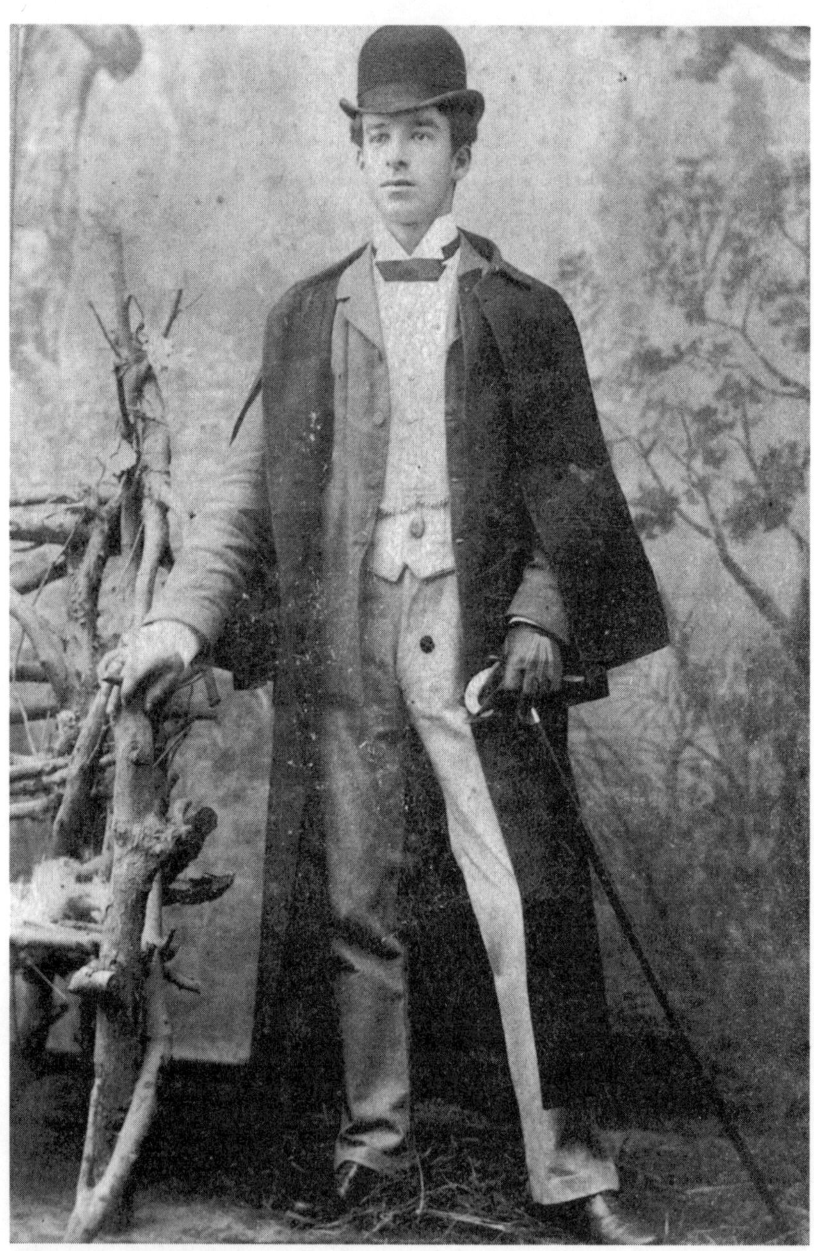

In disguise - 'Gerald Shaw', ca. 1894

regions of New South Wales. Even then – at the tender age of eighteen or nineteen – Harry Thomson had wanted to put his name behind him, a name he discarded for that of Gerald Shaw.

Mary Agnes and Gerald had a difficult voyage to New Zealand, travelling steerage in wild weather. By the time they disembarked in Auckland, Mary Agnes's patience was at an end. Describing her arrival in a letter sent back to Sydney she wrote that it was hot and the customs men insisted on opening all her bags and boxes. In an audible whisper she told the waiting cab driver to tell the customs man she had a pound of opium in her sock if he'd like to inspect her. He just laughed and went on searching her things. Mary Agnes reported that she said 'all the French prayers she knew for his future welfare.'[1]

In her expectant condition, Mary Agnes spent some weeks recovering, but by March she was beginning to enjoy Auckland. She laughed at its horse-drawn trams, marvelled at how cheap the tomatoes were and how delicious the fish.[2] It helped that she had some early success. She sang a Spanish waltz at City Hall; Gerald sang 'London Bridge'. She appeared with the Amy Vaughan Company as Alice, the protagonist's love interest in *Dick Whittington Up to Date*, a burlesque version of the English folk tale. According to the *New Zealand Observer* it closely followed the original. Amy Vaughan played Dick, cruelly treated in his early London days by a cook and her husband. In the *Up to Date* version Dick gets his own back, thrashing them when he comes across the pair in Africa, posing as missionaries. 'Surely', commented the *Observer*'s reviewer, 'the author never prescribed such a thing as a man punching a woman.'[3]

Seeking news of her sons, Mary Agnes wrote to her husband. She gossiped about an Australian journalist in New Zealand whose wife 'left him for good and he says she is leading a terrible fast life in Melbourne, driving about in a carriage painted to death'.[4] But she didn't tell Ted about her own 'fast life' with Gerald Shaw, her partner in more ways than one. Instead she boasted of her successes. She was, she said:

> ...determined to make a go of it now I can tell you for I was sick unto death with one confounded piece of misfortune and another on 'the other side'. That's the way we speak of Australia over here.[5]

Yet she still had her worries and in subsequent letters entreated her husband not to allow teachers to push Reg too hard at school. Leslie was far from strong and she hoped the boys were taking plenty of cod liver oil. She said she was comforted by her trust in Mrs Nicholls, the housekeeper, whom she believed to be 'as fond of the boys as if they were her own'. She sent her love to her sons, to Ted and to Mrs Nicholls.

Of her own situation she said only that she was 'getting quite fat again'. She didn't explain why. She said she'd had offers from various theatrical troupes, though she intended to tour New Zealand with a company of her own. 'But', she wrote, 'the travelling here is very bad in the winter so I may not go out for a while on my own account.'[6] Five months pregnant, Mary Agnes knew she'd have other things to occupy her well into spring. Her theatrical alter-ego Claire Delmar vanished from the New Zealand stage.

Gerald continued to perform in Auckland, with Amy Vaughan's Company and with John Fuller – singer and founder of what would soon become a major theatrical empire in Australia and New Zealand. Then Gerald teamed up with a Professor Henri Frith in a small variety show:

> Professor Frith, in conjunction with Gerald Shaw, went through several feats on skates, some clever and some amusing; and Professor Henri contributed an exhibition of chair and table balancing which was well worth going a long way to see, Professor Henri first of all balanced on his chin five chairs, then an ordinary sized table, and then a ladder, with a boy on one of the top rungs. The rest of the entertainment was also highly appreciated.[7]

Though somewhat upstaged by Henri Frith, Gerald decamped with him, and Mary Agnes, to the south of the north island. He and the self-styled professor travelled around, performing at Napier's Theatre

Royal, in Wanganui and in Hawera. Then they joined the Australian Merrymakers Burlesque and Variety Company, formed by magician George Percy Hausmann.

Meanwhile Mary Agnes saw out her pregnancy in Palmerston North, on the windy Manawata Plain. A small agricultural centre overlooked by mountain ranges on two sides, Palmerston North lay at the heart of a newly created network of rail lines, connecting it to the port of Napier and to the capital city, Wellington. She found lodgings in Main Street, close to the station and bordering The Square, a 17-acre park at the heart of town. The Māori called it Te Marae o Hine, 'The Courtyard of the Daughter of Peace'. It was in these lodgings that Gladys was born, though she was certainly no daughter of peace.

Gladys made her very first entrance on 29 September 1895 while her father was about 80 miles away in Wellington, appearing with the Australian Merrymakers. Gerald was filling in as 'Mr Interlocuter', minstrel show host. It was a step up for him to be master of ceremonies in the Merrymakers show, even for only one or two nights. Normally a bass singer – or basso – Gerald's commanding presence made him the best choice to replace manager and principal artist Percy Shannon, who had fallen ill.

American in origin, minstrel shows were seen throughout the western world in the nineteenth century. Brought to Australia and New Zealand by entertainers from the United States, popular minstrel troupes were soon imitated by locals. Their shows followed a three-part format. In the first act a straight man – the Interlocuter played by Gerald at Wellington's Criterion theatre – was seated in the centre of a semi-circle of performers in blackface. Furthest away were the endmen, traditionally called 'Tambo' and 'Bones'. The comedy of their repartee with 'Mr Interlocuter' was based on uneducated misunderstandings of the more genteel interlocuter's words.

In the third and final part of the program, after individual items which made up the second act, minstrel shows offered a farce. Shortly before Gladys's birth, the Merrymakers performed *The New Woman*. Just as minstrel shows perpetuated racial stereotypes for decades after the American Civil War, so they satirised the issue of women's rights, even after the matter of women's suffrage had been settled – at least in New Zealand. Two years earlier, in 1893, women there were first in the world to win the vote, still years away for most women in the as yet unfederated colonies of Australia, and decades away for their sisters elsewhere in the English-speaking world. Courtesy of her New Zealand birth, Gladys was the first female child of her line born with the right to a future vote. Her mother might have dreamed of being an independent 'new woman', with both a career and a vote, but her daughter Gladys was one from the moment she drew her first breath.

It was two months before her birth certificate was issued. When it was, it didn't mention anyone called Gerald Shaw, basso, theatrical manager and casual 'interlocuter'. Nor did it mention a Mrs Shaw. Legally, if not biologically, Gladys's father was draper Edward (Ted) Connolly, the husband Mary Agnes had left in Sydney. Whatever it said on her birth certificate, Muriel Gladys Warrington Connolly would henceforth be known as Gladys Shaw.

Gerald's youthful ambitions were not all that compatible with his new role as father and breadwinner. Being a performer and theatrical manager meant many absences, during which Mary Agnes looked after her new baby unaided, in a town far from home. Isolated and worried about her boys in Sydney, she'd heard nothing from their father nor from Mrs Nicholls since moving to Palmerston North.

Eventually two letters reached her, one of them accompanied by a photograph.

Her grim-faced boys seemed alone and defenceless, so small were they in comparison to the low-slung cottage and neat picket fence behind them. Mary Agnes was moved to reply to her husband, confirming something of what he must surely have suspected during the months of his wife's absence:

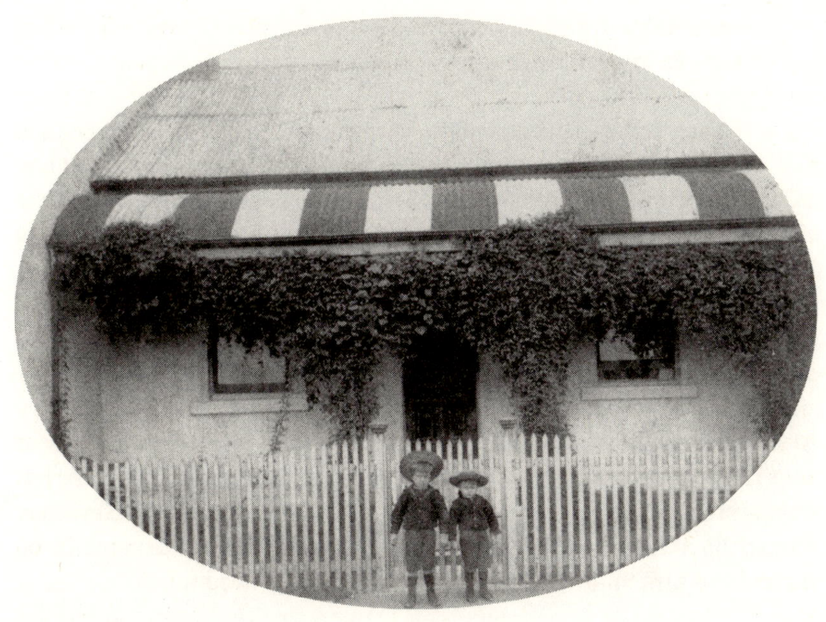

Reg and Leslie Connolly, ca. 1894

Palmerston North
February 13th 1896

My dear Ted,
You will be surprised to hear from me after so apparently a long silence ...I hope you have been able to succeed in the business you have taken and also to keep Reg at a good school. Well old boy I have had a hard and severe battle myself since I landed in New Zealand. You will understand a little of it when I tell you I have a little daughter six months old and have had to follow up my business and provide for her and myself. She is a beautiful child and very like Regie when he was a baby. Thank God she is healthy and sweet tempered and I am able almost to feed her on the breast. Her name is Muriel Gladys Warrington and she was born almost on the stage. I will bring her up to it as she shows signs of being

> remarkably intelligent. If you can by any possibility manage to raise £5 and let me have it I shall not forget it.
>
> I have some engagements to fulfill in Auckland and I want the money to help me get there and then I intend coming to Sydney. Thank Mrs Nicholls for the photo of the boys. I shall write to her later on...Give my love to Mrs Nicholls and my boys and tell them I will try and send them a photo of their little sister.[8]

But there would be no voyage to Sydney. And perhaps no photograph of baby Gladys either. Ted had lost his job at Horderns and had neither the money – nor perhaps the inclination – to send help. Though Mary Agnes posted similar requests to her father and her sister, both later said they were unable to locate her. Mary Agnes had apparently left Palmerston North without leaving a forwarding address. She may simply have neglected to tell her family that their replies should be directed to Mrs Shaw, as she was known in New Zealand.

She hadn't gone very far from Palmerston North. In Feilding, just 12 miles away, 'Claire Delmar' returned to the New Zealand stage when Gladys was eight months old, singing 'For All Eternity' and 'Whisper and I Shall Hear You'. Gerald contributed some very Victorian songs – including Arthur Sullivan's 'The Lost Chord'. Two weeks later, this sedate and sombre musical program was abandoned, and 'Shaw's Surprise Party' formed. It was joined initially by Charles Hugo, a well-known blackface comedian and man of ill repute, then by a Japanese contortionist named Kadame. Gerald contributed a dramatic parlour song, 'Anchored', while encores were demanded of Claire Delmar, who sang about mistaking a stranger for her beau in a number made famous by British music-hall legend Marie Lloyd.

> The wrong man, the wrong man
> Wasn't it awful rum?
> The wrong man, the wrong man
> Oh Jerusalem
> I never was in such a plight before
> Pity me if you can

I thought I should fall
I'd given them all
To the wrong, wrong man.[9]

Mary Agnes must have wondered whether she too had taken up with a 'wrong, wrong man'. When she registered the birth of another child at the end of 1897, it was as if Gerald didn't exist. Like his sister, the new arrival was legally the offspring of Mary Agnes's estranged husband, Ted Connolly. But rather than acknowledge his real father Gerald – or Harry – by choosing at least one of his names for the baby, her new son became Keith Warrington Connolly. His middle name, one also given to his sister Gladys, was a nod to John Warrington, Mary Agnes's own disliked and distrusted parent. Back in New South Wales, John advised his son-in-law Ted to seek a divorce.

At only twenty-four, Gerald was enjoying the thrills of performance and becoming an enthusiast for the gambles and novelties of the entertainment business. He strove to anticipate popular tastes and was an early adopter of technologies and forms transforming popular theatre as the twentieth century approached.

He first saw films in New Zealand, where Alfred Whitehouse began showing moving pictures around 1895. Whitehouse used Thomas Edison's kinetoscope with which, according to the *Hawera and Normanby Star*, Mr Whitehouse was doing great business in June 1896. 'Nothing but wonder was expressed. The kinetoscope has not taken long to make itself known, and no doubt Mr Whitehouse will be kept pretty busy for the next few days'.[10]

Among Whitehouse's customers was Gerald Shaw. In Hawera as the advance representative of the Hugo Buffalo Minstrel Company, he tried out this early form of cinema in an individual viewing booth – then the only way to see pictures that moved. They were not projected until a few months later, when 'Professor' George Percy Hausmann, magician and founding manager of the Australian Merrymakers, used a 'kinematograph' to show films to a packed auditorium at Auckland's Opera House.

By 1898 Gerald had watched films screened with the aid of a dozen such machines touring New Zealand's North Island. He also saw the shows of John Fuller's popular Myriorama Company. Using an old lantern plant acquired from the Sydney School of Arts and imported to New Zealand, Fuller, with the aid of sons Walter and Ben, used magic lantern slides to create a sense of movement. Their programs mixed projected images with vaudeville acts.

Gerald would soon learn how to employ more modern machinery himself, featuring moving pictures in programs he directed, managed and promoted. But first he would relocate his family.

After Keith's birth, the Shaws mostly lived in the suburbs of Auckland. In Ponsonby, Eden Terrace and Onehunga, 'Mrs Gerald Shaw' directed popular concerts. Mary Agnes and Gerald were among six artists who sang, and Mary Agnes performed a piano solo. But when they failed to turn up for their advertised show in Devonport, disapproval was swift. 'Breaking faith with audiences is not calculated to increase the popularity of the company, and the management by now should be cognisant of that fact', commented the *New Zealand Herald*.[11]

The Shaws had worn out their welcome.

3
A Trip to the Moon

Now a family of four, the Shaws left New Zealand for the wild west of Tasmania. Amid the copper, gold and silver–lead mines of the West Coast Range, in the theatres of booming Queenstown and Zeehan, Gerald Shaw and Mary Agnes, appearing as Claire Delmar, performed with a troupe named 'Patey and Shaw's Merrymakers'. In the opening months of a new century the company offered a farce and individual acts to packed houses at Queenstown's new Academy of Music. And Gerald collected £3 19s thrown on to the stage during his rendition of *An Absent Minded Beggar*:

When you've shouted 'Rule Britannia',
when you've sung 'God save the Queen',
When you've finished killing Kruger with your mouth,
Will you kindly drop a shilling in my little tambourine
For a gentleman in khaki ordered South?[1]

Kipling's poem, set to music by some Australian women and more famously by Arthur Sullivan, was used throughout the Empire to raise money for charities known as 'Patriotic Funds' that supported troops fighting in the Boer War and the families of those killed and maimed. Unfortunately, Gerald failed to give the proceeds of his performance to the Queenstown Patriotic Fund before leaving town. When complaints reached him in Zeehan, the next stop on the Merrymakers' tour, Gerald responded in that town's newspaper, objecting to 'the cavalier treatment shown us by two gentlemen in their respective positions as the secretary and collector of the Queenstown Fund.'[2] The money was hastily forwarded to the Zeehan newspaper and another benefit concert deferred. After appearances in Burnie, Devonport, Penguin and Ulverstone, Gerald and Mary Agnes left Tasmania and headed to Victoria, where their efforts to support soldiers fighting the Boer in South Africa were somewhat better received.

In April 1900, this time advertised as 'Shaw's Merrymakers and Myriorama Company', they appeared at the Mechanics Hall in rural Camperdown, west of Melbourne. Their company's first and only program featured a film, *The Transvaal War*:

> Shaw's Myriorama Concert Company appeared in the Mechanics Hall on Tuesday evening and last evening. The entertainment comprised a number of splendid lantern views of war scenes in South Africa, and some cinematographe pictures. The audience was roused to enthusiasm when portraits of Her Majesty the Queen and Lord Roberts were thrown upon the screen. The entertainments were interspersed with songs by Madame Shaw and Mr Gerald Shaw, both of whom were warmly applauded, their contributions being encored in almost every instance.[3]

The Boer War was the first to be depicted on film – mostly in re-enacted scenes. The cinematographe pictures that Gerald screened could have been battle reconstructions filmed in a Paris park, for Pathe's *Episodes from the Transvaal War.*

For the remainder of the year the Shaws joined forces with an acrobat named Martini to form 'Martini and Shaw's Gaiety Company'. It was also known as 'Martini and Shaw's Circus and Variety Company', which, given that it sometimes included a donkey and a 'lady boxer' named Mahatma, may have been a more appropriate label. Whichever title it took, audiences enjoyed the company whenever it appeared in country towns of Victoria and South Australia. In Mount Gambier:

> The members vied with one another in making the evening a success, and it is difficult to say which performer merited the

greatest praise. The acrobatic performances of Martini were again thrilling, and his marvellous feats brought him rounds of applause. Mr. Shaw's songs – patriotic, comic, etc. – were all encored, the audience enthusiastically joining in the choruses…the sentimental songs of Madame Shaw were much appreciated, and they had to respond to numerous encores. Mahatma, the lady boxer, was also in evidence, and the male audience were not slow to realise that they in the future might have to submit in a muscular way to petticoat rule.[4]

In Charlton and Kerang, Mary Agnes was singled out for more praise:

> In some instances, as in the case of 'Ora Pro Nobis', ['Pray for Us'] her voice is heard to especial advantage and comes as a direct inspiration. The hush which fell upon the audience on Saturday night during her rendering of this beautiful number was a remarkable testimony to her powers of song, the silence being such as could be felt and being broken only by the silvery notes of the gifted songstress.[5]

But it was Barney who stole the show:

> Barney, the talking donkey, is quite the funniest thing of the show, however. A droller or more mirth-provoking sight surely never greeted mortal eyes. The man or woman who could sit unmoved before such a spectacle must be devoid of all humour.[6]

In Mildura the ensemble was described as:

> …really one of the finest travelling in country districts. Not a few residents will be secretly pleased that the uncertain state of the Darling River has occasioned the Company's early return and that they will perform again next Monday and Tuesday before passing on up-river.[7]

Meanwhile, Ted Connolly was looking for his wife in all the wrong places. Detectives searched for Mary Agnes in New Zealand in 1899 and learned that she and a man who may have been named Shaw had departed. Further inquiries failed to locate them. In June 1900, whilst Mary Agnes was far away in South Australia, Ted's solicitors advertised in Sydney newspapers. Receiving no response, Ted was free to petition for a divorce without naming a co-respondent or serving papers on his wife.

When 1901 began with Australia's six colonies uniting in a federation, Mary Agnes may not have known she'd been divorced. She was with her new partner Gerald and their children in the prosperous central Victorian city of Bendigo. There Gerald, and a business partner named Frasier, refurbished the Masonic Hall and renamed it the New Gaiety Theatre. The New Gaiety Company was formed to appear on its stage, followed by Gerald's next venture, Hunt's Imperial Vaudeville Company. Gerald and Mary Agnes, appearing as Claire Delmar, were two of its twenty artists, 'only a few of whom,' reported the *Bendigo Advertiser*, 'can have any claim to the magnificent designation 'star'.'[8] New artists were hastily added to the bill, and the following week the same newspaper changed its view. Hunt's Imperial Vaudeville Company, it said, now offered an entertainment that 'went with more 'go' than usual.'[9]

Kate Fanning was one of the few performers among those assembled by Gerald who could have claimed at least minor star status. Described in confrontingly racist language as a 'coon' singer, she performed songs that caricatured African-Americans. Intended to amuse by mocking their apparent lack of sophistication, while paradoxically setting toes tapping with their complex, syncopated rhythms, 'coon' songs were hugely popular on music hall and vaudeville programs in the late nineteenth and early twentieth centuries. In the United States they were written and performed by both black and white artists. In Australia they were often sung by women and children – usually in blackface. The most famous Australian 'coon' singer was another Fanning – Maud, older sister of Kate and an enormously popular artist between the 1890s and 1940.

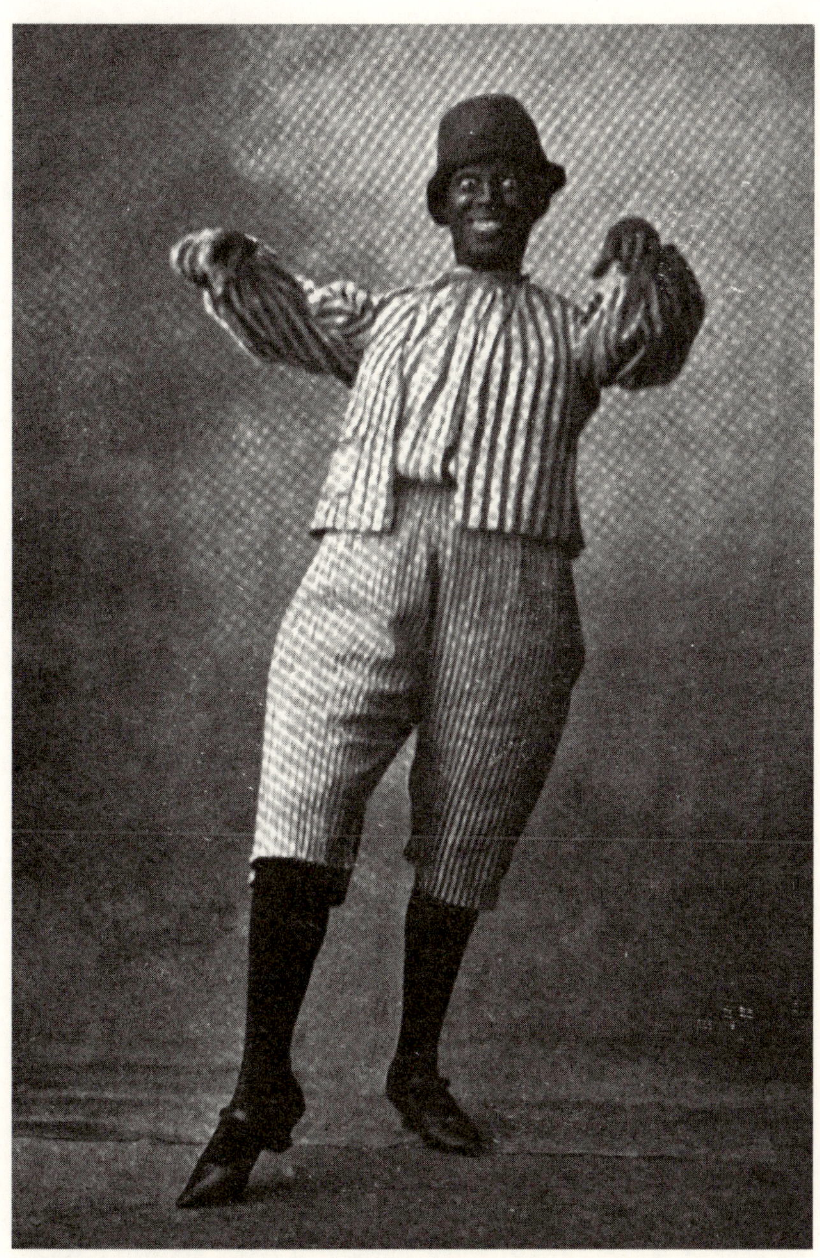

Maud Fanning in blackface, 1890

Kate Fanning also sang 'coster' songs, items performed in a mock cockney accent and from the perspective of costermongers – traders who sold fruit, vegetables and seafood from their barrows. As well as singers, Hunt's Imperial Vaudeville Company included trick cyclists, comedians, a juggler and an English whistling comedian named Ted Box. Performances were well attended, though in the week of Bendigo's horse races Gerald had his work cut out for him as manager:

> The audience and performers at the new Gaiety Theatre last evening were subjected to a great deal of annoyance by the shameful conduct of a set of roughs who elected to spend the night at the variety entertainment. Towards the end of the first act the interruptions became so pronounced that the performance was brought temporarily to a standstill, and the curtain was rung down. During the interval two of the most obnoxious of the crowd came into conflict in the lobby, and inflicted a little well-merited punishment on one another. The manager soon arrived on the scene, and thrust the offenders outside, after which the entertainment proceeded smoothly.[10]

Shortly after this incident, the 'Shaw Gaiety Company' left town to entertain more receptive audiences on both sides of the Murray River, in Victoria and New South Wales, no longer colonies but states of Australia, the world's youngest nation.

In Echuca's Temperance Hall, Gladys joined Kate Fanning and other members of the Shaw company, in her first documented appearance.

> One of the features of the evening was the appearance of Baby Shaw, who is only four years of age, and sang "Kitty Mahone" [sic]. The child gave a splendid rendition, and deserved the applause bestowed upon her.[11]

In fact Gladys was almost six. Her brother Keith was nearly four. Both were of an age to be amazed and delighted when Gerald next became manager of the Skuthorp Rough Riders – a rodeo show. Professor Skuthorp was a buckjumper who displayed his talents on a vacant lot in

Melbourne's Flinders Street before heading to other towns in Victoria. Appearing with him were Gerald's former partner Martini, Barney the donkey and Diana, 'the only lady buckjump rider in Australia.'[12]

Gerald hadn't run away from Bendigo to join a wild west show because he'd had his fill of larrikin theatre-goers. He was escaping unpaid accounts for board and lodging with a Mrs Rees, debts which were probably responsible for his next change of name.

By January 1902, Gerald and Mary Agnes were to be found some miles from Bendigo, in the old gold rush town of Beechworth, where they were described as 'well known variety artists Mr and Mrs H.M. Thomson'. Mr Thomson, it was said in the local newspaper, was 'gifted with a splendid bass voice of great power and compass', whilst his wife owned 'a sweetly modulated, well-trained mezzo-soprano voice'.[13] They sang many songs, comic and otherwise, in a show at the Bijou Theatre, sited in the town's Hospital for the Insane. Their program culminated in 'The Beechworth Plum Pudding', a farce of the couple's own making.

Most appreciated was:

> the part in which Mr. Thomson, as a coloured cook, disencumbered himself of half-a-dozen coats and vests, and, much to Mrs. Thomson's (the cook's employer) astonishment, tried to stand on his head on the pudding.[14]

Debts notwithstanding, the family eventually made its way back to Bendigo, where Gerald kept the name Harry Thomson and assumed a lower profile. Mary Agnes returned to the stage as Claire Delmar, playing Lady Capulet in the Wilson Forbes Company production of *Romeo and Juliet*, and Nancy Goodfellow in *The Village Blacksmith*, a musical dramatisation of Longfellow's poem.

Gerald also appeared onstage in small uncredited roles for which he earned 10 shillings on each of three nights a week. For the remainder of the week he was employed in the ticket box at 3 shillings and fourpence a night.

It didn't take too long for Mrs Rees to realise her debtor was back in town, albeit under another name. She took him to court and struck an agreement under which Wilson Forbes would 'garnish' Gerald's wages, deducting money from them until the outstanding amount was paid. When this did not occur, Forbes was called to appear before the court. In his defence, he cited a section of the *Wages Protection Act* prohibiting employers from garnishing low-paid workers' wages. Perhaps unconvinced that acting really was work, the presiding magistrate asked whether an actor should be entitled to the same treatment as other workers. 'Is an Actor a Working Man?' echoed a headline in the *Barrier Miner*.[15]

Though the case was dismissed, it was reported by newspapers as far away as Sydney, where it was noted that Shaw 'was for some time performing in New Zealand with his wife, Miss Claire Delmar'.[16] Had Ted Connolly's detectives still been on the case, they might at last have been able to locate his missing Bunny.

Mary Agnes was appearing in Adelaide with Wilson Forbes's company when accounts of the legal proceedings were published. Using her pseudonym, Claire Delmar, she played a milliner named Madam Prudence in *Camille*, her performance spoiled for one reviewer by her unexplained occasional lapse into broken English. She was more successful in *Leah the Forsaken*, taking the small role of Dame Groschen: 'a capital indication of her success may be gathered from the remark of a child in the audience, "Oh, mother, what a funny lady!"'[17]

Mary Agnes also appeared in *East Lynne* in which she 'successfully, and perhaps unavoidably, burlesqued the part of Cornelia'.[18]

Cornelia – the melodrama's domineering spinster sister – is not its heroine. That is Lady Isabel Carlyle, who leaves a decent though dull lawyer husband and their children for an aristocratic suitor. He deserts her, and she bears their child. Later a disguised Lady Isabel takes the position of governess in the household of her former husband and his new wife. There she sees one of her sons die, and in a famous line cries 'dead, dead and never called me mother'. Satirists of melodrama everywhere mocked those words, though Mary Agnes may not have appreciated the joke. She hadn't seen her own oldest sons – now aged thirteen and twelve – for more than seven years.

The Shaws stayed on in Adelaide after Wilson Forbes and his company left. In May, a benefit concert for Mr and Mrs Gerald Shaw was held at Adelaide's Central Hall. Though it contributed little to her upkeep, it was Gladys's second reported stage appearance. Despite being almost seven years old, she was billed as 'Baby Shaw' who 'delighted the audience with her songs "Kitty Malone" and "The Sheeny Coon"'.[19] 'Kitty Malone' was probably ' Sweet Kitty Mahone', an Irish-American song, the same number Gladys sang with such success in Echuca. 'The Sheeny Coon' parodied a black, Jewish American serenading his Rachel:

You're no common dolly,
No you're my shuck-ol-lolly,
I'm yer little Ikey Mo',
The Dandy Sheeny Coon.[20]

It was not an unusual 'coon song'. But even discounting the repugnant racism of the whole genre, it seems an unsuitable choice for a small child's repertoire. Yet these two songs would be Baby Shaw's signature numbers for the next couple of years. And Gladys would go on to make a career of being inappropriate.

Mary Agnes and Gerald eventually funded a return to New South Wales, where Mary Agnes's father, John Warrington, had died the previous year. Yet she kept her distance from remaining family members, including her oldest sons and her sister Maud. With her new family she settled in Penrith, some 30 miles from Sydney, supporting her young children by teaching piano and voice while Gerald staged concerts at the Temperance Hall. Mary Agnes, 'Baby Shaw', Gerald and a singer named Jack Tipping sustained an entire program of musical numbers, blackface sketches, jokes and farce. Gerald even gave 'amongst other things, an exhibition of high kicking'.[21]

Toward the end of 1903 'Shaw's Society Entertainers' recruited another family to add to their show for appearances in Bathurst and Mudgee. 'The Marvellous Vertos', husband and wife, headlined the company's program.

Percy Verto was an old acquaintance of Gerald's. His real name was George Hausmann, the very same Professor Hausmann who formed the Australian Merrymakers with which Gerald was appearing when Gladys was born, the same Hausmann credited with first projecting films in New Zealand. He had returned to Australia as a magician, picture-show man and escapologist, with a new name, 'Verto', and a new wife and assistant, Millie Richardson. Millie had been on the stage since her childhood in Christchurch, touring New Zealand and Australia as an actor and singer with Pollards Lilliputians. She joined Hausmann's company in 1898 and soon married the proprietor.

Her husband achieved notoriety on and off the stage. In early 1900 Verto was hailed as a hero when fire broke out in the smoking carriage of the Broken Hill Express, threatening twenty or so passengers:

> The ladies in the car behind were terrified. Attempts were made by some of them to throw themselves out of the train. The men had to place themselves in the doorways and use force to drive the frantic women back.[22]

Meanwhile Verto climbed along the outside of seven moving carriages to warn the guard, 'then the brakes were immediately applied and the train brought to a standstill'.[23] In Melbourne, the magazine *Table Talk* congratulated him; 'the young actor deserves great credit for this opportune display of bravery'.[24] It was indeed opportune, a sensational way to promote Verto's growing reputation as an escapologist – 'the handcuff king'.[25]

At eight years old, 'Little Gladys (the clever child performer)' took 'a prominent place in the program' of Shaw's Society Entertainers.[26] But between items, she watched from the wings at the School of Arts as Verto plied his magic, and Millie Verto appeared as 'La Petite' in her fabulous electric cloak. Percy Verto also screened *A Trip to the Moon*, a miraculous French film by Georges Méliès. Gladys had seen moving pictures before, mostly documentary footage of trains, mountains and busy city streets. But *A Trip to the Moon* transported her – and the art of cinema – much further. She saw a rocket ship land in the eye of the man in the moon and laughed at the strange gymnastics of the lunar people. All around the world audiences were enchanted. And so was Gladys.

When the Shaws returned to Penrith late in 1903, Mary Agnes enrolled to vote in the first national election in which women were permitted to do so. Aboriginal, Torres Strait Island women and others considered 'aboriginal natives' of Africa, Asia and the Pacific Islands, did not have the right to vote. For their white sisters, enrolment was voluntary.

Mary Agnes, a 'new woman', wanted a say in who would govern the world's newest nation. Perhaps she voted for Nellie Alma Martel, a Sydney elocution teacher. Nellie was also an accomplished speaker and president of the Women's Social and Political League. Standing for election to the Senate, she became one of the earliest women to appear on a ballot paper anywhere in the world. Though an unsuccessful candidate, Nellie would go on to become an influential figure in the English campaign for women's right to vote, a battle that would take another fifteen years and a world war to win.

Even in Australia, where women were both candidates and voters in the election of 1903, it would be forty years before they were among those elected to the national parliament.

4
The Marvellous Shaws

Gerald was hired by the Hawtrey Comedy Company to make arrangements for its tour of Perth and goldfield towns of the west. He gathered up his family and in Melbourne boarded a boat for a voyage of almost 2000 miles. Arriving in Fremantle in June 1904, the Shaws disembarked in a port throbbing with all the trade and traffic of a gold rush. Western Australia's population had more than doubled in the last decade of the nineteenth century and for an opportunist like Gerald the possibilities seemed endless. Not only might a man find wealth on the goldfields, he could also make his fortune entertaining the hordes who came seeking riches. When the Hawtrey Company departed after a couple of months playing to packed houses, Gerald, Mary Agnes, Gladys and Keith stayed behind.

Gerald had agreed to oversee the renovation of Perth's Cremorne Gardens, a theatre and open-air venue behind a Perth hotel. The venture was the brainchild of Hawtrey Company manager Leonard Davis, who would soon return to the west with a new company of entertainers. In the meantime Gerald was his spokesman. He announced that he was 'repainting and decorating the gardens', and that 'the lane leading to the gardens will be asphalted and brightly illuminated. The premises will in future be known as the Palace Gardens'.[1] It was not the only theatre project underway in the city. Construction of His Majesty's was nearing completion. An extravagant theatre designed with a domed roof that could open to air the auditorium on hot evenings, it would be the largest theatre in the country.

While work continued at the Palace Gardens, Gerald also organised concerts at the Crystal Palace Skating Rink, where he and Mary Agnes both sang. This time Gerald's was the agreeable voice noted by reviewers. At his very first Perth performance, the audience demanded an encore.

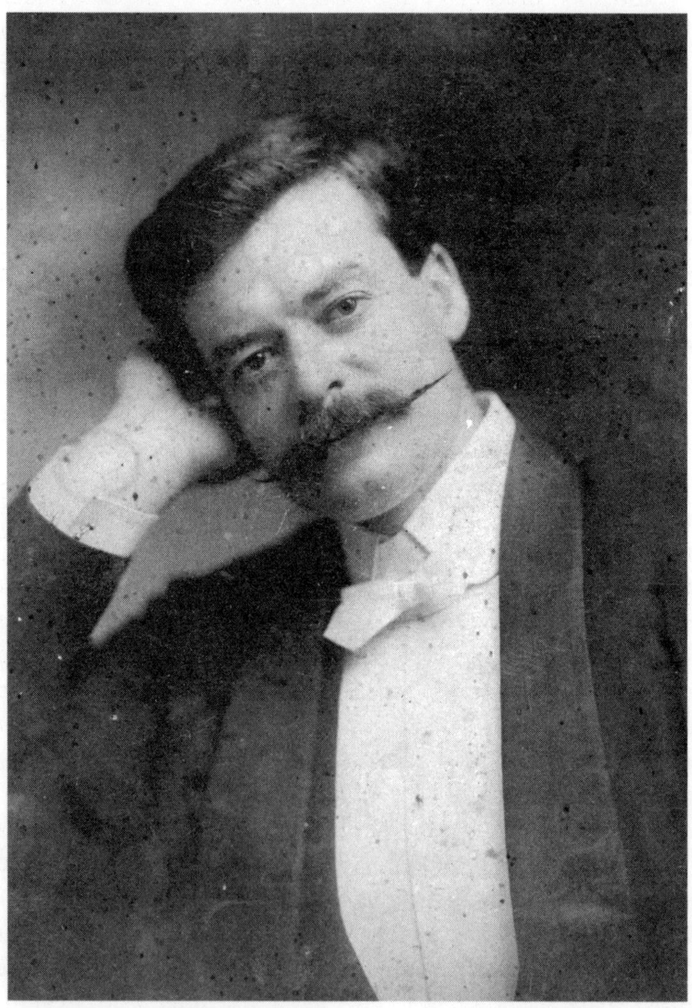

A 'popular basso', Gerald Shaw, ca. 1904

On 5 November 1904, the Palace Gardens and the Palace Entertainers opened 'before a very large attendance'. The *West Australian* reported:

> ...no end of costly ability has been expended in refurnishing, redecorating and replanting these grounds throughout, while the quality of the entertainment has been lifted out of all recognition. Dante, the brother of the dead magician, was easily the most astonishing performer of the evening. He is neat and artistic in his work, has a good address and successfully carries off some really wonderful tricks. He concluded his mystifying 'turn' with a weird suspension of a girl in the air.[2]

Singers, dancers and comedians also contributed, among them Gerald Shaw with his illustrated songs, precursors of the music video, made possible by the 'wonder-moving Chronojector...Edison's latest invention for producing moving pictures':[3]

> The pictures displayed by the aid of the Chronojector evoked tumultuous applause, while those exhibited in illustration of the song 'When the roses bloom again', sung by Mr Gerald Shaw, appealed to the audience by their beauty and appropriateness.[4]

The new Palace Gardens and its program were crowd-pleasers. One night more than 2000 people crammed into the available seats, while those who couldn't be seated established an impromptu gallery on the roof of the pub next door. But on 25 January 1905 the Palace Gardens projectionist went missing. Percy Abrahams simply vanished from his room at the Metropole Hotel, and the chronojector from reviews of Palace Gardens shows that followed.

Gerald too soon disappeared. He'd earlier borrowed money from the next-door publican – on behalf of manager Leonard Davis, he said – to pay workers and some costs of renovation. He failed to repay all of the money and the ensuing dispute ended in court. There was a confusing account of legal proceedings in the newspaper, but no further mention of Gerald Shaw in connection with the Palace Gardens.

Instead he and Mary Agnes cobbled together a living wherever they could. Styling herself as 'Madam Marie', Mary Agnes taught singing, voice production and piano. And Gerald carried on wheeling and dealing, devising an assortment of money-making schemes, few of which earned much at all.

He sang with a variety party that played in Perth theatres and, more lucratively, on paddle steamers SS *Decoy* and the *Zephyr*. On Sundays they ferried around a thousand people on the Swan River to the Applecross Hotel, and then the few miles back to Perth. Artists would perform an item on each leg of the journey and from the verandah of the hotel, where patrons had around half an hour for refreshments before the return trip that deposited them back in Perth in time for the last trains and trams of the day. The band on a rival vessel, the *Westralian*, played 'We Shall Meet in the Sweet By and By' and 'Way Down Upon the Swanee River' when overtaking the slower *Decoy*. And when, as sometimes happened, the *Decoy* became stuck on a sandbank, its passengers would miss their last rides and find themselves walking home.

Despite such hazards, Gerald liked these al fresco entertainments. On Christmas night in 1906, he organised a sacred concert featuring his family. He ferried the audience to Perth's Botanic Gardens, where he lit a stage for the occasion. Early in the new year he repeated the show. His ventures were not confined to Perth; for the next three years he led his family a merry dance around towns and mining settlements all over the southern half of Western Australia.

He promoted his daughter as 'Little Gladys, the Child Wonder, youngest performer in Australia':[5]

> Little Gladys, with her engaging ways and really clever dances, established herself as a popular favourite. In such songs as 'Skylark', 'Barney' and 'Oh, Mr. Station Master' she scored brilliantly, and in her dances her every movement was followed with rapt interest by the crowd.[6]

An even younger artist joined the family show when Keith became the 'Pocket Comedian':

> It requires no small amount of talent for a family, comprising two adults and two children, to give an entire evening's entertainment without wearying an audience. That is, however, what the Shaw family did on the two occasions they appeared at the Town Hall. Opening on Tuesday night to a large audience, they submitted a musical programme which occupied two hours and a half, and right up to the end encores were demanded...A welcome element of humour was supplied by Master Keith, aptly described as the 'Pocket Comedian'. This young gentleman was thoroughly self-possessed and reeled off comic song after comic song with a facility and clearness that was remarkable. He caused no end of fun and the audience insisted on his reappearance over and over again. Little Gladys completed the quartette and pleased hugely with a number of serio-comic songs tunefully given. Both concerts were enjoyable, and they formed an agreeable holiday attraction.[7]

In Greenbushes, a small timber and mining town, the Shaws quickly won local recognition for their appearances in a fundraiser for a new hospital. And Mary Agnes earned special praise for her role in organising and appearing in a concert that made more than £20 to help a newly widowed neighbour. Gladys and Keith were, unusually, photographed with other children in Greenbushes. On the back of that image, now faded beyond recognition, someone – perhaps Mary Agnes – noted that the youngsters were the Smiths and that the photograph was taken at their home.

Greenbushes was a far cry from the Sydney of her early success, yet by the age of forty-three Mary Agnes may have developed more modest ambitions: to settle somewhere and have a home, neighbours, and friends for her children. They were now eleven and nine years old and though Mary Agnes had given them an education herself, especially in music, they'd had precious little schooling.

But Gerald had other plans – schemes requiring his presence in Melbourne. The Shaws were soon on the move again, making their way back to the eastern side of the continent, entertaining audiences in South Australian and Victorian towns along the way. In Mount Gambier, 'Master Keith provided the humorous element', whilst 'Little Miss Gladys Shaw's' best numbers were reported to be '"If the Man in the Moon Were a Coon" and "The Sheeny Coon" and another, "Mignonette" with which she scored her success of the evening. She also took part in several dances with Master Keith'.[8]

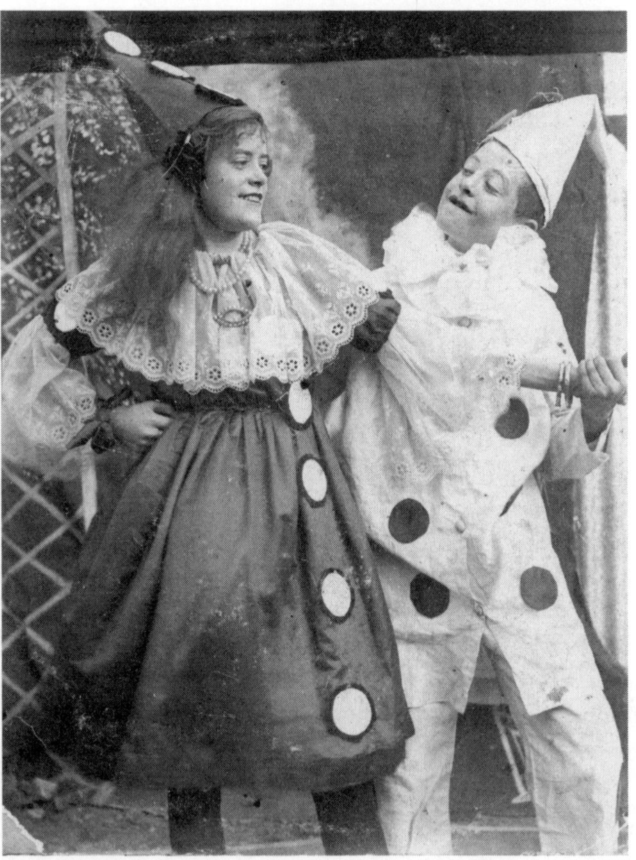

Little Miss Gladys and Master Keith, ca. 1909

Meanwhile their father was plotting an entirely different kind of show. In Melbourne he issued a prospectus to raise capital for his latest enterprise, one for which he – Gerald Shaw – resumed the identity of Harry Morewood Thomson.

According to the *West Australian*:

> Sunnyside Prospecting Company was formed in Melbourne for the purpose of despatching to Western Australia Messrs. H. Morewood Thomson and John Duffy to secure gold-mining leases in a new belt of auriferous country discovered by Mr. Thomson, lying between the Murchison and Coolgardie goldfields, and to acquire the Golden Mile leases, formerly known as Cheriton's Find, about fifty miles south of Southern Cross. The locality of the newly discovered find made by Mr Thomson is certainly vaguely enough indicated.[9]

Having raised at least some of the funds needed, Gerald returned to that vague location. He left his children and Mary Agnes, pregnant again at forty-four, to make their way to Sydney.

There Gladys and Keith would meet their half-brothers Reg and Leslie, now young men of nineteen and eighteen years. They must have appeared grown-up to Mary Agnes's younger children, who found companions closer in age among their cousins. By now Maud had five children, the youngest of whom was only four. Into this newly reacquainted family Mary Agnes would bring yet another child when she gave birth to Gerald in March 1908.

He was given a mouthful of monikers. Gerald was his father's assumed name and Morewood his father's genuine middle name. Warrington was Mary Agnes's maiden name and Connolly that of a man who divorced her eight years earlier. More than a century later I would thank her for the puzzle of Gerald Morewood Warrington Connolly's name. It held vital clues that helped me unravel the mysteries of a family tree which was more like a thicket – of maiden names, married names, false names and stage names. For most of his life, Gerald junior would be known as Gerry.

Whilst in Sydney, Mary Agnes visited her mother, Mary Gertrude, who remained in an asylum. Transferred from Callan Park to Rydalmere Hospital in 1905, by now she'd spent twenty-three of her sixty-nine years in establishments for care of the insane. As well as the suffering this inflicted upon Mary Gertrude, it also meant that Mary Agnes and her young children endured a poverty unrelieved by help from their family.

Mary Gertrude's properties were still managed by the New South Wales Master in Lunacy, though he had a plan to dispose of them. A letter from the master's office in Chancery Square advised Mary Agnes of a proposal to apply to the Court for permission to sell, 'with a view to discharging the mortgage debt on the property and liquidating the arrears of maintenance due to the Crown for [the] patient's support'. How the properties came to be mortgaged is unclear. I've always wondered whether Mary Gertrude's husband, John Warrington, coerced her into mortgaging her inheritance before she was hospitalised. He paid for her maintenance in state asylums, but since his death payments for her care had been neglected. In any event, money was now owed and the Master in Lunacy was eager to see the debt recovered.

According to Gerald, however, the family's prospects were improving. At the beginning of 1908 the *Sunday Times* reported that he was 'up to his waist in mining', working on the Never Never goldfield leases, 230 miles east of Perth and south of Southern Cross. The paper claimed he'd produced samples of the riches to be found at his mine site (described as his 'show' by the *Times*) '...which if – we repeat IF – they came from the show partnered by Shaw should land him a fortune'.[10]

In Perth he was still known as 'Gerald Shaw', but around the Never Never lease they knew him as Harry. When things began to go wrong, Harry Morewood Thomson was the culprit named in the *Southern Cross Times*.

Under the headline 'Thomson's Lying Masterpiece', the newspaper reported that Harry Morewood Thomson had penned a document attached to a prospectus issued by the Sunnyside Prospecting Company. In it he recounted that a group of Aboriginal people had passed on a tip to his wife. It was corroborated by an old prospector and had inspired his expedition to reach the fields of plenty – by bicycle. 'None but a past master in the art of lying', said the *Times* report, 'could invent and put into cold type the lies about bicycle journeys, hard level country, ironstone outcrops etc.' It claimed that Harry had gone even further, over a period of months embroidering the story of rich gold deposits, 'to hypnotise credulous people and draw from them that which could be conveniently converted into a balm for the dryness which affected the internal membranes of H. Moresulphur Thomson's neck.'[11] The report concluded, 'For barefaced lying, Thomson could give the late Baron Munchhausen a lead of many furlongs and win in a canter.'[12]

Harry Thomson, miner, thought it high time to become 'Gerald Shaw', entertainer, once more. By September 'Gerald' was in Adelaide, appearing at the Tivoli Theatre with George Sorlie, an English-born comedian of West Indian ancestry, later to become famous for his travelling tent shows. Then he moved on to Victoria. Meanwhile back in Perth, where Gerald and Harry were now known to be the same man, it was clear that neither the change of location, nor of name, had rescued his reputation:

> Gerald Shaw, the deep-voiced basso, who did a season at Cremorne a few years back and afterwards was mixed up in a boom wild cat near Southern Cross, was recently located doing a professional perish in a way-back bush township in Victoria. Shaw had a fine voice, but had absolutely no soul or fire.[13]

Mary Agnes's new baby, Gerry, was nearly nine months old when he first met his father. Reunited, the Shaw family took to the road, touring New South Wales, Victoria and South Australia. In Little River, Gerald's mother Fanny added to her will a note about the birth of her new grandchild, who would share any money Fanny might leave. But there would be little family help from that quarter. Gladys, Keith and Gerry had twenty-three cousins on their father's side, and would receive only a tiny inheritance when Fanny died the following year.

The children were doing their best to earn an income. 'The Marvellous Shaws', said the *Riverina Recorder* early in 1909, made a talented company. Master Keith, said the journal:

> ...gives imitations of the leading English and American character comedians such as Little Tich and Dan Leno...The extreme youth of this clever performer, coupled with his marvellous power of imitation, captured all hearts.[14]

Dan Leno had been dead for six years before Master Keith mimicked him in 1909, though young Keith may have seen film of the renowned Leno performing. Little Tich also made films and had appeared live in Perth in 1905, when Gerald, and even seven-year-old Keith might have been in his audience. The West Australian's critic described the English star as:

> ...a comic singer, agile dancer, droll talker, natural comedy actor, and the clever master of 'business' and 'patter.' Imagine these in four feet of irresistible personality, with the activity of a rubber ball, and an idea will be gained of 'Little Tich.'[15]

In Balranald Little Gladys was not as enthusiastically received as her brother Keith and his imitations of famous comedians, but she was also an attraction who 'sings and dances with an ease and grace seldom seen in one so young'.[16] And 'Madam Marie' (Mary Agnes) was described as an American mezzo-soprano who, like Gerald, had enjoyed great success abroad. It seems Gerald was as imaginative when embellishing his family's performing past as he had been in promoting his mining prospects.

Gerry, the youngest member of the family, later recalled that he was 'reared in the wings of a small travelling show...sleeping with

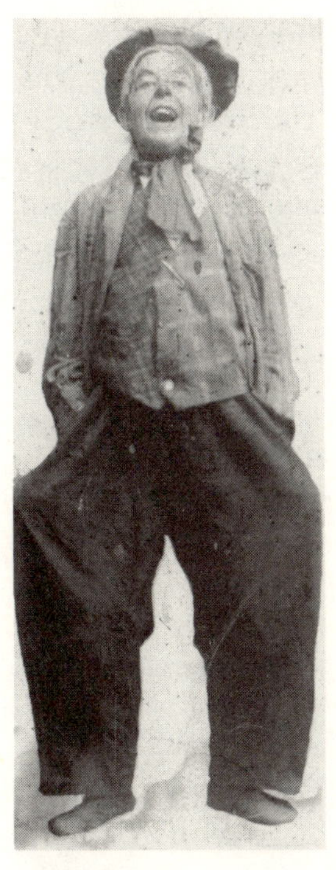

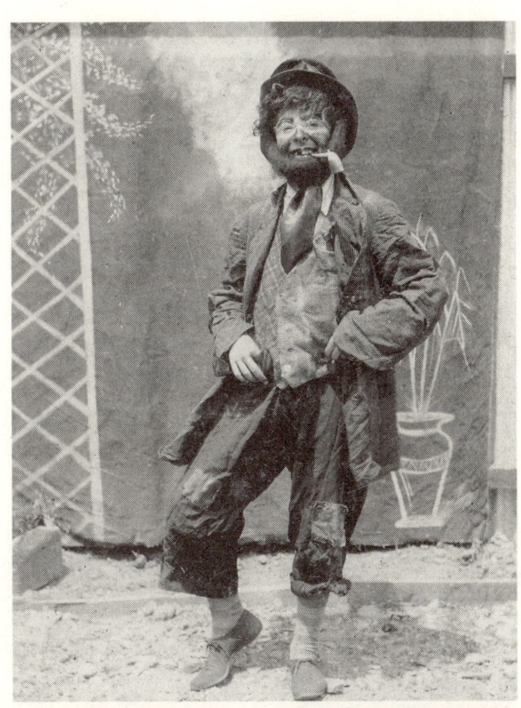

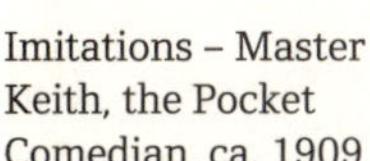

Imitations – Master Keith, the Pocket Comedian, ca. 1909

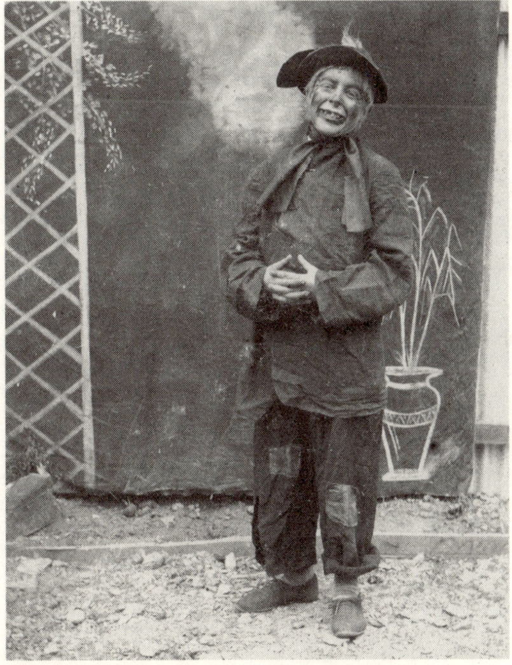

the aid of brandy and milk in a prop basket'.[17] He said of the family troupe:'One thing about our show – we could always come back to the same towns, and that was something of a proud claim in those days.'[18] Gerry was too young to have known about his father's unpaid debts in Bendigo and Perth, nor about his fraudulent mining ventures near Southern Cross.

Mary Agnes had done her best to cloak the family in fresh disguises. Her skill as a dressmaker was such that the Shaw Company's costumes were said to have been made by Zenda, Sydney's best known theatrical costumier.[19] When they were photographed early in 1910, the family and its fellow artists wore costumes loosely inspired by *commedia*

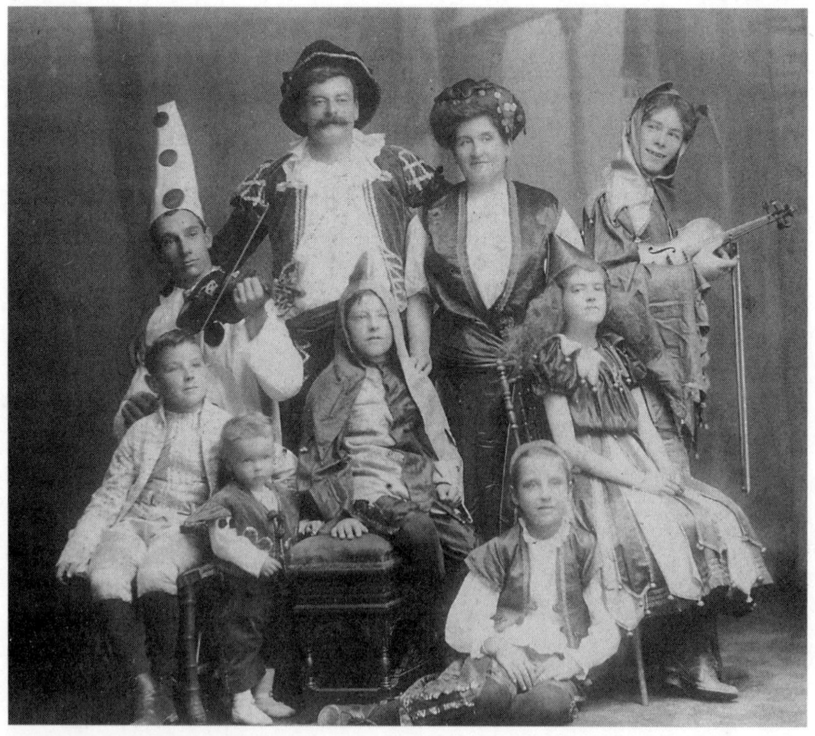

'The English Pierrots,' ca. 1910

del arte. The stock figures of popular Italian comedy had long ago been appropriated by performers around the world, so Mary Agnes's interpretations were more the dress of English pantomime artists than the original garb of the Italians. Indeed, in the backblocks of New South Wales the Shaws were 'The English Pierrots', 'a company of high-class concert and variety entertainers'.[20]

Gladys, a young-looking fourteen-year-old, doesn't look very happy in the English Pierrots' photograph. Maybe she was bored, exasperated by sitting still for the camera. Or maybe she was fretting about her father's latest plan. Shortly after the photograph was taken, the Shaw family returned to Western Australia, a move Keith would later describe:

> ...the big Bullfinch gold rush broke out. Father got gold fever, so away we went – back to the Golden West. We made for Northam...[21]

The Shaws ventured further along the eastern goldfields railway line, shameless Gerald leading them from Northam to Southern Cross. There he went to some lengths to repair his good name – or at least his original one, Harry Thomson. At the Mechanics Institute, in celebration of the king's birthday, he appeared in an entertainment dubbed 'The Prospectors', the format for which was previewed in the *Southern Cross Times:*

> The scheme is to portray first, the camp of a body of prospectors, when round the fire, after the day's work is done, the evening is beguiled by song. Later, all of them having been successful in their quest for gold, [they] return to their homes and foregather at the house of one of their number where, inside the more civilised condition of things, they have a musical re-union.[22]

The same newspaper, the very one that only three years earlier accused Harry Morewood Thomson of being a more accomplished liar than Baron Munchausen, now spoke highly of his efforts in painting a drop curtain for the town's Stadium. It promised to be, said the *Southern Cross Times*:

> ...something unique in the way of design advertising. We have seen the plans and can safely say there is nothing approaching it in W.A., and when completed and hung in position, will add greatly to the finish and beauty of this favorite amusement resort. Mr. Thomson having carried out similar work for Sydney and Melbourne theatres to the entire satisfaction of the various managements, can be relied upon to do full justice to the work he has in hand.[23]

In the nearby town of Marvel Loch, the English Pierrots met with a great reception. Gerald's singing 'evoked unstinted applause', Mary Agnes sang and even yodelled with much 'spirit and dramatic effect', and Master Keith 'kept the audience in roars of laughter.' Little Gladys was praised too:

> A great attraction with this talented company is the appearance of Little Gladys. This gifted little artiste established herself as a warm favorite from the outset, her fresh young voice, combined with her graceful dancing being a revelation, and appealing irresistibly to her listeners, who applauded her to the echo.[24]

Family life, however, was less delightful. Despite Gerald's attempts to be of better character, his old habits persisted. Years later Keith made light of them:

> You know father was a sort of sporting man, and was always playing cards for money. Poker seemed to be his hobby, and he would go without eating any time to play it. In fact, after playing poker the whole family used to go without eating for a while...One peculiar thing about it was, if father did happen to come home from downtown and had been drinking, mother could always tell it instantly. All she had to do was to go to the door and look at him and she would come back and say, 'Boys, your father has been drinking.' Sis and I could never tell. When we went to the door and looked at him we used to think he was dead.[25]

But Gerald did at last strike gold, albeit in a small way. According to Keith:

> the old 'pot and pan' was lucky enough to make a find – yes a handy little nugget worth close on £100. That was at a place called Parker's Range, a little below Southern Cross. So we quit the gold-digging stunt and made for Perth.[26]

Gladys and Keith saw in the new year of 1912 onstage at Perth's Palace Gardens. Gerald was reportedly too unwell to perform, but the 'Prince of the Singers of Illustrated Songs' joined his children in the days after New Year. He sang 'Follow the Crowds on a Sunday', and brought the house down with his big voice, accompanying a film of the weekend's races. These December and January appearances would be the Shaw family's last.

Gerald found himself a new interest – a promising tin deposit at Coodardy in the Weld Range of Western Australia, north-east of Perth. He named it 'Gladys'. Newspaper reports waxed lyrical about the potential for mining in the area, and of the Thomson Coates operation, for which one Gerald Shaw was the spokesperson. His mine soon disappeared from the news, but one venture led to another and out there beyond the rabbit-proof fence Gerald gradually faded from family life. Mary Agnes simply could not or would not follow him any further. She turned fifty in 1914, with a seven-year-old to raise and two teenagers to watch over. It might have been too hard to go on looking after Gerald as well, and to continue trailing him from one disaster to the next.

She could play the piano, sing and even yodel. So she stayed in Perth where, for the next seven years, she gave lessons in voice production, training students for the concert stage. She promoted her services with modest one-and two-line newspaper advertisements in the personal columns, amid notices for seamstresses, graphologists and money lenders:

> Consult me about your voice. Pupils trained for stage. Madam Marie Shaw, Balcatta, the Esplanade, next Technical school.[27]

Mary Agnes no longer had Gerald to embellish her copy, nor to complicate her life. Perched on the western edge of a continent not yet connected by rail, far from her oldest sons, her demented mother and dreams she'd shared with Adelaide Cushman twenty years earlier, Mary Agnes made do. She could take care of herself and her children. Though Gerry was still small and in need of parenting, Keith was almost old enough to look after himself. And Gladys was beautiful, clever and talented.

5
The Tango Girls

As she'd promised years earlier, Mary Agnes had raised her only daughter for a life on the stage. Gladys even assumed the surname of her mother's alter-ego, Claire Delmar, when, in 1914, she became a 'Delmar Sister', half of a duo also billed as the 'Tango Girls'. At eighteen, Gladys Shaw was one half; the other went by the rather blowsy name of Gloria Delmar. Gloria may have been thirty-seven-year-old Madam Millie Verto, wife and onstage assistant of The Great Verto, escapologist, magician, and the picture-show man who'd once transported Gladys to a cinematic moon.

Recently returned from Singapore, the Vertos and the Tango Girls entertained Western Australian towns with films, conjuring tricks, songs and demonstrations of the tango. In the agricultural town of Moora, the dancing of 'the ladies' was highly praised:

> Miss Gladys Shaw, the well-known serio, delighted all by her rendering of two songs, and later on, with Miss Gloria Delmar, appeared in the Tango dance. The ladies went through the different steps with precision, and the elegance of their movements was indeed beautiful, showing that both were adept in the terpsichorian art. They also danced the Hesitation Waltz together, earning the hearty approval of the audience.[1]

This made the tango and those who performed it seem almost respectable. Elsewhere, however, the new dance craze was regarded quite differently:

The Tango Girl

…She is found at Tango breakfasts,
Tango suppers, Tango teas
While she wears a Tango petticoat
And Tango (p'r'aps!) chemise
She will Tango in the morning
In the eve or afternoon,
If she doesn't Tango too in bed
No doubt she'll start it soon.

…Yet she still is discontented
And she'll absolutely swear
That she finds her movements hampered
By the clothes she's got to wear
And she'll not be really happy
I am absolutely sure
Till she's allowed to do the Tango
In the costumes that Eve wore.[2]

New technologies – gramophone records and moving pictures – carried the dance from Argentina to Europe and then to the United States. From there, mass marketing campaigns spread it to all corners of the globe. The tango came to Australia branded as romantic, risqué and decidedly modern. It connected Gladys, at least in her imagination, with exotic, sophisticated life in cities far from Western Australia. The craze didn't last long, but it left its mark on the way young women dressed, and indeed on the way they saw themselves. Their clothes were already changing, but the tango hastened the demise of constricting corsets and hobble skirts.

Gladys wasn't much bothered by any suggestion that she lacked respectability. She may have been inspired by Daisy Jerome, a United States-born comedienne and singer of the English music hall, who specialised in being unconventional. Daisy was known as 'The Electric Spark'. She had a shock of red hair that gave rise to great speculation. Was it natural? Passing through Western Australia en route to Sydney in 1913, she allowed journalists to interview her whilst she remained in her berth aboard SS *Orsova*. Her meeting with the press was merely the first titbit of gossip salacious enough to pique public curiosity, without alienating her admirers. By the time Daisy returned to Perth after a year on the stages of the eastern states, she was most eagerly awaited. Descriptions of earlier appearances preceded her and suggested how she won over her Australian audiences:

> ...Her manner and methods were different. Her personality was remarkable, to say the least, and the means she took to 'reach over the footlights' and 'get the people' had to be got used to. As a matter of fact, they considered Miss Jerome was an 'acquired taste'. But they did get used to her. From amazement and puzzlement the audience went to admiration and appreciation.[3]

Roy Rene (the great comedian also known as Mo) put it more bluntly: 'She was a good artist...She got the crowd all right. She used to give them the stuff semi-blue. I should think that quite a number of people would remember her'.[4] If Perth audiences weren't struck by her lewdness, they couldn't fail to notice her outspokenness:

> 'I went into vaudeville because there is more money in it.' That is the candid confession of Miss Daisy Jerome, probably the most popular vaudeville artist in Australia at the present time. Miss Jerome, after a triumphant tour of the Eastern States, has come to Perth, and will appear at the Melrose Theatre on Saturday night...'Not that my aim is to be a millionaire,' explained the artist when she had finished her second song. 'Were I a politician, I would probably be something akin to a Socialist. I believe, I think, in the equality of all.'[5]

Daisy Jerome's first visit to Australia came as Gladys and her brother Keith were weighing up their own theatrical options. Like Daisy, money determined their decisions. In their father's absence, they needed not only to support themselves but also to contribute to the upkeep of their mother and young Gerry.

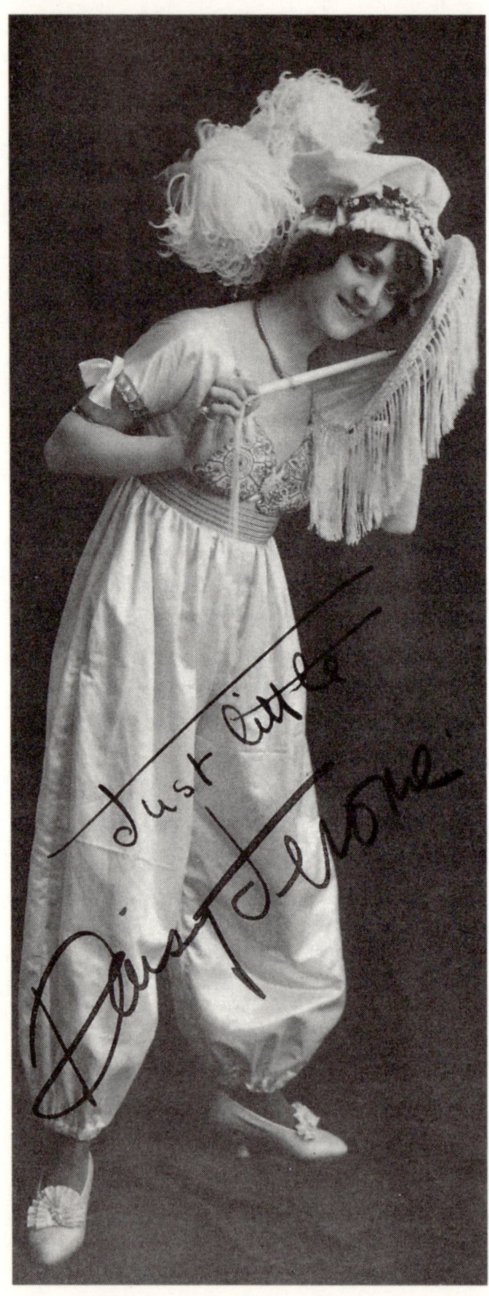

Daisy Jerome, ca. 1914–1923

They were a double act onstage and off, a theatrical partnership, brother and sister. Moving about so much had given them few opportunities to forge other lasting relationships. With her mother busy teaching aspiring entertainers and caring for her youngest child, Gladys had assumed a big sister's responsibilities, watching over Keith from her position as senior of the pair. They didn't have the advantages of formal education, settled family or financial security, but they did have each other.

What they didn't have was Gerald. Although he'd gambled most of the takings on card games and mining misadventures, he had been the Shaw Family manager and promoter. Without him, Gladys and Keith had to find their own work.

While Gladys tangoed her way around the Western Australian wheatbelt, Keith went on the road with the Young Australia League, an organisation formed in WA to foster nationalism and to 'educate through travel'. Selected as one of forty boys to visit North America and the United Kingdom on the League's second overseas tour, Keith first travelled around WA with the entertainers of the party, raising funds for the overseas trip. No longer the 'pocket comedian', at sixteen and seventeen he was billed as a 'clever patter comedian'. Appearing among instrumentalists and acrobats, his performances received enthusiastic reviews. Pictures show him loose-limbed, wearing clown-like make-up, a broom slung over his shoulder.

In August 1914 the declaration of war caused the League to abandon its travel plans. For some months Keith remained part of its entertainment troupe, performing to raise funds for the war effort. But Keith wasn't on board when the League party did finally set sail in early 1915, with a new itinerary that omitted the United Kingdom.

After appearing as a Tango Girl, Gladys was beginning to attract admirers. A young man named Wilbur sent her photographs in which he shone with good nature and good looks. Gladys, it seemed, had well and truly put her child wonder identity behind her.

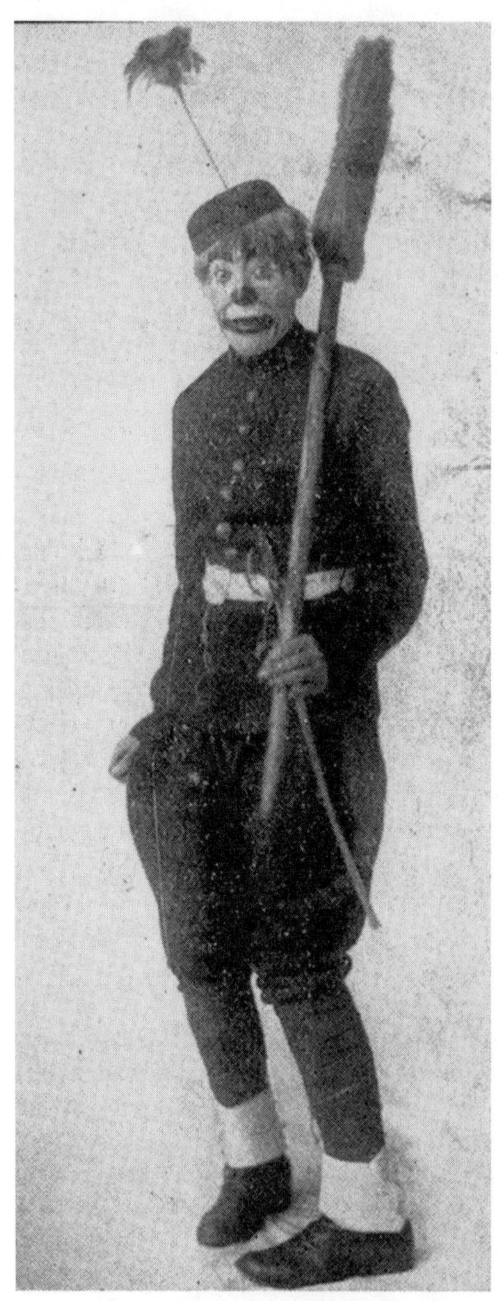

'A clever patter comedian,'
Keith Shaw (Connolly), 1914

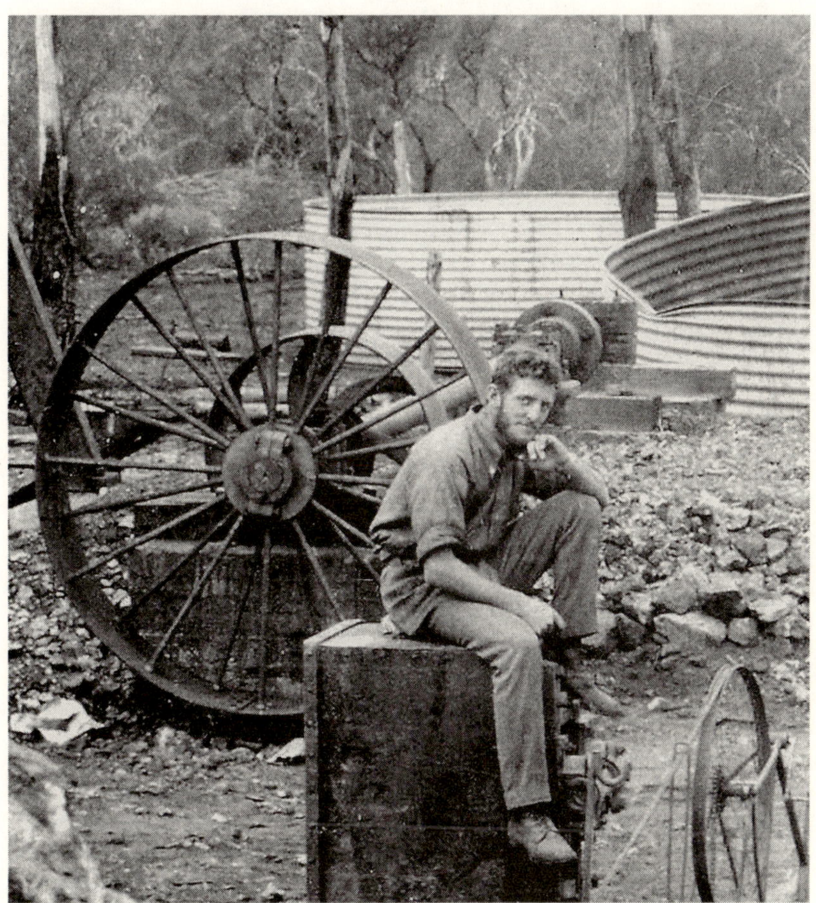

'To Gladdie, from Wilbur', 1915

On the back of his photographs, Wilbur sent his compliments from Warriedar, a few hundred miles north-east of Perth. He dated the images he sent to 'Gladdie'. All were taken in 1915, a year in which young men like Wilbur were thinking about going to war.

Keith however was too young to enlist. No longer an entertainer with the League, he took a new stage name and continued performing. 'Wilf Connolly – the living marionette' appeared out of nowhere in

April at Adelaide's Tivoli Theatre and in Brisbane in June of 1915. Descriptions of Wilf in advertisements and a handful of newspaper mentions evoke a puppet-like performer in heavy make-up, not unlike the picture of Keith Shaw in his League photographs. But following appearances in regional Queensland in July and August, 'Wilf' Connolly was never heard of again. Perhaps Keith then joined Gerald to mine molybdenite, used in steelmaking, at his latest excavation in Yalgoo – 300 miles north of Perth. Mining experience, gleaned during his father's various mineral misadventures, would ultimately qualify Keith for some of the most dangerous work of all.

Two weeks after his eighteenth birthday Keith enlisted, using the surname Connolly rather than Shaw. Suspecting his mother wouldn't agree with his decision to join up, and with no father in Perth to sign the forms, he claimed to be twenty-one, an age at which parental permission was unnecessary. Mary Agnes was recorded as his next of kin and a note on his enlistment papers said his father was seldom at home. In March 1916 he sailed for France, where he was assigned to the 1st Australian Tunnelling Company.[6]

Six months later Gladys turned twenty-one, having returned to live with her mother and eight-year-old Gerry in Perth. They had rooms in a Hay Street boarding house when Gladys enrolled to vote, soon after her birthday. She would cast her first ballot in an historic plebiscite to determine whether conscription should be introduced. Voters were asked:

> Are you in favour of the Government having, in this grave emergency, the same compulsory powers over citizens in regard to requiring their military service, for the term of this war, outside the Commonwealth, as it now has in regard to military service within the Commonwealth?

Gladys and her mother were no doubt torn between the argument for a 'no' vote and the view that only a 'yes' result would help those already fighting. It would be another decade before Gerry was old enough to be called up, but they wouldn't have wanted to see him go to war too. Yet according to those in favour of conscription, young men already fighting – Keith and perhaps Gladys's admirer Wilbur among them – would be betrayed by a vote against it.

Keith had arrived in France in May 1916 and travelled from Marseilles to Hazebrouck, near Ypres, in Belgium. As a tunneller, or 'sapper', he worked above and below ground, digging trenches and tunnels. By October, when Gladys cast her first vote, he was stationed near Hill 60.

Of the six shillings he was paid for each day of service, he kept only one. Another was deferred until discharge, and the remaining four were paid to his mother.

Gladys did her bit to pay her own way, working as a cashier at the Grand Theatre, one of five dedicated cinemas opened in Perth during the war. It boasted *a modern scheme of ventilation* and a design *to accommodate any rush*.[7]

Between shifts in the cashier's booth at the Barrack Street entrance, Gladys saw films which showed continuously throughout the day and into the evening. She experienced war through newsreels – usually of British origin – of patriotic parades and the good-humoured labours of boys like Keith, casually smoking cigarette after cigarette as they dug trenches, moved ammunition and supplies, and marched endlessly through the French countryside. It was footage that largely avoided ghastly truths of death and mutilation in bloody, muddy, rat-infested bunkers.

One film, *The Battle of the Somme*, did include scenes of battle and something of their aftermath.[8] British Prime Minister Lloyd George said at its London premiere:

> I am convinced that when you have seen this wonderful picture every heart will beat faster in sympathy with its cause and purpose. Mothers, wives, sisters and affianced ones, your hearts will beat, your voices will speak in honour and glory of the living

> and the dead. You are great and powerful. This is your mission. See that this film reaches everyone.[9]

In Perth it screened at the Pavilion in Hay Street in the lead-up to the 1916 plebiscite. Six thousand people saw it in just one record-breaking day of its extended season. On 28 October 1916 Australians answered 'yes' and 'no' to conscription in almost equal numbers, though in the end the 'no' vote prevailed and Prime Minister Billy Hughes could not implement his compulsory call-up plans. But Western Australia recorded the highest 'yes' vote in the land.

At Hill 60, south of Ypres, Keith excavated tunnels and laid mines which were exploded at the beginning of the Battle of Messines in June 1917. The explosion was felt as far away as London; some said even Dublin. By September he was in the Hooge crater, in an area where 11 000 Australians were killed or wounded in little more than a week, many of them in the Battle of the Menin Road on 20 September.

Australian photographer and official war cameraman, Frank Hurley, was there too. Venturing up the Menin Road on 17 September, he described it as 'the Valley of Death...It is the most gruesome shambles I have ever seen'. At Hooge, where Keith and the First Australian Tunnellers were excavating dugouts to make new headquarters, Hurley reported:

> It is a wretched job as they are working 25 feet below the surface level and most of the time knee deep in mud. From the roof trickles water and mud, which they jocularly term 'hero juice' on account of it percolating through tiers and tiers of buried corpses.[10]

In Perth, Gladys knew nothing of this. News of casualties fuelled her fears for Keith, but the tunnellers' role on the western front remained largely secret and unremarked. Newspapers emphasised the heroics of Australian soldiers in combat, rather than the horrors they experienced underground and in the trenches. Frank Hurley's film *Fighting in Flanders* might have given Gladys some idea of what her brother was enduring, but it didn't screen until the war was over.

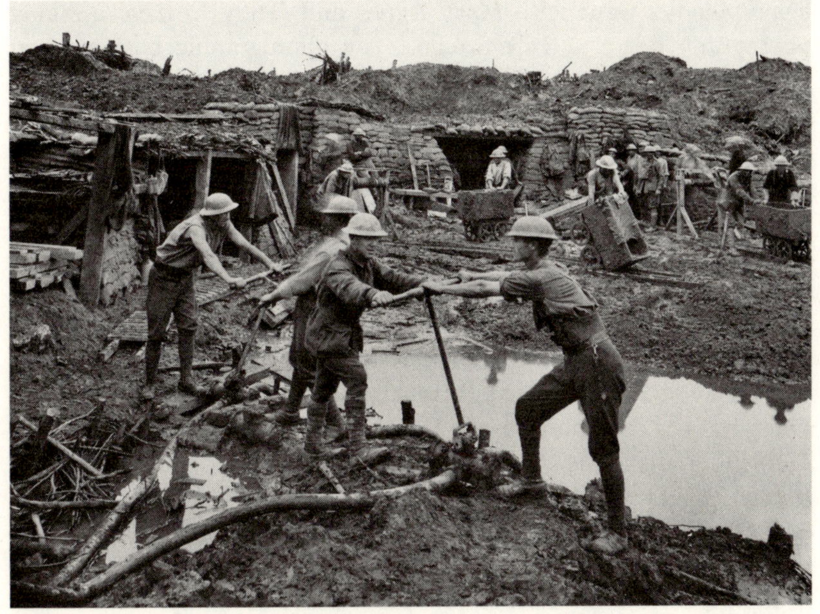

Excavating at Hooge, Frank Hurley AWM E01396

Nor would she have seen the photographs I found in Grandma Elsie's zither case. They were Hurley's images of Hooge, reproduced years after the war. They showed Australian soldiers at work, pumping water out of muddy trenches. On the back, in pencil, Keith had scrawled 'September 18, Hooge'. It was the day before the dug-outs were handed over to troops who would enter the third battle of Ypres.

I don't know why Keith had those images. It's hard to make out whether he is actually among the troops Hurley filmed that day, though the records show that he was there. Maybe, many years later, Keith needed visual proof that his experiences on the Western Front weren't a nightmare or some terrible hallucination.

By the time of a second conscription plebiscite in December 1917, Keith had been at the front for eighteen months. Shortly before voting again, Gladys went with Mary Agnes and Gerry to have a family photograph taken at Falk Studios. The photographic business had expanded considerably since Sarah Bernhardt and Adelaide Cushman had their portraits made in Sydney some twenty-five years earlier. Now it had branches in Sydney, Melbourne and Perth. Australian families flocked to these and hundreds of similar studios, to have their wartime images recorded. Some were sent abroad to comfort husbands, sons and brothers at the front; others froze in time the faces of young men who would be lost forever, killed or damaged beyond recognition.

Australia again said 'no' to conscription at the end of 1917. Having survived Passchendaele, Keith remained in the danger zone of the enlarged territory known as the Ypres Salient. There the 1st Australian Tunnelling Company constructed and repaired dugouts across an 8-kilometre front. Though the winter was relatively mild and there were rum rations at the end of each underground shift, there was little respite from German explosive and mustard gas shellfire. In January 1918 he received the photograph of his fatherless family.

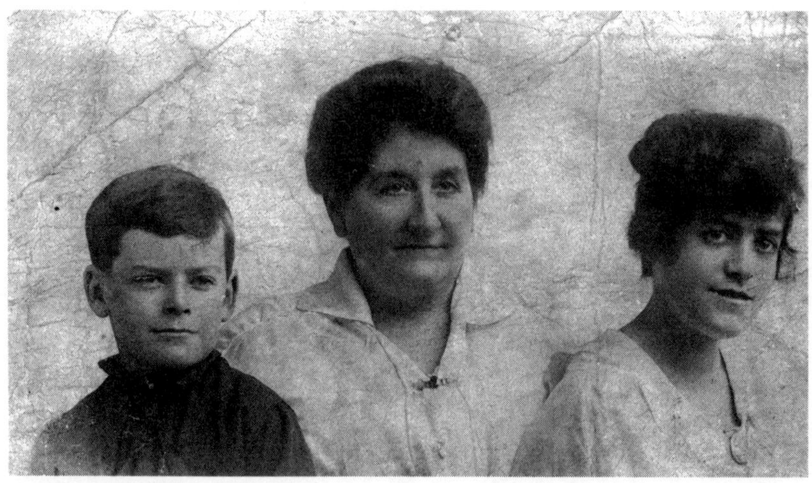

Gerry, Mary Agnes and Gladys, 1917

6
Heaven Will Protect a Working Girl

At Perth's Grand theatre, Gladys sold tickets for programs that included newsreels and war propaganda. But most patrons handed over their money for Hollywood features starring Charlie Chaplin, Mary Pickford, Theda Bara and Australia's own Louise Lovely.

Also screening in Perth cinemas were Australian productions – mostly filmed plays and war dramas. Though there were fewer local films than before the war, in 1917 Gladys might have seen *Mutiny on the Bounty*, *The Church and the Woman*, *The Martyrdom of Nurse Cavell* and *The Joan of Arc of Loos*. They starred famous names like Lottie Lyell and Vera Pearce, and a less well-known young woman named Jane King. Gladys would have seen her play Emilienne Moreau, a true French wartime heroine, in *The Joan of Arc of Loos*. Jane played Emilienne as a warrior who not only tended the wounded, but also lobbed grenades at enemy snipers. Then, inspired by a vision of an angel of war, she rallied retreating Allies. 'Waving a bullet-swept flag and the tricolor of France, and singing the Marseillaise, she turned the tide of battle from the shame of defeat to the glory of victory'.[1] Moreau won both a medal and her man.

But audiences were wearying of war-mongering, or wary of it. *The Joan of Arc of Loos* didn't win stardom for Jane King.[2] Indeed her depiction of a female combatant offended some cinema patrons. The angel, played by Jean Robertson, was singled out for more praise. *The Joan of Arc of Loos* failed at the box office.

Front of house at the Grand, Gladys was doing her best to succeed *in* the box office. Her time there was later recalled in Perth newspaper, the *Mirror*:

> Many years ago in the ticket seller's box in the Barrack-street entrance to the Grand Theatre, a young lady attended daily to hand over small bits of cardboard in exchange for various pieces of silver. In between times, in the off moments, said g'rleen used to amuse her fellow usherettes and ticket taking belles by giving remarkable imitations of Theda Bara (then a boom on the screen), and piercing their ears by shrill but clever whistling imitations. That girl was Gladys Shaw.[3]

The ticket-seller's box was never going to be big enough for Gladys. She was twenty-two and eager to be on the stage once more, even if it meant using her absent father's connections to secure theatrical engagements. She would keep his phony surname, with which she'd earned a small degree of celebrity as Little Gladys Shaw 'the child wonder', and a little more as 'a dashing serio and instrumentaliste'[4] when she'd appeared as a more grown-up performer shortly before the war.

Percy Dennis, bookmaker and entrepreneur, engaged Gladys for a season at Kalgoorlie's Palace Theatre in July 1918. He must have thought her father's name still counted for something, as he dropped it into advance publicity for Gladys's return to the stage:

> Gladys Shaw, on Dennis' goldfields bill, won vaudeville fame as Baby Shaw a few seasons ago, and was popular on every stage in the West. Brother Keith is on active service with the Tunnellers, and Pa Shaw, well known as Gerald Shaw, the showman, has molybdenite interests near Yalgoo.[5]

This publicity effort was penned by a writer who either didn't know or wasn't telling the whole truth about Gerald's circumstances. He'd again reverted to the name Harry Thomson, with which he'd started out in life. And his name was not the only thing he'd changed. The year before Gladys returned to the stage, Harry Morewood Thomson married Cecilia Law Hutchison in Wollongong. By 1918 he was nowhere near Yalgoo, but in East Gippsland in Victoria, managing the revival of a gold mine.

Nonetheless his daughter was a hit on the Western Australian goldfields circuit. At Kalgoorlie's Palace Theatre 'shrieks of laughter again followed the antics of Miss Gladys Shaw whose ability as a burlesque and patter artiste is undoubted'.[6] Returning from the goldfields to the coast, she continued working for Percy Dennis at the King's Theatre in Fremantle. There she took a small role in Arthur Morley's 'oriental revue', *The Island of Spice*. Though advertised as a revue, it was more like a one-act musical comedy. Sometimes known as 'revusicals', such revues with storylines were developing as a uniquely Australian theatrical form.[7] Where revues consisted of comic sketches, musical and novelty acts sometimes loosely linked by theme, the revusical folded those ingredients into a crude plot.

Gladys – whose mother Mary Agnes was once a burlesque artist, and whose father Gerald appeared in many a minstrel show farce – was familiar with the theatrical antecedents of the revusical. She might have learned more by following the career of Daisy Jerome, star of *Come Over Here*, the first revue show of its type produced in Australia. Gladys was well prepared to play her own part in the story of the revusical's rise and fall, as well as that of May, 'a tourist in Rubiana' in *The Island of Spice*.

She'd not long finished an engagement with Percy Dennis's Frivolities company at Perth's Shaftesbury Theatre, when news of the armistice arrived. Local reaction was described by a journalist moved to lyricism:

> When the third boom of the Observatory gun had sounded, people knew that Rumor had made her exit and Fact had entered. Then, in every home, humble cottage alike with splendid mansion, broke forth the music of the heart. Streets quickly began to fill with people, there was a rush citywards, trams carrying such crowds as had never been carried before, and leaving thousands by the wayside.[8]

The celebrations were memorable – especially for those associated with the Shaftesbury. There were few arrests for anything more serious than drunkenness, but hundreds of young men wrecked the Shaftesbury Theatre's iron gates.

The end of hostilities elicited no such exuberance from Keith and his fellow tunnellers in Belgium. Captain Oliver Woodward described their response to the announcement of war's end:

> …officers and men moved quietly about from one group to another giving and receiving a handshake among comrades. It was an occasion too great for words…we felt to the full the real comradeship of war and the realisation that the distasteful task had ended.[9]

Keith would remain in Belgium for a further three months. He turned twenty-one during his third European winter, spent clearing bombs, mines and other explosives.

After the armistice Gladys returned to the goldfields. In Boulder she sang in the vaudeville part of a show which starred Bostock's menagerie with its performing tigers, 'educated monkeys' and a trained elephant. By February 1919 she was acting again, in *The Haunted House*, a farce performed for Gordon's Vaudeville Company in Northam. On the same bill, her 'whistling chorus and comic song, Heaven Protect a Working Girl' [sic], 'established her a favourite, and for each item she had to bow to an encore':[10]

A village maid was leaving home. With tears her eyes were wet.
Her mother dear was standing near the spot.
She says to her, 'Neuralgia dear, I hope you won't forget
That I'm the only mother you have got.
The city is a wicked place, as anyone can see,
And cruel dangers 'round your path may hurl;
So ev'ry week you'd better send your wages back to me,
For Heaven will protect a working girl.

You are going far away, but remember what I say
When you are in the city's giddy whirl.
From temptations, crimes, and follies,
Villains, taxicabs and trolleys,
Oh! Heaven will protect a working girl.

Her dear old mother's words proved true, for soon the poor girl met
A man who on her ruin was intent.
He treated her respectful as those villains always do,
And she supposed he was a perfect gent.
But she found diff'rent when one night she went with him to dine
Into a table d'hôte so blithe and gay,
And he says to her, 'After this we'll have a demitasse.'
Then, to him these brave words the girl did say:

'Stand back, villain! Go your way! Here I will no longer stay,
Although you were a marquis or an earl.
You may tempt the upper classes
With your villainous demitasses,
But Heaven will protect a working girl.'[11]

Unlike the mother of this burlesque hit, Mary Agnes didn't caution her only daughter. Instead she encouraged her. Gladys was only beginning to realise her mother's dreams.

She was making her own way in the world of entertainment and developing her skills, especially that of whistling. It was a talent for which she'd be known for decades to come, though it wasn't particularly ladylike. But neither was Gladys. Indeed, like many young women of the time she was testing the boundaries of acceptable female behaviour.

Perhaps the most extreme example of a Perth woman putting those boundaries to the test was Effie Fellows, male impersonator. Just two years older than Gladys, Perth-born Effie appeared as 'Freddie Manners' for Fullers' Theatres in Australia and New Zealand from 1915. She described her start as a male impersonator:

> In about the year 1912, the feeling arose within me that my nature resembled muchly what is known as a 'tomboy', and the desire to deceive everybody led to a girl pal being invested with full power to cut my hair. This she did, and then I stepped into the male attire.[12]

Effie performed in India and South Africa in 1916 before travelling further afield with her partner Piquo, the Acrobatic Clown, who would become her first husband in 1917. Her marriage might have surprised the author of a 1918 article in Perth's *Truth*, which not only made assumptions about Effie's sexuality but also accused lesbians of sybaritic and predatory behaviours:

> Our own Effie Fellows is also a case in point, known to us all, as it were. The feminine invert goes in for manly games, wears her hair short, and takes to men's occupations in general. She satisfies her pathological appetite by masturbation which, if occasion offers, is mutual. Her sexual craving is often much exalted and she then becomes a veritable Don Juan. Women of this kind have been known who held sexual orgies, and induced a whole series of young girls to become their lovers by initiating them into the practice OF MUTUAL MASTURBATION.[13]

Taking the name Bobby Folson, Effie entertained audiences in the United Kingdom, Europe, the West Indies and the United States, where she appeared alongside Al Jolson, Sophie Tucker and Stan Laurel. After returning to Australia, she was known for her signature tune, 'I've Never Seen a Straight Banana'.

Gladys, however, was more vamp than gender bender. She danced the tango, impersonated Theda Bara and admired Daisy Jerome. She earned her own living, exercised her right to vote and had no male protector – no father, older brother or husband around to cramp her style. Why shouldn't she whistle?

As a child, Gladys had shared stages with English whistling comedian Ted Box, and later with an American whistler named Harry Saunders. His was a popular skill, especially in times when newly invented

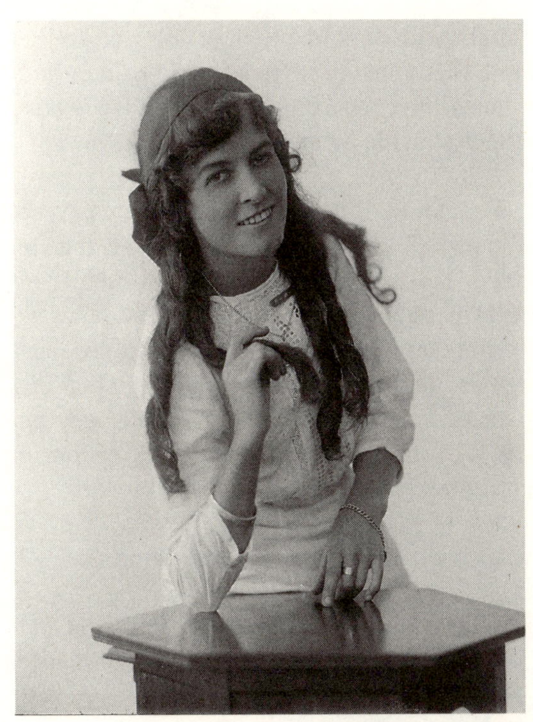

Effie Fellows, ca. 1915,
SLWA 151694PD

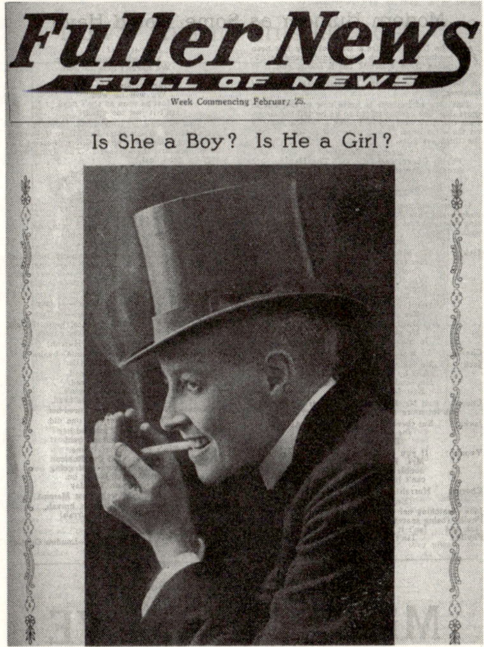

Effie Fellows, 1922

recording technologies brought whistlers like George Johnson to the ears of the world. In the late 1890s Johnson's 'The Whistling Coon' and 'The Laughing Song' were bestselling recordings in the United States, and widely thought to be the first made by an African-American.

'Lady whistlers' were not so common. But in the United States, Alice Shaw, 'La Belle Siffleuse', started something of a fad for female whistlers. She recommended the practice: 'Whistling for half an hour after meals is…the best possible aid to digestion. Try it, weak chested, slender-throated sisters mine, and profit by my experience'.[14] American music teacher Agnes Woodward formed a ladies' whistling chorus which toured in its own yellow bus. She established the California School of Artistic Whistling. And in the United Kingdom, a Miss Errol Stanhope became known as 'England's Lady Whistler'.

In late nineteenth century Australia things were a little different:

> The lady whistler is as yet almost unknown here. True, girls and young ladies blessed with brothers often get almost unconsciously into the habit of whistling a little, sometimes prettily and well. Australian girls are not, however, given to much puckering up of pretty lips for a whistle. In this respect, as in some others, the American woman has got ahead of her sisters…In spite of the emancipation of the sex, which is supposed to have taken such root as to leave little care for aught that is not masculine in its trend, I think a long time must elapse before we get quite accustomed to women and girls whistling.[15]

Like cycling, whistling was something young women were discouraged from doing. As well as disapproving columnists, there were proverbs to deter them;

> A whistling maid and a crowing hen,
> Are liked by neither gods nor men.

Yet women could not be prevented from whistling, just as they would not be kept from their bikes once they'd begun to enjoy the freedoms of cycling. And despite claims that 'lady whistlers' were unknown in Australia, the then colony of Victoria had one of its own: Daisy Chard. Her real name was Rebecca Cohen and she made her stage debut at the age of three as 'Fascinating Daisy'. She appeared in a visiting minstrel show and learned to sing and to whistle 'The Whistling Coon', which she turned into her own hit number. A highly versatile performer, she was also an actress, singer and audience favourite in 1890s Australia. She appeared with most of the leading Australian companies before her retirement from the stage around 1907. Gladys might not have seen Daisy perform, but she would have heard about her. Daisy appeared in Bendigo when 'Baby Shaw' was also there, preparing to take her earliest theatrical steps. And on the Western Australian goldfields where Gladys spent so much of her childhood, 'Daisy Chard' was at one time the nickname for a musical whistle.[16]

Another Daisy whistled for Australian audiences in the late 1890s. Daisy Merritt, later to become more famous for her comedy work, was a dancer and serio-comic who was sometimes billed as the 'Champion Lady Whistler'.[17] She performed around Sydney and then left for North America. When she returned some years later, she was reported to have whistled 'the "Stars and Stripes" with a spirit and force unusual in a lady'.[18]

Gladys would not cross paths with Daisy Merritt until the 1920s, by which time she'd forged her own reputation as a siffleur. In Katanning's town hall in 1919 she whistled the national anthems of the Allies 'in a most charming manner.'[19] She was announced as 'Premier Comedienne and Queen of the Whistlers' for Gordon's Vaudeville Company. On that same program she was also advertised as stage director of the company's 'Screamingly Funny Revue', *The Insurance Agent*.[20] Gladys was making the most of an Australian entertainment boom.

As the economic hardships of the previous century receded from memory, developing communications and transport technologies brought new ways to be entertained. Australians increasingly sought fun and distraction in the venues of a modern age. Purpose-built picture theatres opened in larger towns, and communities everywhere accommodated the latest dance crazes in halls, hotels and cafes. Across the land, the syncopated rhythms of ragtime, then jazz music, movies and vaudeville competed for popularity.

Emerging entertainers like Gladys honed their stagecraft in some of the nation's more out-of-the-way places. South of Perth, in Katanning and Albany, she polished her performing skills to the delight of local audiences. Not long after Federation and in times of war and its aftermath, these were spectators who saw themselves as Australian. They responded enthusiastically to local performers, artists whose vocabularies and accents were like their own. These new comedians, dancers, singers and actors gave them revues and routines about people and places they knew.

Foreign entertainers, numerous and prominent on the major Australian theatrical circuits in the pre-war years, were not so available during and immediately after the war. Local companies and entrepreneurs were forced to search out new Australian acts. Many of the artists they recruited were women like Gladys – filling gaps left by a dearth of imported talent, and by men who had left the stage to join the war effort.

Keith was finally shipped from Belgium to the United Kingdom in February 1919. He spent two more months there before boarding SS *Soudan* for the long journey home. Photos taken in Glasgow, where he took leave, show a robust man who looks older than his twenty-one years. He and his mate, Todd from Subiaco, stare into the camera.

Millions died on the western front, 46 000 Australians among them. Many thousands more were wounded. No wonder then that survivors Keith and Todd look hollowed out, solemn and stunned. On the back of the photograph, Keith scrawled a message to his mother, warning her that the photo was not a good likeness. By the time he reached Australia his hair had turned white.

Keith was fortunate to disembark in Fremantle on 21 June. The *Soudan*, on which he'd travelled, was a 'clean ship', free of the

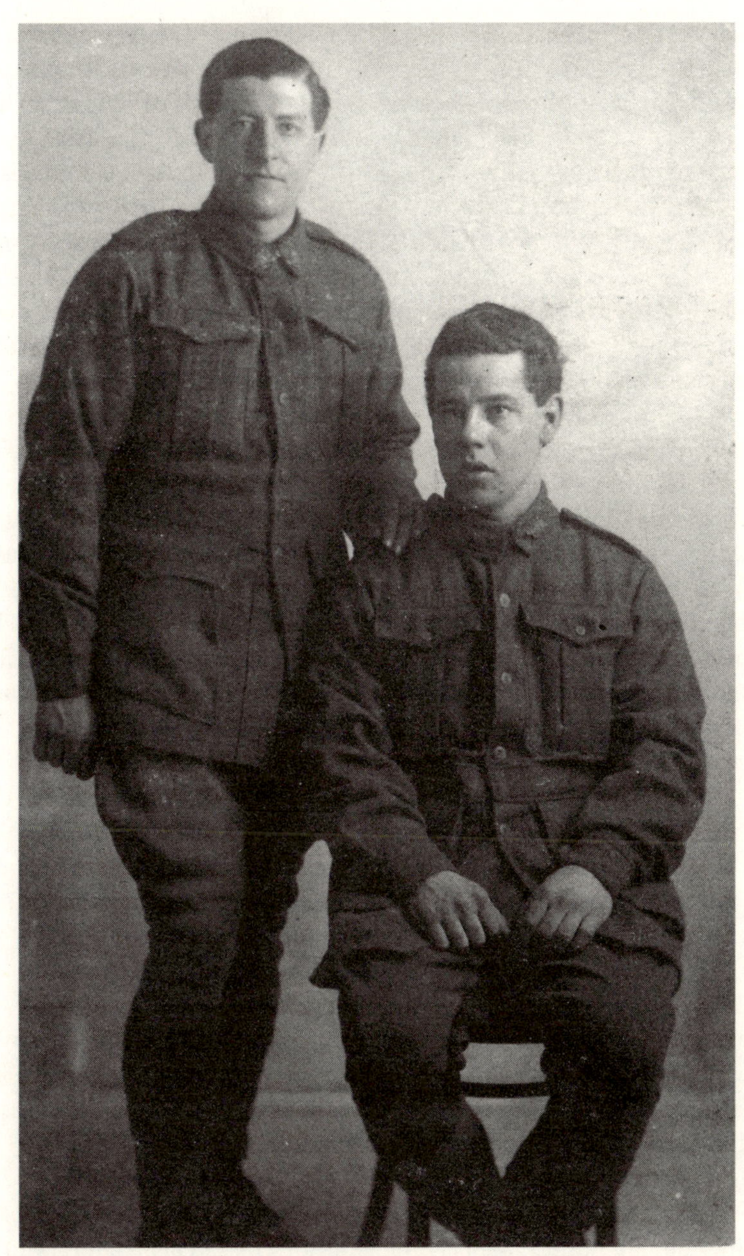

Keith and friend Todd (seated), 1919

influenza that forced other vessels into quarantine. Western Australia itself was declared a quarantine area a fortnight earlier and in the two weeks since the outbreak became official, 137 cases had been reported.

Returning Australian troops brought the Spanish influenza home late in 1918. Though comparatively well controlled in Australia, it killed more people worldwide than did the First World War. In Australia nearly 15 000 died in a year, many of them young adults. Almost a third of Australians were infected. Schools, theatres and even churches were shut, face masks were compulsory, interstate borders were closed and quarantine camps established.

Ventriloquist Sydney James and his troupe the Royal Strollers, also known as the Pierrot Pie Company, were due to open in Perth in April. Delayed in Adelaide when the epidemic prevented western-bound steamers calling at South Australian ports, the company finally departed on the new transcontinental train. But it too was held up, in Kalgoorlie, where all of its passengers spent a week in quarantine. The experience inspired one detainee to pen a poetic account of camp life, published soon after the train with its entertaining passengers finally arrived in Perth on 11 May:

Oh, the camp, the Quarantine Camp,
Looking for germs with a hurricane lamp;
Sleeping in tents with the canvas all damp,
Your head has the 'flu and your legs have the cramp.
Nobody cares if you rave or you ramp,
You're taking pot luck in the Quarantine Camp.[21]

Having added their bit to the general good humour of the camp by staging a concert on their final night in quarantine, the Pierrot Pies went on to play to packed houses in Perth. The company sailed for India in early June, not long before Keith's homecoming.

Left behind was its business manager, Charles Weston, who assembled a new company under the original name of The Royal Strollers, which he invited Gladys to join. Weston secured an engagement for the troupe to premiere, 'by special arrangement with Sydney James', in Newcastle, New South Wales.[22] For the first time as an adult performer Gladys, now twenty-three, would leave her mother in Western Australia and take her place on the stages of the eastern states.

In New South Wales, at Newcastle's Victoria Theatre, her many talents were soon on display:

> Miss Gladys Shaw showed that she possesses quite a number of accomplishments and a keen sense of humour. She is a whistler of high skill, and this was apparent in the air of Those Endearing Young Charms. From this she merged into rippling ragtime melody, and concluded with the refrain of My Hero, the concluding notes of which rang through the house. Miss Shaw also delighted the audience with her narrative of her misfortunes as a domestic servant, and her grotesque dancing was a clever finish to her turn for which she was given a flattering recognition.[23]

Gladys literally breathed new life into the rhythms of ragtime. Though it was a musical style familiar to audiences who'd seen minstrel shows tour the antipodes, its interpretation by a whistling woman was unexpected. Her dancing was equally surprising. 'Grotesque dancing', later known as eccentric dancing, was performed by comedians whose apparently uncontrolled limbs pitched them from one side of the stage to the other. Mostly they were long-legged and male. Gladys was neither. She was an unusually uninhibited, some would say wild, young woman.

By August she was attracting attention in Brisbane:

> Miss Gladys Shaw cleverly whistled a few tuneful melodies. This young lady later figured in a comedy turn, presenting a sketch of a slatternly domestic drudge, who sang and danced with abandon, and altogether was irrepressible.[24]

What followed seemed to prove an old theatrical superstition that whistling on or offstage in a theatre brings bad luck. The Royal

Strollers learned that shortly after departing Australia the company's founder Sydney James had died of a burst appendix. Then, only hours after the company's opening night in Brisbane, its leading comedian Fred Arthur was taken ill. He died in hospital less then a week later. Within another fortnight so too did the wife of manager Charles Weston.

Days after Fred Arthur's demise, Keith replaced him as Royal Strollers comedian, a break he later recounted in Perth's *Mirror*:

> That was a short time after my return from the war. The company were in Brisbane at the time and had suffered a sad loss from their ranks in the person of Fred Arthur...Fred was known as the 'Shabby Genteel'. This was the vacancy that was responsible for my re-entry into the profession.[25]

Keith's account of events was not wholly accurate, for his name had already appeared in advance publicity for the Royal Strollers Brisbane season. But he didn't join the Strollers onstage until Fred Arthur was in his grave.

After years of family breakdown, hardship and war, brother and sister were at last reunited, though not as a double act. Keith, his hair blackened, was paired with Freddie Webber, not Gladys, in 'mirth-provoking numbers' that, according to the *Brisbane Courier*, proved 'highly popular'.[26]

Freddie was a multi-skilled performer. At home, in Charters Towers, Queensland, Master Freddie Webber was known as 'the college boy'. He was a singer, dancer, comedian, composer and a talented instrumentalist who played piano, banjo, mandolin and cornet. Only eighteen when Gladys and Keith met him, he'd already appeared with rising stars like the American comedian Paul Stanhope, and popular comedy duo Stiffy and Mo.

Though he performed with Keith, it was Gladys who became close to Freddie. Once the Royal Strollers season in Brisbane ended in October,

Gladys and Freddie went on to work together, with Blanchards Entertainment Company on the New South Wales north coast.

Keith moved to Sydney in search of further work. There Leslie, his half-brother, was gravely ill. Never a strong child, in his teens Leslie developed renal tuberculosis, a life-threatening disease in a time before antibiotics. Now he was in North Shore Hospital. On the very same photograph Keith had received two years earlier in Belgium – the Falk Studios image of Mary Agnes, Gladys and Gerry – Keith scrawled a message to Les. It simply said, 'Les, from Keith, 18/10/19'. Two days later Leslie died. He was twenty-eight.

That picture, with both its wartime and peacetime messages, found its way into Grandma Elsie's zither case. It may have been returned to Keith after his half-brother's death, or perhaps it never reached Leslie in hospital. But on the other side of the continent, Mary Agnes may have found some comfort in the knowledge that Leslie had two brothers, Keith as well as her first-born Reg, close by when he died.

Keith found work in Sydney at the Princess Theatre near Central Station, headquarters of leading theatrical entrepreneur, Harry Clay. In the first half of 1920 he appeared with a company that included George Wallace, then a comedian just beginning to capture the attention that would propel him to national fame.

In more provincial theatres Gladys was being noticed too. She was said to have 'a number of accomplishments' which 'met with flattering receptions', while 'Master Frederick Webber, a musical college boy, proved to be a wonderful instrumentalist. He introduced songs of his own composition, at the piano, one item being Down on Manly Beach' [sic].[27]

When sheet music for that song was published, it pictured both Gladys and Freddie on the cover. Webber and Shaw, it proclaimed, had enjoyed 'immense success' with the song. Freddie was credited with both words and music, but autographs on a surviving copy suggest a division of labour that had Freddie responsible for melody and Gladys for comedy:

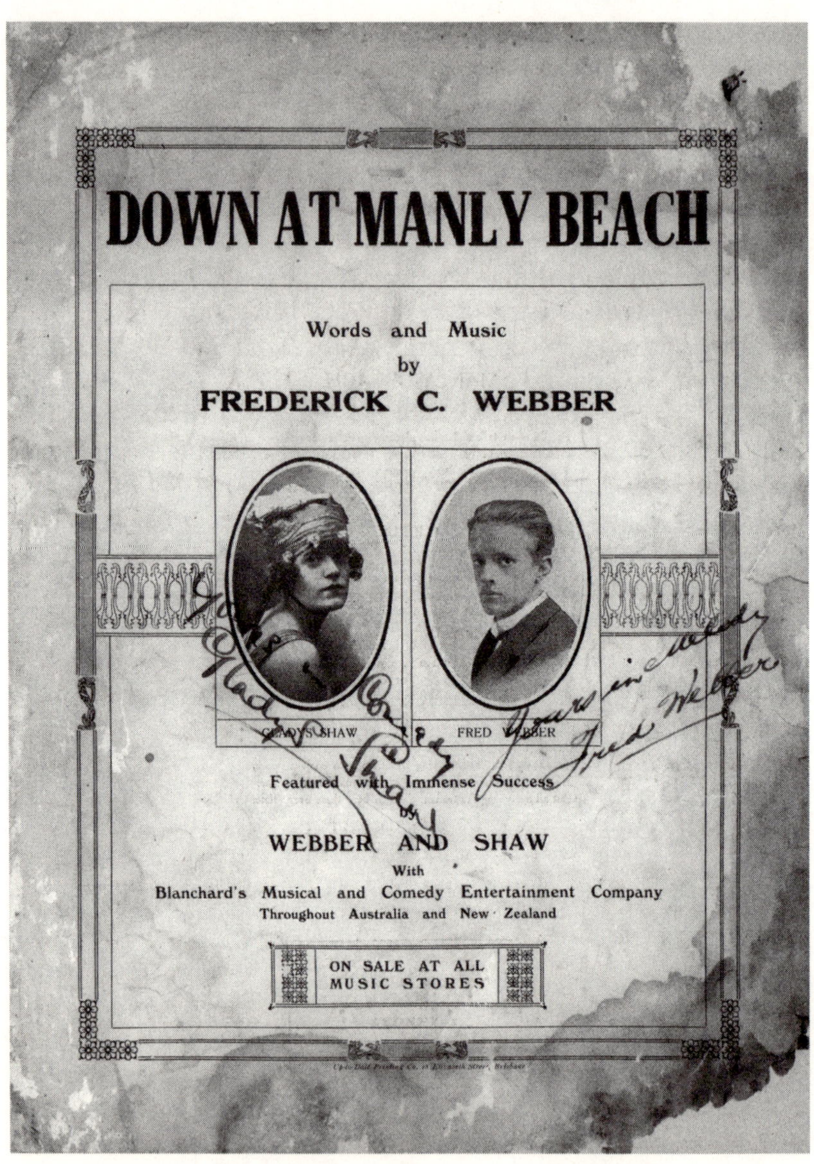

Comedy, melody and Manly Beach, ca. 1920

People often talk about the places they have seen –
Honolulu, Dixie, or wherever they have been:
They can have their beauty spots away in foreign parts,
But there's one place that's held most dear in all Australian hearts.

Manly by the sea
That is the place for me;
Down among the breakers,
With the merry-makers,
Sporting in the surf,
I've been in Old Tennessee,
But now I'm sure you'll agree,
Ev'ry young Tom Dick and Harry,
Love to surf with Maud and Carrie,
Down at Manly Beach.

Sunday afternoon will find the girls upon the beach,
When a tourist comes along he thinks each one's a peach
English girls and those from Paris are, no doubt, sublime,
But all our young Australian girls can beat them every time.[28]

How things had changed. When Mary Agnes left her dreary life in Manly almost thirty years earlier, ocean bathing was still prohibited during daylight hours. Now her daughter was singing and jesting about 'young Australian girls' and men 'sporting in the surf' together.

Freddie's connections secured the pair their next engagement, with the Fullers Company. In Melbourne at the Bijou Theatre, then in Adelaide at the Majestic, 'Webber and Shaw displayed their accomplishments as songsters and musicians especially Miss Gladys Shaw, who possesses a fascinating stage appearance, together with a taste for chic costumes'.[29]

It's unclear whether she had more than a professional relationship with Freddie. He was her junior by five years, but the age difference may not have bothered Gladys, who was a very youthful-looking twenty-four. Her mother had set something of an example by living 'in

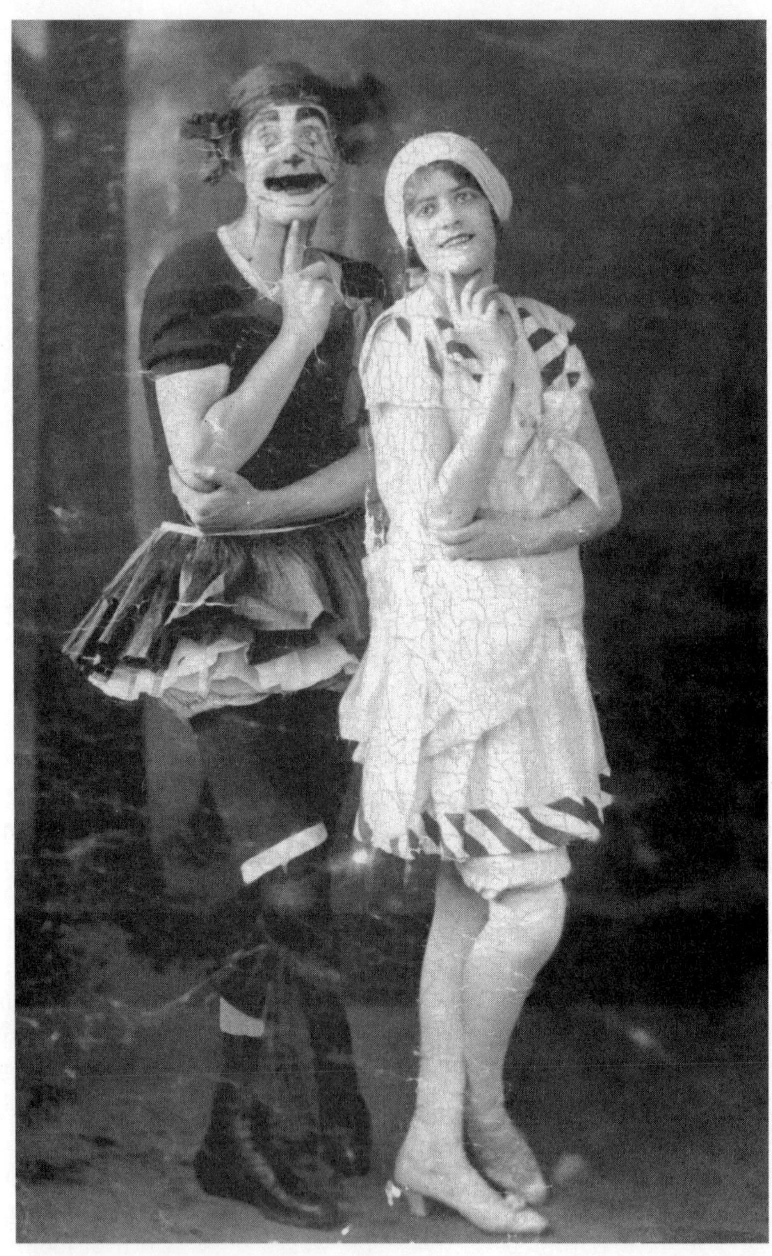

'Chic costumes', Freddie and Gladys, ca. 1920

sin' with a younger man for so many years, and intimate relationships between unmarried colleagues, unthinkable in most quarters, might not have been thought so scandalous in the theatre, where 'moral' standards were considerably more flexible.

But that might not have been the kind of relationship either had in mind. Both had their hearts set on careers as entertainers. Freddie said his ideal work would be in film – as a female impersonator.[30] He never achieved his dream, but continued as an instrumentalist for decades. Eventually he married, but he left his wife shortly after the arrival of the couple's child. They reunited, only to divorce after a couple more years. According to Freddie's wife, who claimed her husband had deserted her, 'he preferred to live with his mother'.[31]

Whatever the nature of the partnership between Gladys and Freddie, it would take the pair across the Tasman Sea, making Gladys the second woman in her family to sail for New Zealand with a younger man.

7
Laugh and the World Laughs With You

Twenty-one years after her family left New Zealand, its professional reputation under a cloud, Gladys returned. She did her best to restore the Shaws' good name.

In her very first New Zealand appearance in Wellington, just 80 miles south of her birthplace, she 'rather surprised her hearers with her marked powers of ability as a siffleur'.[1] Visiting His Majesty's Theatre nearly a century after that performance, I could see why.

Now called St James, the theatre is home to the national ballet company. I called in early on a weekday afternoon when the only sign of life in the foyer was a young woman behind a ticketing desk.

I climbed a wide staircase and at the very top opened a door into a magical world of red upholstery, gold trim and honeyed timber. From up in the grand circle, seats cascaded down through the dress circle and stalls to the stage. Far below, technicians were rehanging lights, shouting instructions to one another as long sections of rigging were manoeuvred into place.

Determined to build the best theatre in the land, John Fuller and his designer Henry E White made the world's first entirely steel-frame theatre. They limited the number of pillars and arranged seats in a shallow curve, giving all audience members the best of views, even those seated where I now stood, at a dizzying height above the stage.

Only then did I begin to understand the power of Gladys's whistle. Audio amplification was still some years away, but even without it her sound was strong and clear enough to soar up and around and through the darkness, thrilling even those in the cheap seats at the very top. No wonder she surprised them.

And whistling was not her only talent. In New Zealand she won equal praise for her singing, her dancing and her skills as a comic actress. Unlike their Australian counterparts, New Zealand's reviewers didn't mention her physical charms. It was an omission that may have said something about the attitude to women in a country that early on had shown appropriate respect for women by granting them the vote.

To the south, in Christchurch, the most English of antipodean cities, Webber and Shaw appeared in the town's oldest theatre, the Opera House. It had been the site of significant meetings during the previous century's campaign for women's suffrage. Once they'd won the vote, 600 women went to the Opera House in order to enrol to use it and became the first women in the world to participate in electing the government of their nation.

Gladys, born two years later, her right to a future vote already secured, might not have known the Opera House's history. But she must have been impressed by its size. Its gallery alone held 600 members of an audience that could number more than 2000. There Gladys presented 'some splendid whistling solos, but was deafeningly applauded for a clever character song, Heaven Will Take Care of a Poor Working Girl [sic]'.[2]

Playing to the feminist sensibilities of their audience, Webber and Shaw then delighted Christchurch with their rendition of 'Everybody Works but Father':

Everybody works but father
And he sits around all day,
Feet in front of the fire –
Smoking his pipe of clay,

Mother takes in washing
So does sister Ann,
Everybody works at our house
But my old man.[3]

All over New Zealand they appeared in the first part of Fullers' vaudeville programs. In Auckland the *Observer* said, 'Fred Webber and Gladys Shaw sing, whistle, dance, and play the cornet, make jokes, make laughter, and make good'.[4] The second half of the show usually featured revues produced for Fullers' Theatres by entertainers like Bert Le Blanc.

Le Blanc's Travesty Stars was one of the two most popular Fullers' troupes of the day – the other being the legendary Nat Phillips's Stiffy and Mo company. Both featured 'Hebrew' comedians, like the Mo character famously played by Roy Rene, whose acts included gags and behaviours of supposedly Jewish origin. Californian-born Le Blanc came to Australia in 1913 with the American Burlesque Company. He formed a comic partnership with another American performer, Jake Mack, and the pair created their alter-egos 'Ike Cohen' and 'Morris Levi'. They were hugely popular, appealing to Australian audiences largely because of a larrikin quality to their characters.

In New Zealand Gladys watched them in a show titled *Do It Now*, in which 'as two would-be speculators, the principals, Le Blanc and Mack, with truly Yiddish get-rich-quick notions, create some droll situations, which are enhanced by the tangled love affairs of the other members of the company'.[5] Though New Zealand reviewers may have been less sexist than their Australian counterparts, it seems they were no less anti-Semitic.

Do It Now was another revusical, a form Gladys had encountered when working with Arthur Morley in Western Australia. Morley, Paul Stanhope, Le Blanc, Nat Phillips and Roy Rene (aka Stiffy and Mo) were among well-known performers and producers who collectively developed and promoted this form of popular theatre in the early decades of the twentieth century. It was a genre with roots in

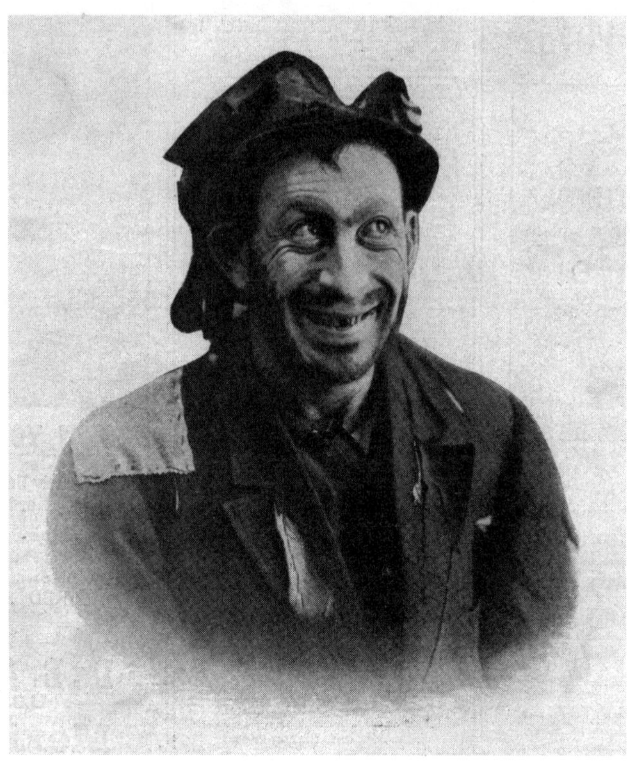

Bert Le Blanc, 1913

English 'tabloid' musical comedies, but the incorporation of American burlesque traditions and a focus on two principal comedians distinguished the revusical from its overseas precursors.[6]

At around an hour in length, with slight and ridiculous plots, these mini musical comedies were all the rage in Australian and New Zealand theatres of the 1920s, when movies were still silent and radio was in its infancy. Alongside male comics who contributed to the development of the form were women who played leading parts in writing, producing and performing revusicals – among them Gladys Shaw.

Gladys and Freddie returned to Sydney after almost six months in New Zealand:

> a very cordial welcome was given to Webber and Shaw who, although lacking physical robustness, are a bright and artistic young pair, who dispense wholesome enjoyment, and crack merry jokes at each other's expense. Cornet playing, whistling, dancing, and a vocal sketch, 'I've Got Everything I Want, But You', were the main features of their contribution.[7]

Then, just as her parents had done after leaving New Zealand, Gladys went to Tasmania, where Freddie may have had connections. In Hobart a Charles Webber leased the Temperance Hall, a substantial venue in Melville Street where Gladys and Freddie were favourites for months. They were, said one newspaper:

> ...without equal. One is always certain of getting a very pleasant half hour or so from their inexhaustible repertoire. Comedy, song, musical items and eccentricities are included in their items and it is with feelings of regret that they are allowed to give way to another turn.[8]

Yet it was Gladys and Freddie who were left with regrets when, despite well-received appearances in Hobart, they found themselves badly out of pocket.

Family or not, Charles Webber failed to pay the pair all that he owed them. He claimed an insufficiency of funds. Although he lived in a fine and well-furnished house, he didn't even have enough equity in his pianola to pay the £59 and 15 shillings he owed Gladys and Freddie.

When they took legal action to have their earnings paid, Charles Webber told the court:

> There were a number of artists left over whom he could not settle with, but he offered them £5 each and their fares to the mainland, which they would not accept. He had several interviews with them,

> and they all agreed to stand together and not to take extreme steps, but Fred Webber and Gladys Shaw accepted a position in Launceston, and issued a summons against him, to the consternation of the other artists as well as himself. He admitted that he had a luxurious home with expensive furniture and a £300 pianola, but unfortunately it was not his, as he had only paid a £20 deposit on the furniture and one £5 instalment, and £40 for the pianola.[9]

Gladys and Freddie spent February and March performing in Burnie, Devonport and Launceston to earn their passage back to the mainland. By the time they reached Sydney there wasn't much room for them at Fullers, where contracts usually ran from January to the end of June. They made only a few appearances before setting out across the continent to join Gladys's family in Western Australia. Perhaps her relatives would prove more helpful than the Webbers.

Mary Agnes and young Gerry were still living in Perth, and Keith had returned as 'the magnetic comedian' with Brooks Amusement Company, playing at the Shaftesbury Theatre.

His contributions to the entertainments on offer there were sometimes controversial:

> There are a few 'patriots' left even now. One grubby-looking specimen rose in his place at the Shaftesbury on Wednesday night and roared at Keith Connolly because the comedian cleverly lampooned Billy Hughes. The 'patriot' caused his own wife to burst into tears, but as his abusive lingo continued, Connolly retorted 'So's yer ole man'. This caused the roof to fall once more, and the 'patriot' departed from the building. Shame on yer, Keith Connolly, breakin' up the 'appy 'ome like that! The 'paytriot' who resented the Billy Hughes lampoon cleared out of the house and left his sobbing wife alone. Then wifie retired too and apparently missed the 'patriot' in his tantrums, for the Hughesite barracker returned alone a few minutes later to find his wife's vacant chair. No home can be happy when Billy Hughes comes into it.[10]

During the war, Prime Minister Hughes had forged a new political party out of supporters of conscription in both the Commonwealth Liberal and Labor parties. Though his attempts to introduce conscription were defeated in two plebiscites, the Nationalist Party Hughes created held government either alone or in coalition from 1917 to 1929. The man himself was widely viewed as a 'rat' for deserting the Labor Party, and was equally mistrusted by many on the conservative side of politics. He would be forced from leadership of the Nationalists in 1923.

But in 1921, when he was the subject of Keith's send-up, Hughes was still Australia's prime minister and the Nationalists governed the country. Eleven days before Keith spoofed their federal leader they'd won a second term in government in Western Australia, where they ruled in coalition with other conservative parties. It was a poll most notable for electing Edith Cowan, the first female member of parliament in Australia. Though women remained unrepresented by politicians of their own gender at the federal level, Cowan – a Nationalist – became state member for West Perth.

She was well known as an advocate for women and their rightful place in public life, but she also represented a political party that subscribed to an Australia wedded to the British Empire. It was an idea that had taken eighteen-year-old Keith from his mother and sent him to a hell on earth on the Western Front. Now he was back close to her in Perth, Mary Agnes must have seen the psychological scars he wore. Though she might have supported Cowan's efforts on behalf of women, I doubt that Mary Agnes voted for her.

Like so many returned soldiers, Keith spoke little about what he'd experienced on the Western Front. Instead he said, in an interview with Perth's *Mirror* newspaper:

> Laugh and the world laughs with you, weep and you weep alone; that's my motto. As a matter of fact, I get paid by the management to make their patrons laugh – so why should I be sad?[11]

He had plans to try his luck in the United States:

> I have a particular liking for 'straight' parts, such as I am playing in Elton Black's revues at the present time; therefore, my main goal in the business is to 'click' with a big show over in the States in this class of work. So I anticipate saying farewell to the 'low' comedy style of working which at present earns me some fine receptions at the Shaftesbury Theatre.[12]

Despite laughing off his sadness, Keith had gone to war a comedian and returned a straight man. He wanted to play the one who never laughed, who was serious no matter how funny his partner was.

Scottish comedian Elton Black, Keith's stage partner in 1921, was indeed witty. Hired to perform and produce at the Shaftesbury, his salary was said to be substantial. Black was an entertainer with talent and long experience. In Perth Keith appeared opposite him in many skits and revues:

> For the final revue the stage was transformed into a remarkably realistic scene of the Goodwood racecourse, and for twenty minutes the attention of the audience was closely held by the clever comedy production entitled 'Sure Thing'. Keith Connolly appeared in the role of the evil doer 'Jay Bird', who has laid £5,000 against the success of the thoroughbred 'Sure Thing', and accordingly drugs the jockey. How this plan is eventually frustrated by 'Dopey Do Little', the racecourse detective (Elton Black), who himself takes the mount and wins the race, found an extremely comical denouement.[13]

It was the beginning of a long career during which Keith would go on to win most praise for his work as a foil for some of Australia's legendary comedians.

In April 1921, Gladys and Freddie reached Perth and also joined Elton Black's show. Gladys, in particular, was well received:

> Gladys Shaw is frank and engaging. She blithely confided the joyous components of the latest craze, 'Jazzola', while many a laugh was raised by her travesty of The Gipsy's Warning, wherein she narrates her experiences as a result of disobedience of the fortune teller's wise prediction. Her whistling numbers also won loud applause, the act being one of the most successful of the evening.[14]

Continuing a theme started when she sang about heaven protecting working girls, Gladys parodied the 'Gipsy's Warning' lyrics. This folk song, popular in both the United States and the United Kingdom, was yet another cautionary tale for young women:

> Gentle lady, do not trust him, though his voice is low and sweet,
> Heed not him who kneels before thee, gently pleading at thy feet.
> Now thy life is in its morning; cloud not this thy happy lot.
> Listen to the gypsy's warning, gentle lady, trust him not.[15]

Gladys's treatment of songs of advice to women played with old ideas about female chastity and virtue. Her versions of them turned their lyrics into wry and sometimes deeply ironic words better suited to times when young women were testing newfound freedoms. Like Gladys, they'd joined the workforce in wartime. They hadn't made the same money as men, but they'd earned the right to live life more on their own terms. And Gladys had her mother's example before her. Mary Agnes had trusted a man who was not her husband. Nonetheless she'd had something of a stage career and continued to make her own way in the world even after the 'wrong man' was long gone.

After so many family separations, the early 1920s were better years for Mary Agnes and her children. In Perth, where as 'Madam Marie' she persevered in earning her living as a singing teacher, Mary Agnes must have been proud that her performing children, Gladys and Keith, had returned as minor celebrities in the closest thing they had to a 'home town'.[16] Even her youngest son was beginning to attract attention. At only thirteen, Gerry appeared with Keith in *Sleeping Beauty*, the Easter pantomime at the Shaftesbury Theatre. The following month he was onstage at the Melrose with pupils of Carters

Vaudeville Academy in *Boy Blue*. One review said he'd 'afforded a happy interlude with his droll sayings and comedy intrusions'.[17] The *West Australian* was less complimentary; 'as a pert, saucy page Master Gerald Shaw showed aptitude for the stage, but it was a pity his elders had taught him to sing a vulgar song'.[18] Though Mr Branson Carter authored and produced the pantomime, it may not have been his influence that counted. Gerry now had Gladys and Keith back in the west to lead him astray.

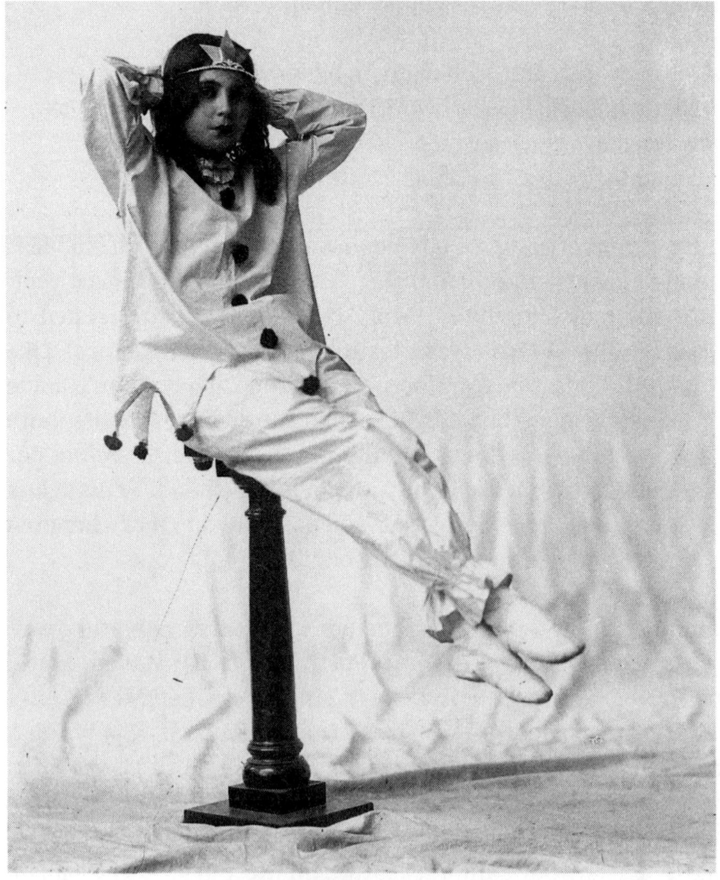

'Little Elsie Hosking', ca. 1917, SLWA 153862PD

At the Shaftesbury, Keith would sway another young performer too. Elsie Hosking, a juvenile character singer, was among the concertina players, whistling pianists and comedians on the Brooks Amusement Company program.

She was well known in Perth. In the last years of war and for a time after the armistice, she was sometimes called 'Little Elsie Hosking' or the 'The Little Urchin Singer'.

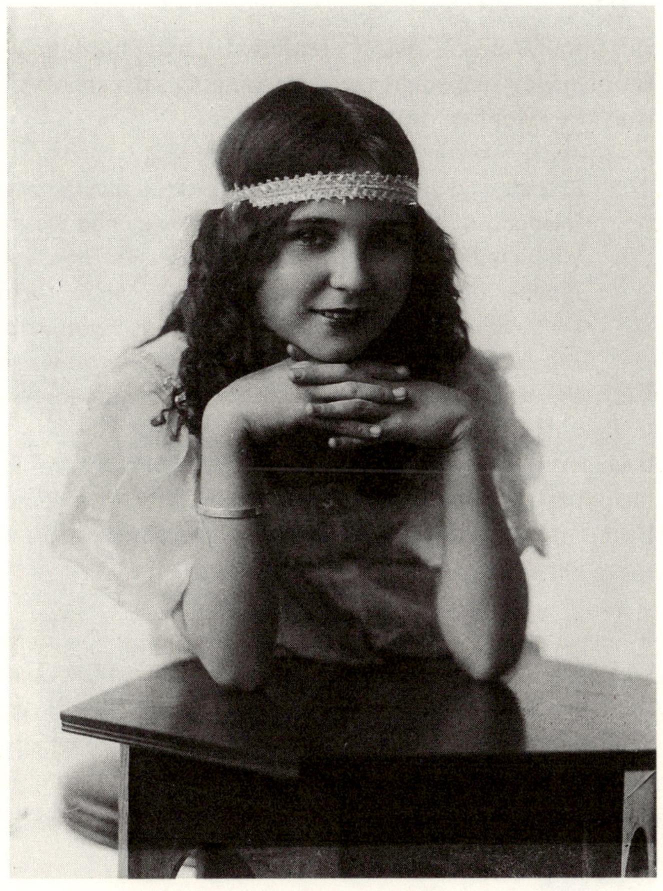

'Little Elsie Hosking', ca. 1917, SLWA 153772PD

Elsie was a favourite at charity shows, welcoming returned soldiers home with songs like 'Rosy's Cosy Bungalow'. Long before her romance with my grandfather Keith, my Grandma Elsie was billed as 'Perth's Little Idol'.[19]

She was equally successful on the professional stage. Arthur Morley – with whom Gladys had also worked – included her in a 1919 line-up at the Melrose Theatre, where the then eleven-year-old was described as 'that clever child vocalist', who, said the *West Australian*, 'gave complete satisfaction'.[20]

Her father, Andy Hosking, certainly believed his daughter was clever. He managed her stage career, arranging appearances at which she won praise for her 'dreamy' songs:

> Probably no one secured a better reception in the new bill that was introduced last week than the winsome child Elsie Hoskings [sic], whose popularity, which she established during the war in a record number of charitable performances, is being further enhanced. Last night, the dainty serio sang with sweet expressiveness a dreamy melody, Alabama Lullaby, and so great was its appeal that the artist had to render an encore number to satisfy the audience.[21]

It helped that Andy had been associated with several Perth theatres, including the Shaftesbury, vaudeville venue and sometime cinema. He'd long dabbled in the entertainment business, while holding down a day job at the Gas and Electric Department.

By all accounts he was gentle and charming, if somewhat nervous. Well known and well liked about town, he was the kind of man who thought the best of everyone. His work and his theatrical pursuits kept him out of the fray at home in East Perth, which left his wife Ethel, armed with her considerable reserves of common sense and good humour, to calm the currents of resentment between her two daughters, Lydia and Elsie.

According to my father, the sisters did not get on. After we watched Jane Campion's debut feature *Sweetie* in 1989, Dad told me he thought his mother Elsie was something like the film's protagonist. Sweetie bore little physical resemblance to my grandmother. She is large and untidy where Elsie was neat and petite. But Sweetie's situation resonates. She is capricious, attention seeking, perhaps mentally ill, but her father believes her to be the 'artist' of the family. To her only sister, she is overpowering.

Elsie specialised in sentimental songs, but also danced and performed in revues. Amid comedians and bevies of dancing girls, she appeared in one Brooks Company show:

> in the leading part of a tableau representing France's gratitude to Australia, designed by M Seguy, and gracefully executed by six young girls, who give a finished exhibition of fencing. Light rapiers flashed and scintillated with marvellous speed and dexterity, and

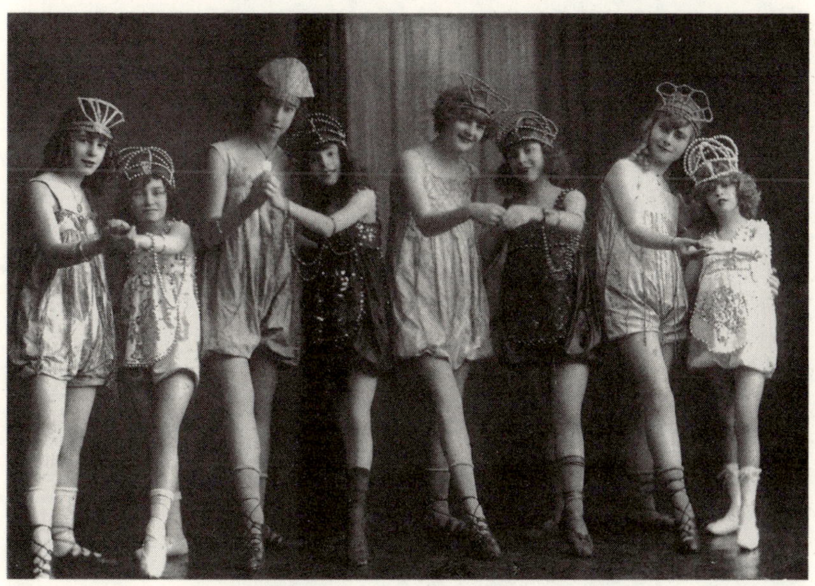

The artist of the family – Elsie Hosking, second from left, ca. 1919.

> when the screen closed with an allegorical representation of France embracing Australia the audience cheered again and again.[22]

Shades of Emilienne Moreau, the brave woman of Loos. Armed women must have been more acceptable after war's end than when Jane King played the militant French heroine back in 1916.

But Elsie's reputation in Perth was mostly made by her singing of sweet songs, which were especially well received by audiences with memories of war fresh in their minds. In 1921, aged only thirteen, she did her best to impress a dashing returned soldier, Keith Connolly, when she sang more of them – including 'He's Coming Home', 'Bubbles' and 'Let the Rest of the World Go By':

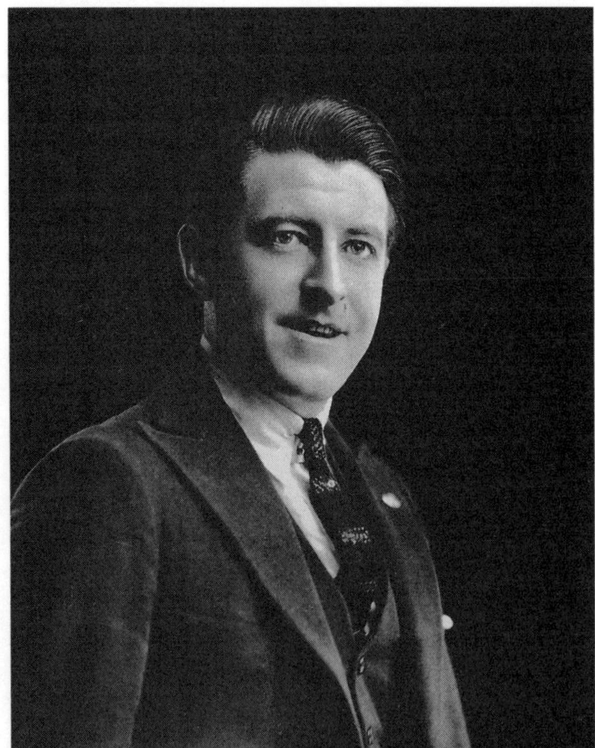

Returned soldier and 'magnetic comedian,' Keith Connolly, ca. 1921

We'll find perfect peace, where joys never cease
Out there beneath a kindly sky
We'll build a sweet little nest somewhere in the west
And let the rest of the world go by...[23]

Meanwhile, all was not well between 'Webber and Shaw' whose act was said to be 'a decided acquisition to Shaftesbury'.[24] Freddie's poor health may have had something to do with growing tensions. And he may not have been happy about Gladys developing a closer performing relationship with her brother, or that Keith chose to announce the fact in the local press. With six weeks remaining on his Shaftesbury contract, Keith declared he and Gladys had 'arranged to try a "double" out shortly' and were 'thinking very seriously of heading for South Africa, where things in our line are very rosy'.[25]

Toward the end of July, the *Mirror* reported that:

> Freddie Webber has concluded his Western engagement and leaves within a few days for his home town – Sydney. Fred enjoys far from what might be called tip-top health, so a complete rest from the boards would do him no harm.[26]

But he didn't leave Perth for some weeks, nor before laying charges against Gladys, accusing her of stealing two books of theatrical scripts. When neither Freddie nor Gladys showed up at the City Court, the case was struck out without being heard. The following week the *Mirror* reported that the matter 'was settled out of Court to the entire satisfaction of Mr. Webber. He has the assurance of his many Perth friends' best wishes for his future success'.[27]

The truth remains mysterious, but my guess is that Gladys was not a thief. The books of scripts may have been their own work, hers as much as his. After all, as they'd suggested when autographing the sheet music for *Down at Manly Beach*, Gladys was responsible for comedy and Freddie for melody. She wasn't about to let him take all the credit, nor perhaps all of the skits and jokes they'd written together. In days before photocopiers, it's hard to imagine how Gladys and Freddie resolved the problem of sharing their scripts. Perhaps, to keep the peace, Gladys let Freddie keep both the books. Or maybe they simply agreed to take one each.

> The initial turn of Keith Connolly and Gladys Shaw, as a 'double', at the Shaftesbury Theatre this week, was the means of even furthering their already bulky reputation. Their act was dipped deep in 'localities', and that fact, plus a nifty eccentric dance, made their act the hit of the bill.[28]

Brother and sister act, Gladys and Keith – 'the topical two'– won many fans during what turned out to be a long engagement at the Shaftesbury. For a show that changed each week, they wrote patter that lampooned local identities and events. They sang comic duets and performed an eccentric dancing act which proved the 'hit of the programme'.[29] And in 'a humorous ensemble…Gladys Shaw led the ladies of the company in what may well be described as a riot'.[30]

Keith's idea about touring South Africa vanished when Perth 'clamped them to its heart'.[31] The most enthusiastic of local newspapers, the *Mirror*, observed that Gladys had been seen at the races, remarked on Keith's dazzling array of neckties and reminded readers that Gladys was once 'one of our Movie Girls at The Grand'.[32] Then it commissioned a series of articles by Keith himself. In four overblown pieces he related amusing events from his theatrical life. He wasn't much of a feature writer, but he did his best to make them witty and the series at least proved that he had his father Gerald's knack for self-promotion.

Keith promised he'd 'rake up some of my war experiences' in a fifth article, but it didn't appear. The *Mirror* apologised to readers and explained that he was '…struggling under "flu conditions"'.[33] Keith's recollections of war were never published. Maybe it was too hard to make light of such dark times. Among the papers in Grandma Elsie's case I found only an army paybook, a postcard and Frank Hurley's photographs of tunnellers at work on the Menin Road. There were no other clues to suggest how Keith remembered his time on the Western Front.

Gladys didn't go unmentioned in Perth papers, though she did no interviews. Nor did she write articles. No personal letters or diaries survive, if they ever existed. So I don't know whether she was sad or relieved about the rift with Freddie Webber. Or if she had misgivings about forming a new double act with Keith.

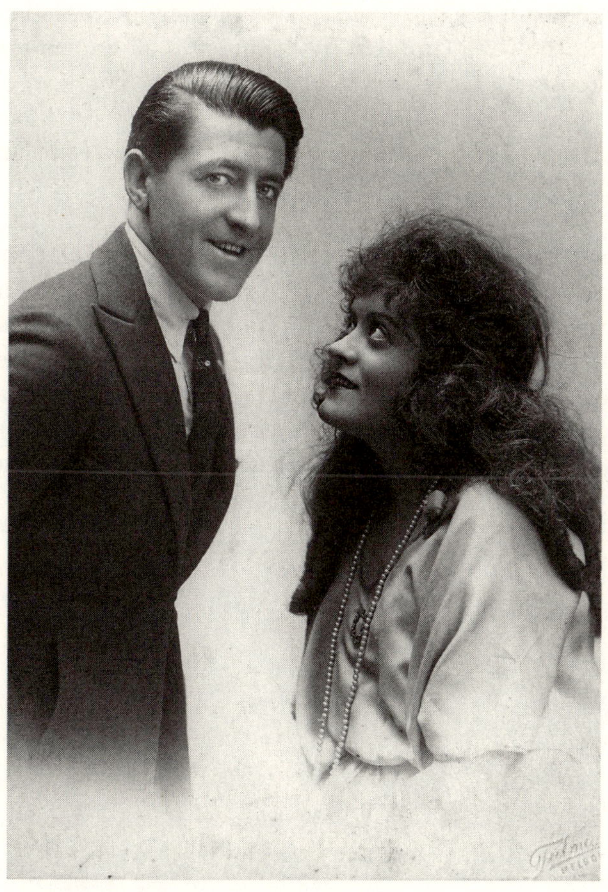

'The topical two', Gladys and Keith, 1921

After being swindled in Hobart, it was clear she was in need of more professional management. Neither heaven nor Freddie had protected Gladys the working girl from Charles Webber's insolvency. Perhaps a brother could be better trusted to look after her interests. He had big plans and the chutzpah to publicise them. And after so many years of performing together as children, they were well matched, equally versatile and ready to make their mark.

Gladys may have felt too that she owed Keith whatever she could offer by way of loyalty. Unable to protect her younger brother during the war years, perhaps she had some survivor guilt about whistling in the cashier's booth at the Grand while Keith endured the misery of the Western Front.

On 10 September 1921, brother and sister boarded a steamship bound for Sydney:

> This page loses one of its best friends to-day, when the Karoola sails away with comedian Keith Connolly on board. Keith has been for the past few weeks a frequent contributor to this section, with a series of humorous articles about his life, which have caused much comment. On the stage – it would be a hard task to select a harder working, more versatile, or cleverer performer than the same Keith. His sister, Gladys Shaw, is making the trip by the same boat...[34]

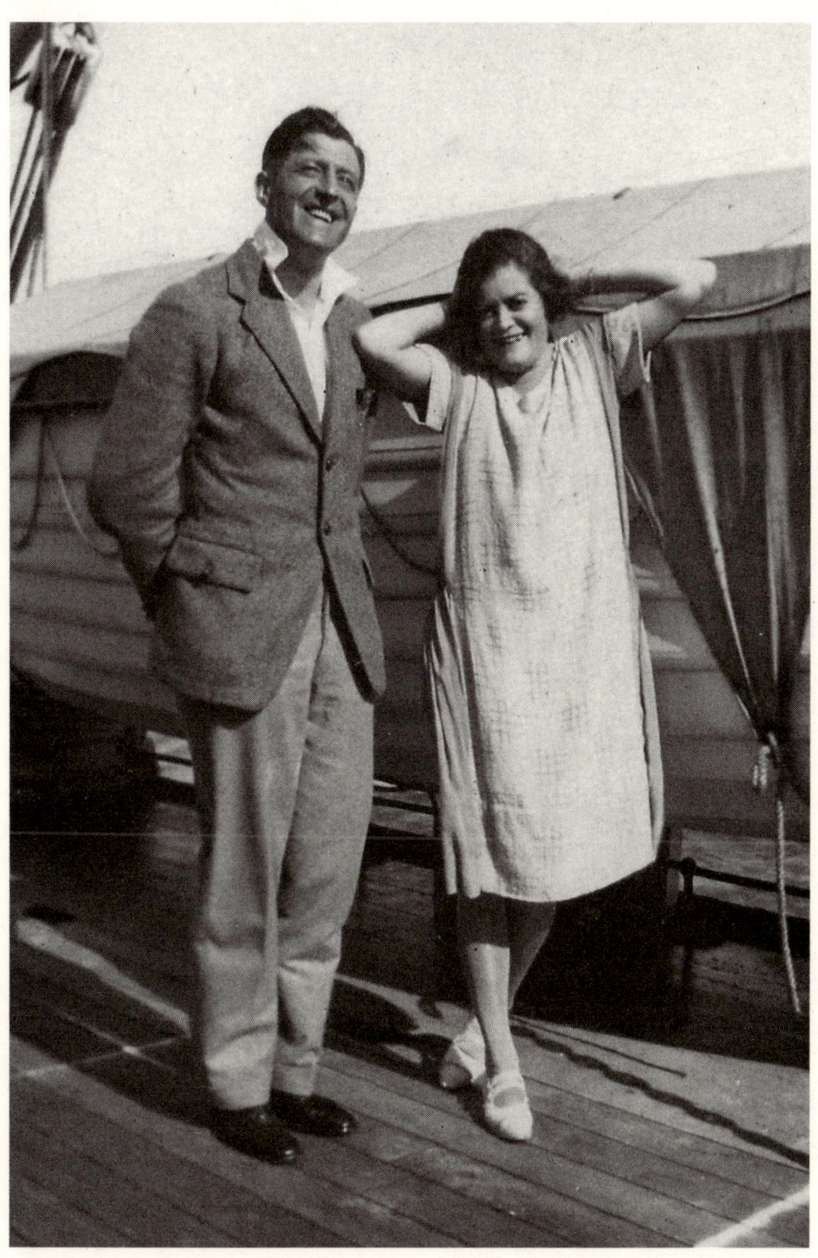

Bound for Sydney, Gladys and Keith, 1921

8
Matrons, Maids and a Murderess

Ten days after arriving in Sydney, Keith and Gladys were onstage at Fullers' Theatre in Castlereagh Street, in the heart of the city. By mid November they were in New Zealand as 'Gladys Shaw and Brother Keith'. Their comic singing and tap-dancing routines were among many acts in a crowded Fullers' program, but an Auckland reviewer remarked that it 'went with a swing' and 'Gladys Shaw proved a successful fun-maker'.[1]

Their big break came a few months later, in April 1922, when they were recruited to Australia's leading vaudeville act – Nat Phillips's Stiffy and Mo Revue Company:

> It is extremely doubtful if there are any other comedians in vaudeville or in any part of the world, for that matter, as popular as Stiffy and Mo, the clever burlesque stars appearing at Fullers' New Theatre. Since their return to Sydney these breezy fun-makers have created such a demand for seats at this theatre that the management are daily establishing fresh records.[2]

Stiffy and Mo didn't want Gladys for her whistle. They hired her for her comic talents as a character actress, one who could also dance and sing. She was exactly the artist they needed:

> Stiffy and Mo are an all-Australian company…They prefer Australians to the imported fun-maker. They find them more

> versatile – more adaptable – and when a new show has to be staged every week the adaptability of the Australian is a winning factor.[3]

Performers as resourceful as Gladys were often the product of show business families like her own. As a child she might have lived on the margins but, as promised, Mary Agnes had indeed raised her daughter for a stage life. And for all his unreliability Gerald and his fellow performers had played their parts in developing the Shaw children's abilities. They had grown to be talented all-rounders, accomplished and experienced beyond their years. By the time she joined Stiffy and Mo, Gladys had already been on the stage for twenty-one of her twenty-six years. Now her further education was about to begin – in a family of her own making, a family of entertainers who would nurture and extend her talents.

Nat Phillips was a jack of all trades theatrical – a producer, director, performer, musician and writer. With his wife Daisy Merritt he toured the United States, the United Kingdom and Europe before returning to Australia, where Fullers engaged the couple in 1912. Roy Rene, also known as Mo, joined them in 1916, when Stiffy and Mo's double act, and their revue company, were born.

Decades before Gladys came to know her, Daisy Merritt was a Sydney whistler, comic, dancer and teacher of dance. Then she met Nat, more than ten years her junior. Like Gladys's own mother, Mary Agnes, Daisy left her husband, her children and her country for a younger man and a theatrical life. Daisy and Nat spent seven years abroad as partners offstage and on. When they returned to Australia in 1912, it was Daisy who played opposite Nat as he developed his famous character, Stiffy the Rabbitoh.

Begun in similarly scandalous fashion, Daisy and Nat's partnership would prove more enduring than that of Gladys's parents. They were all that Mary Agnes and Gerald Shaw might have been.

Gladys may have recognised in Daisy the same determination that drove Mary Agnes to pursue desires that placed her beyond polite

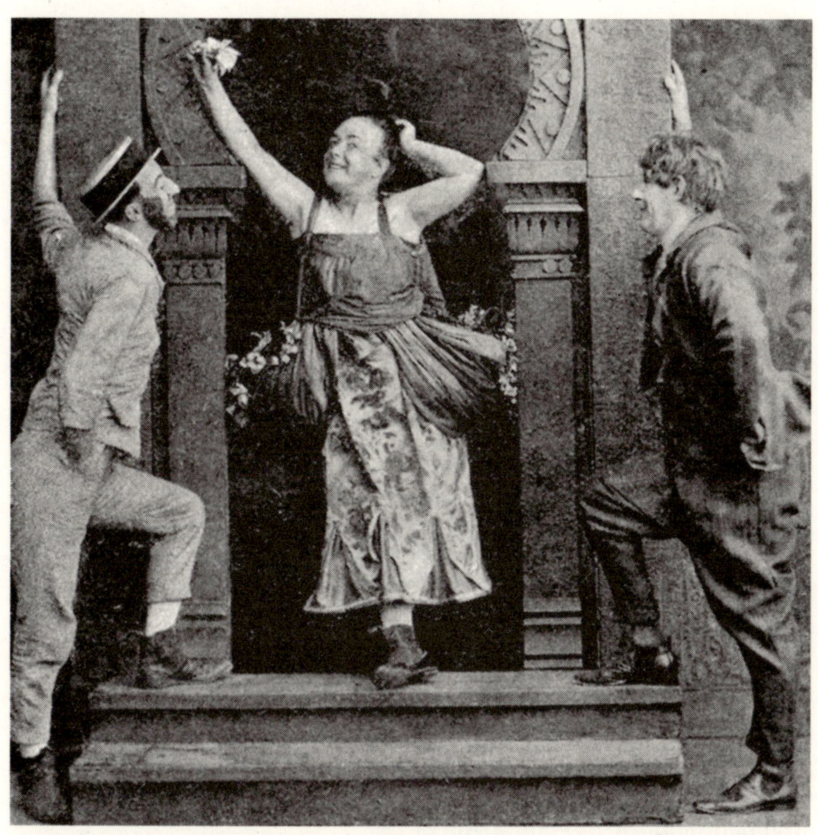

Daisy Merritt, between Mo (left) and Stiffy (right), 1919

society. Like Gladys's own mother, Daisy had made painful choices and Gladys knew something about their cost. Both the older women had married and divorced in New South Wales, the last Australian state to abolish the principle of father-right in determining custody of children.[4] Its courts took a dim view of adulterous women and their fitness as custodial mothers. Mary Agnes and Daisy might have left marriages to lead more creative and fulfilling lives as much as to be with new partners, or escape their husbands, but they were judged for their adulteries – by society and the legal system. Neither was in a position, financially or in the eyes of the law, to petition for custody of their children. And so Daisy and Mary Agnes bore the grief of separation from their offspring and the stigma of being mothers who 'deserted' their families.

Unlike Mary Agnes, Daisy had no children with her new partner. Instead, she and Nat created a family of promising young artists. Well known for their generosity and their talents, they gathered together many of the brightest and best of a new generation of performers. Among them were husband and wife Mike Connors and Queenie Paul, who joined the company shortly before Gladys and Keith. Later Nat and Daisy would take on young Elsie Hosking, and Stella Lamond, who became a star of stage, radio and then TV. According to her daughter, Toni Lamond, Stella said that 'all she knew about show business she learned from them'.[5]

By the time Nat and Daisy took Gladys and Keith under their wings, Daisy had already handed the role of Stiffy's onstage partner to Roy Rene. Stiffy and Mo became the most famous of the era's great comic duos, which included Bluey and Dopey, Dinks and Oncus, Ike Cohen and Morris Levi, and the gloriously named Mutt and Chopp.

Excluded from this galaxy by virtue of her gender rather than any lack of talent, Daisy continued to take roles in the company's revues and pantomimes. Roy Rene said of her:

> She was a real low-comedy woman and she used to lead me on with her ad-libbing. I never could resist it when Daisy got going. She knew how to bring out the best, or shall I say the worst, in me. Sometimes I've actually fallen down on the stage in laughter at some of the tricks Daisy used to get up to. I used to make my legs collapse under me as if they were india-rubber, and then I'd bang my right leg on the floor and laugh and laugh, and the audience would laugh and laugh too. But Nat used to stand in the wings scraping his feet with rage and telling me to stop fooling and get up. His eyes would disappear into his head with rage, and then I'd be even more helpless laughing at him, and the audience, who couldn't even see what I was laughing at, used to roar.[6]

One of Daisy's sons, having worked with the Stiffy and Mo company when he was an adult, remembered things quite differently. He claimed that his mother was the one frustrated by improvisations. Stiffy and Mo's sketches, he said, 'were always censored by Daisy before the act went on stage, but the written script and the spoken script were never the same. To Daisy's despair the two comedians threw away their carefully-rehearsed lines and madly ad-libbed'.[7]

In 1922 Daisy gave Gladys her place in the company's celebrated revues. It was a temporary handover, possibly precipitated not by Daisy's own need for a rest, but by the poor health of her ageing mother Amelia. Whatever the reason for it, Daisy's absence made Gladys the company's character comedienne. It would prove to be her biggest break yet.

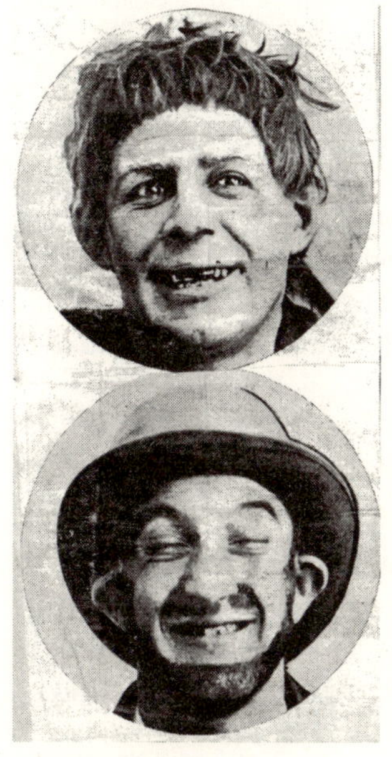

Stiffy the Rabbitoh (top) and Mo (bottom)

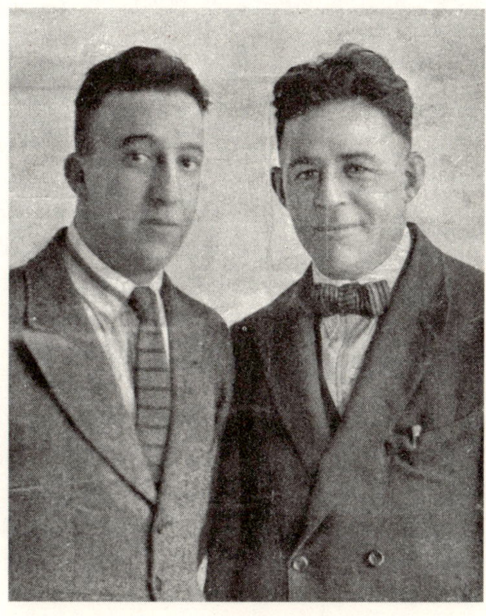

Without their makeup, Stiffy (right) and Mo (left)

Stiffy, played by Nat Phillips, was a 'rabbitoh', a seller of rabbit meat and supporter of South Sydney's rugby league team, a character sometimes described as an urban larrikin, the Paul Hogan of an earlier time. Roy Rene's character was Mo, a Jewish caricature with heavy make-up and an Aussie twist.

Stiffy and Mo were the constants in their stories. Their characters varied little, whatever situation or role they played. They frequently wore the same oversized, ragged clothes when performing. Even when they changed attire it was usually for something equally shabby: singlets, footy guernseys, old boots and trousers held up with string. Around them their colleagues appeared in numerous parts and an assortment of costumes.

Gladys played maids and matrons – of society and hospitals. She was a shopper, hotel manager and charwoman. In *The Plumbers*, she played a Mrs Pinetree, a character described in Melbourne's *Age* newspaper as a 'nagging wife…ably portrayed by Gladys Shaw',[8] in a story filled with nonsense, dance and song:

[…Enter Stiffy, Mo and Mrs Pinetree]

MRS PINETREE: Now look here, I tell you what I want. You see my husband is very jealous and I want to cure him of it. Now how would you like to work for me? I can find you both a billet. [To Stiffy] You can have a situation as a butler.

STIFFY: What have I got to do?

MRS PINETREE: Not much. First of all you get up in the morning. You clean the master's bicycle. My bicycle. Clean the front door step. Clean the knocker, the knob, water the garden, help the cook, mow the lawn, do the messages…

STIFFY: [On the floor] Stop counting, I'm out. Eh, you haven't any clay in your backyard have you?

MRS PINETREE: What do you want clay for?

STIFFY: I thought I might be able to make you some bricks in my spare time.

MRS PINETREE: You won't have any spare time. Have you had any breakfast?

STIFFY: I had a set of smalls.

MRS PINETREE: For heaven's sake what's that?

STIFFY: What's a set of smalls, Mo?

MO: A set of smalls is a ting vhere dey hide two pies under six peas and bet you a zack you can't find the pies.

MRS PINETREE: Well you go down to the cook and she will get you something to eat.

MO: Eh, what kind of tart's the cook?

MRS PINETREE: The cook's a woman and not a piece of pastry. And now you go down to the kitchen. [Exit Stiffy. Mrs Pinetree turns to Mo] And now I want you to do a different kind of work. As I told you before, my husband is very jealous and I want to cure him. Now do you think you could make love to me?[9]

The last of the revues in Gladys's first Sydney season with Stiffy and Mo was *In Society*, in which, not unusually, she played a maid. The *Sunday Times* was impressed:

> Miss Gladys Shaw (a most comely damsel in private life), sacrifices her beauty on the altar of art to give us the most amusing study of Polly, a comic slavey with operatic yearnings.[10]

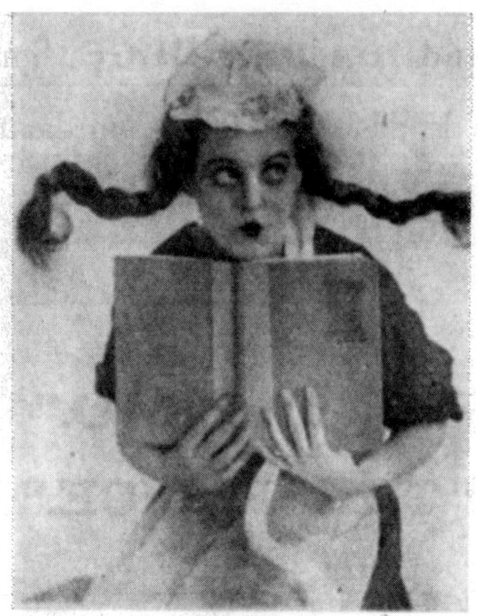

Fuller News, 1922

Gladys Shaw, a Clever New Zealand Character Comedienne playing comedy parts in the Revues staged by Stiffy and Mo at Fullers' New Theatre, Sydney.

Stiffy and Mo's revue was not the only drawcard that night at Fullers' New Theatre. The other big attraction – starring in the first half – was Daisy Jerome, back in Australia, 'electric and vimful as ever':

> 'I'm just the same old Daisy – only six years older', she said. And then she gave her audience the same audacious little Daisy of yore, tireless, restless, and temperamental, with the happy, hail fellow-well-met sort of knack that gets the simplest songs over.[11]

It was exciting enough for Gladys to appear on the same stage as the famous and admired Daisy. To also be praised for her own performance by a reviewer who thought Daisy 'magnetic' and 'compelling', must have been thrilling. But Gladys had little time to enjoy her triumph. Stiffy and Mo's company had a punishing schedule:

> Stiffy and Mo deserve their success. Sheer hard work is theirs from daylight to dark. As they give two shows every day of the week (Sundays excepted), and stage a fresh revue every Saturday, they have to rehearse every morning, consequently they practically live at the theatre.[12]

As producer, Nat demanded rehearsal. Roy Rene's approach was more relaxed. He'd take Nat offerings of his favourite small fried sausages in an effort to make his partner 'forget to go mad at us for not being at rehearsal...I never did like rehearsing, and learning a script is no good to me'.[13]

Which meant those performing with him had to be on their toes. In her first four months with Stiffy and Mo Gladys rehearsed each morning, before appearing in two shows every day except Sunday. Outside in Castlereagh Street, Sydney's short autumn turned to winter while indoors Gladys practised lines and songs for roles in sixteen separate revusicals. She brought her characters to life in the familiar surrounds of the Castlereagh Street theatre, where she and Keith had appeared earlier that same year. Designed by Henry E White, architect for many Fullers' projects, Fullers' New Theatre in Sydney had two levels. Its Wellington cousin, His Majesty's, had three tiers, but the Castlereagh Street premises were similarly promoted as 'a theatre that has no worst seat', one with 'a perfect stage view'[14] from everywhere in the house.

Gladys's reputation was growing:

> ...in Gladys Shaw the Fullers have a real find. This talented girl, still a youngster, is thoroughly at home in revue...She is naturally humorous and it is doubtful if she could be serious even if she tried.[15]

In August 1922 Stiffy and Mo's Revue Company moved on to Melbourne and the Bijou Theatre – a more tattered venue than its Sydney equivalent. It too would soon be given a makeover by Henry E White.

Gladys, however, was given a far from shabby reception. The *Sporting Globe* said:

> New Zealand does not give the stage as many actors and actresses as most countries, but when a New Zealander scores before the footlights, he or she has exceptional ability. Gladys Shaw is no exception to the rule. . . .Gladys Shaw is a genius at characterisation, and her clear-cut comedy cameos in the 'Stiffy and Mo' revues at the Bijou Theatre are sheer delight.[16]

These words and others like them kept turning up in press mentions of Gladys for the next couple of years. Perhaps Fullers seized upon and repeated the praise of journalists, or maybe even then the nation's scribes were simply parroting press releases.

Whichever was the case, it's clear that at the height of her career Gladys was identified as a New Zealander, despite growing up and living in Australia. Was she simply complying with a Fullers marketing strategy, or was she choosing to identify with a country that had early shown its appreciation of her as an entertainer? Perhaps she understood she'd won recognition for her talents there partly because New Zealand was more willing to tolerate confident women. Those who emerged from the temperance movement to become first in the world to achieve women's suffrage had not been shy – and neither was Gladys.

The country of her birth had its dark side. Sometimes thought of as melancholy and brooding, perhaps as a result of its weather and sparse population, New Zealand has, nonetheless, produced its fair share of comedians. Only four years after the end of the most destructive and wasteful of wars, New Zealand-born Gladys declared her commitment to the uplifting possibilities of amusement. Unlike her brother, who sought straight roles after his return from war, Gladys put her faith in hilarity to keep the darkness at bay. 'Miss Shaw frankly admits that she never wants to invade the dramatic realm, not even in a comedy part. "My idea of life", she says, "and particularly stage life, is lights and laughter".'[17]

In Adelaide, following their ten-week, ten-revue season at Melbourne's Bijou, Stiffy and Mo's company again produced *In Society*. The *Register*'s reviewer certainly responded to its brightness, though any semblance of story was lost on him:

> Like all revues of this type 'In Society' is devoid of any plot. The various characters are introduced with the object of giving the several artists the best opportunity for displaying their vocal or histrionic powers, as the case may be. The principal aim of the composer is to amuse, and if a continuous roar of laughter was to be taken as a criterion of success, then the author of 'In Society' certainly attained his objective…One of the best numbers in the revue was the duet, Excelsior, by Keith Connolly and Gladys Shaw. It evoked a burst of applause.[18]

The company returned to Sydney in December so that Nat could produce *Mother Goose*, the end-of-year pantomime for Fullers. But Gladys and Keith remained in Adelaide, appearing for Fullers as Gladys and Keith Shaw, the versatile pair back to their old tricks:

> They scored a success. The lady siffleuse of exceptional ability, and the male performer, in addition to possessing an excellent voice, is a very capable dancer. Their opening duet, My Home Town Is A One-Horse Town, was very amusing, and Keith Shaw did well with his song, She's Fat, Fair, And Forty [sic].[19]

'Fair, Fat and Forty' was a British music hall number, performed and recorded in the UK by Australian-born star Florrie Forde, who was somewhat older than forty when she made the song her own:

I'm fair, fat and forty
I'm feeling full of vim
The boys just won't leave me alone
I'm something to cuddle, not skin and bone
My chassis may be bulky but the steering gear's okay
Oh, I'm fair, fat and forty
Getting younger every day[20]

While Florrie Forde's version of the song balanced self-deprecation with a kind of genial defiance, it's unlikely that Keith's version was as benign. Sexism, ageism and fat-shaming were vaudeville constants, as was the kind of racial caricaturing of 'Yiddisher Comedians' Bert Le Blanc and Jake Mack, who also appeared in Fullers' Adelaide holiday season program. Australian entertainers in the nineteenth and twentieth centuries amused their audiences with a great deal of material we'd find offensive today.

Early in the New Year Gladys and Keith appeared with other members of the Fullers' 'family' in Brisbane. Among their fellow performers

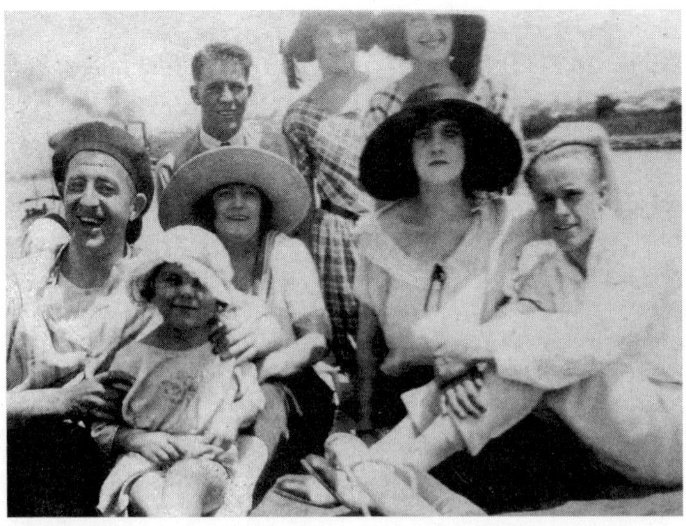

Fullers friends – Keith, Gladys (left), and Freddie Webber (right), 1923

was Freddie Webber, from whom Gladys had parted eighteen months earlier. Bygones, it seems, were bygones.

In March of 1923 Gladys and Keith rejoined Stiffy and Mo for what would become one of the most successful theatrical tours in New Zealand history. 'Long established in popular favour on the Australian vaudeville stage, "Stiffy" and "Mo", as Messrs. Nat Phillips and Roy Rene choose to be called, have descended upon New Zealand with the set purpose of dispelling all gloom', announced the *New Zealand Herald*.[21]

In Auckland for almost four months, the company performed in fifteen different revues, with Gladys often mentioned for her work in them. In *A Sporting Chance* she was daughter of an old inn landlord played by her brother; 'Polly, played by Miss Gladys Shaw, the girl who had hopes of some day becoming a 'dukess', was a cleverly-conceived and genuinely funny character'.[22]

When the company moved on to Wellington hundreds of patrons were turned away from His Majesty's Theatre during the opening week of Stiffy and Mo's *The Lords*. It featured 'Mrs. Porter, in which role Gladys Shaw is welcomed back'.[23] She'd returned to the town and the very theatre where she'd once surprised audiences with her whistling. Wellington found her comic acting no less impressive.

For seventy weeks Stiffy and Mo's Revue company entertained New Zealand audiences – in Auckland, Wellington, Dunedin, Christchurch, then Auckland and Wellington again.

> They (Stiffy and Mo) were a success everywhere, except in Dunedin. They say the only way to get a joke into Dunediners is to tell it to them in their youth, and then it is quite possible they may recognise it and laugh before old age has destroyed their hilarity glands...[24]

Keith felt similarly. He sent Mary Agnes a postcard with a picture of himself in costume on one side and on the other a message: 'Dear Mum,

Keep this photo with the others as in later years they may become very valuable when it gets known that I nearly made Dunedin laugh…'

In Auckland, *The Policemen* was the last revue the company produced and some reviewers thought it the most clever:

> All the performers acquitted themselves most creditably; but most worthy of comment was the work of Miss Gladys Shaw, who appeared for the first time during the season in a serious part, which suited her even better than the comedy roles in which she has previously appeared.[25]

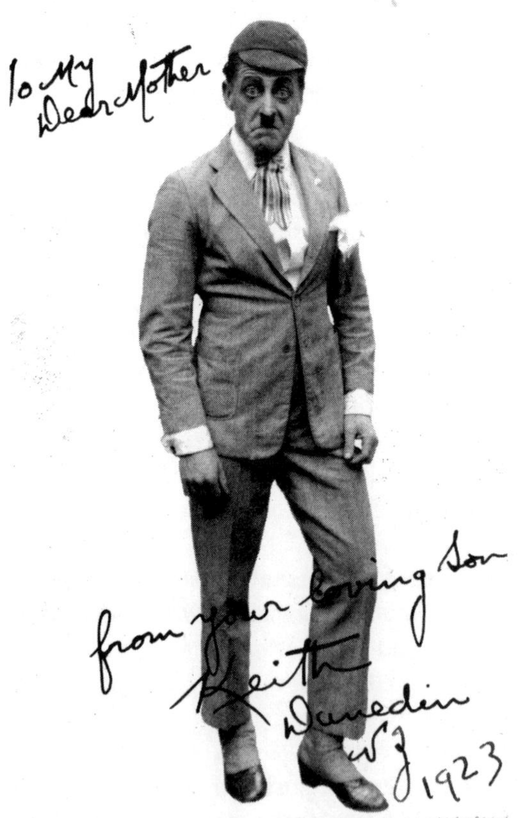

Trying to make Dunedin laugh, Keith Connolly, 1923

Despite previously suggesting she had little interest in dramatic roles, Gladys had won praise for her acting. It wasn't acclaim for her caricatures of domestic servants and society matrons. In *The Policeman* she played a murderess.

> Stiffy and Mo have returned to Fullers – in other words, Standing Room Only! For it is quite useless to attempt to buy a seat at the last moment when these two favourites are on the bill. Roy Rene and Nat Phillips must surely be the biggest money makers the Fuller firm has ever had.[26]

Back in Sydney after its marathon seventeen-month tour of New Zealand, the company opened at the end of August 1924 with *The Sailors*. Soon Gladys was back to the now-familiar round of Pollys and Marys, Mrs Pinetrees, Mrs Porters and, more notably, Mrs Mush. 'A word must be said for the series of clever character acting provided by Gladys Shaw in this company. Her Mrs. Mush, a charwoman, in yesterday's revue was delightful'.[27]

There were neither charwomen nor murderesses in a revival of *The Bunyip*, the end-of-year pantomime Nat Phillips (aka Stiffy) produced for Fullers. Written by pianist and songwriter Ella Airlie, *The Bunyip* was first staged with great success in 1916. Its cast numbered around 250 people. It featured corroborees and bushfires and told the story of Princess Wattleblossom, transformed into a bunyip by an evil gnome. But Gladys took no part in this latest version of the extravagant show. Instead she and Keith were whisked off to Adelaide to join a program headlined by another highly profitable Fullers act, comedian George Wallace, at the tail end of a record-breaking engagement.

In Adelaide their 'act of mirth and merriment'[28] included patter, dancing and another old music hall favourite:

You can't judge a woman by her clothes,
The dainty little furbelows and bows,
You can't judge a woman by her blouses,
The tight black skirt or Harem trousers,
She looks lovely when she's got em on
With a little bit of powder on her nose,
But you can't judge a chicken by the parsley round the dish
And you can't judge a woman by her clothes.[29]

With barely a break, they moved on from Adelaide to Melbourne, where they rejoined Stiffy and Mo for more rehearsing and performing twice a day, six days a week. It was a punishing routine for all concerned. A reviewer for the *Age* noted a 'lack of freshness about some of their gags and jokes', though conceded that 'they were very popular with the audience'.[30] Appearing again in *The Plumbers*, Gladys played Mrs Pinetree for what turned out to be the last time. In May 1925 Stiffy and Mo's Revue Company opened in Adelaide – without Gladys and Keith.

Rene's contract was soon to expire – major Fullers artists were usually on contracts that ran from January to June – and Gladys and Keith must have seen the writing on the wall. They left for Perth, their own performing partnership intact. Barely two months later Stiffy and Mo parted ways:

> Speaking of the Stiffy and Mo partnership he [Nat Phillips] said that it had been mutually dissolved after a period of nine years. He considered that both the public and the performers can have too much of any one turn and also that in the theatrical business a change is as good as a holiday.[31]

At Perth's reopened and newly named Luxor Theatre, previously the Shaftesbury, Gladys and Keith were welcomed back with a warmth reserved for Perth's homegrown success stories. Journalists wrote of Gladys as if they knew her, recalling her days as an amusing and delightful ticket seller at the Grand.[32] The *Sunday Times* declared, 'There is an irrepressible vein of comedy in the make up of Gladys that should carry her far on the road to fame in the realm of vaudeville'.[33]

The siblings' singing, dancing and comic patter act headed a new program at the Luxor, which was again under Andy Hosking's management. As was his daughter Elsie, no longer 'Perth's Little Idol'. Now seventeen, she was known as Elsie Hosking, 'dainty soubrette'. She'd graced the newly launched Luxor stage only a few weeks before Gladys and Keith reappeared in Perth.

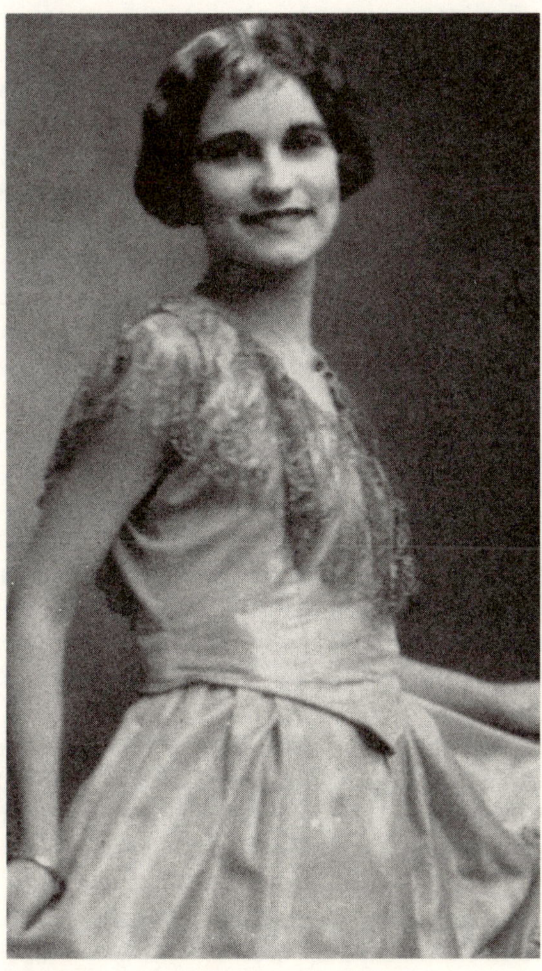

'Dainty soubrette', Elsie Hosking, ca. 1925

They were soon joined by Roy Rene and his first wife, Dot Davis, with whom Gladys and Keith performed in revusicals, some familiar from the Stiffy and Mo days: *The Sailors, The Club, The Waiters* and *In Society*. On busy nights, hundreds of people were turned away. Gladys and her brother were still working hard, appearing in both parts of the program – singing, dancing and pattering comically in the first, and in the second half playing in revues with Mo. But at the Luxor there was just one show a day and a matinee on Saturday.

Meanwhile Stiffy – otherwise known as Nat Phillips – was in Adelaide building a new company, 'The Whirligigs', with his wife Daisy Merritt. Queenie Paul and Mike Connors remained with him as he rapidly regrouped, allowing barely a week between his last show with Mo and the first Whirligigs production. Nat was working harder than ever:

> Three days is all he allows for the rehearsing of a new revue which he himself maps out on Sunday. Hard work, he stressed, is the only ladder to success in the stage world. 'On my morning off', he remarked, 'I have an enthusiastic game of golf and when I can I like a good boxing match. It may not be exactly what one would call resting but it acts as a brief respite from the daily round'.[34]

Something of a whirligig himself, Nat was going full tilt. If he had Shakespeare's jester Feste in mind when he named his company, he wasn't heeding the Bard's words; 'the whirligig of time brings in his revenges.'[35] In October, Nat took the Whirligigs to Sydney. That same month Mo opened in Melbourne's Athenaeum Theatre in the comedy *Give and Take*.

Gladys and Keith remained in Perth. They no longer had family there – Mary Agnes had left the west with her seventeen-year-old son Gerry some months earlier and was now living in Sydney. But their 'home town' had other attractions. For one thing, in Perth they were stars:

> It is not very often that any vaudeville act becomes so popular with a Western Australian audience that it is in a position to appear nightly for six months, but such has been the record of the popular

act, Connolly and Shaw, at the Luxor Theatre. They arrived in Perth last May for a six weeks' season at the Luxor Theatre, but at the end of the contract they were further signed up on account of their popularity, but now, after completing six months at the one theatre they are compelled to finish up this week to enable them to fulfil other engagements.[36]

They didn't announce where they would next appear, instead revealing a surprise offstage engagement, and another of the reasons Keith, in particular, had found the Western Australian capital so attractive:

> All who are acquainted with local stage artists will be interested to know that the clever and versatile Elsie, second daughter of the well-known Mr. Andy Hosking, will shortly wed Keith, only son of Mrs. and the late Gerald Connolly. The latter will be remembered as being the fine basso-baritone, who sang so splendidly at the old Cremorne and Palace Gardens 20–25 years ago, under the name of Gerald Shaw, and who was later on associated with mining ventures in and around Southern Cross. Mrs Connolly ... was at one time a well-known teacher of singing in Perth, while the musical and histrionic accomplishments of the bride are too well known to all for repetition. We wish success to the happy couple.[37]

Elsie, Keith's reason for lingering in the west, was only seventeen and thought too young to marry. She would remain in Perth for the foreseeable future while Keith returned to Sydney. Despite Elsie's charms, he was still ambitious for the kind of celebrity that couldn't be won far from the big city lights of Sydney and Melbourne. And in the Western Australian capital he'd already won a name for himself.

No matter that it wasn't his name to make. His father was indeed the Gerald Shaw referred to in the report announcing Keith and Elsie's engagement. But Gerald was neither a Shaw nor a Connolly, and he wasn't dead. Just as he'd long ago discarded his identity as the swindling Harry Thomson, Gerald had now also jettisoned his guise as head of the entertaining Shaw family. Harry Thomson had been reborn as director of a company with plans to revive a Queensland tin mine, and was the father of three small children.

His older offspring had no contact with their father. Nor had Gladys and Keith seen their mother while they were touring with Stiffy and Mo. By the time they returned to Perth, Mary Agnes had gone 'home' to Sydney, where her own mother was now eighty-six years of age and still institutionalised – in Rydalmere Hospital for the Insane.

Transferred there from Callan Park in 1905, Mary Gertrude had spent twenty years at Rydalmere, an overcrowded hospital offering little effective treatment. Patients were dressed alike in shapeless blue or grey, often restrained and put to bed by 5.30. Rydalmere was, said a Doctor Edwards who worked there in the 1920s:

> ...an introduction to the 'lunatic asylum' at its worst...the wards were dingy and antiquated...even more repelling and soul-killing inside. Most of the rooms were painted a dull green or a peculiar unattractive shade of brown. Nearly all floors were washed every morning and the damp bare boards for hours afterwards added to the asylum smell of urine, faeces and unwashed bodies.[38]

Mary Agnes wrote to Doctor Prior at Rydalmere. She told of her return to Sydney and sought news of her mother:

> I am not in a position to make a home for her. This is a boarding house, but I feel it would not be the sort of restful home she needs, as she will be 86 years of age on 5 April and it is 40 years this month since she was taken to Gladesville. After so many years of seclusion the noise and bustle of city life would only agitate her. A cottage with a garden in a quiet suburb would be a peaceful home for her if I could afford it.[39]

Poor Mary Gertrude. Described by the doctor as 'frail physically', 'mentally weak' but 'quiet and no problem', she'd become one of those 'so accustomed to life within the hospital, and so dependent on the services that it provided that they were unwilling or unable to leave. These patients were known as "asylum-sane"'.[40]

Even if sixty-year-old Mary Agnes had the strength to care for her damaged, feeble mother, she lacked the money to do so. The Master in Lunacy continued to hold three of the five properties bequeathed by Mary Gertrude's father, two of them having been sold to pay for the costs of her care. Her daughter's idea of a safe haven for her mother would remain a dream whilst the master continued to control Mary Gertrude's remaining assets.

Mary Agnes was herself in need of a better home. Contact addresses she left at Rydalmere Hospital were those of theatrical boarding houses in inner Sydney, less suitable accommodation for an older woman than they may have been for her peripatetic children.

9
Speed and More Speed

When Elsie and Keith revealed their engagement at the end of the Luxor season, Gladys announced holiday plans. In Fremantle, she boarded the SS *Centaur*, bound for Java. She would have needed a break, having worked continuously in the nation's most popular shows for the past four years.

Success suited Gladys and so did the times. It was the flapper era, when young women might behave as they pleased. They worked in offices and shops and went to cinemas, theatres and dance halls. They wore their hair bobbed, their skirts short. They smoked and drank and danced suggestively. They were thought frivolous at best, hedonistic and immoral at worst. But they were full of life. Flappers were also, by definition, young. Though she looked and acted the part, Gladys was no girl. She'd recently celebrated her thirtieth birthday.

Her holiday was brief. Gladys sailed back into Sydney barely six weeks after leaving Western Australia for Java. It was almost a year since she'd seen the harbour city. In her absence houses that once stood on its northern shore had vanished to make way for construction of a bridge. The miracle of radio was slowly beginning to infiltrate the city's remaining homes, and a different kind of music was in the air.

Three years after the first radio broadcast in 1923, very few Australians were licensed to own a radio set. But the hesitant beginnings of broadcast didn't slow the spread of international entertainment crazes. Before radio reached every home, before Australia had a significant recording industry and before movies spoke, live performance and imported recordings kept Australians up to date with the latest musical and dancing fashions. North American entertainers brought jazz across the seas. Some toured Australia for months at a stretch, spreading musical and dance fads and inspiring local performers. By 1926 when Australia's population was 6 million, 'a Melbourne music company estimated that there were 1600 jazz bands working in Australia'.[1] Among them was 'Keith Connolly's Syncopating Jesters', formed in the last weeks of 1925.

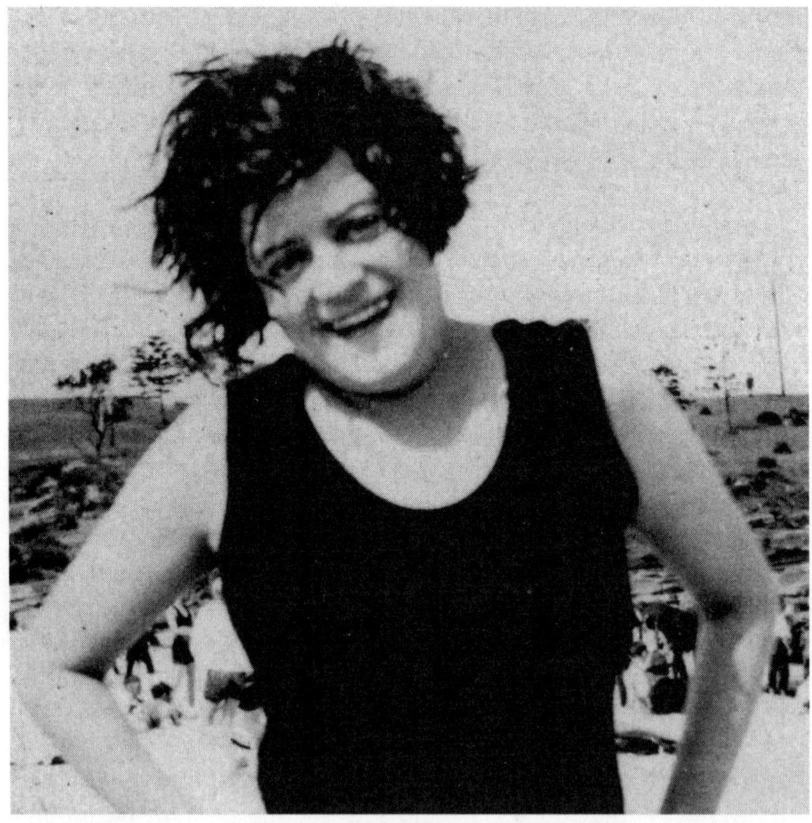

Gladys at 30, 1926

While Gladys was away, Keith had returned to Sydney, where he selected and rehearsed six musicians, including his younger brother Gerry. Between them the male instrumentalists played the saxophone, trumpet, clarinet, violin, drums, banjo and piano. When his whistling sister returned, Keith's band was complete. The Syncopating Jesters made their debut at the Haymarket Theatre, where they appeared twice daily, before screenings of the film *Peter Pan*. By January the band was performing at the Tivoli in Brisbane, where Gladys appeared as 'Ruby Connolly'.

> Spirited jazz music on a multiplicity of instruments was the keynote of the performance by the Syncopating Jesters. There was nothing dull in their work, and they showed a complete mastery of the art of syncopation. Each of the eight members is a comedian, dancer and instrumentalist, and one of the most vivacious is Miss Ruby Connolly. Her principal contribution was a whistling turn, which won for her the warmest applause. Keith Connolly was at his best in vocal jazz music, and as a dancer he was particularly nimble and entertaining. The Jesters gave something new and enjoyable, and they should be popular at the Tivoli for the rest of the week.[2]

Gladys may have used the name 'Ruby Connolly' in order to differentiate her musical persona from that of Gladys Shaw, character comedienne. She might have been filling in time with whistling and music-making until she found another opening as a comic actress.

In the band's early days Gladys wasn't always there in photographs. Keith named the ensemble for himself, and may have wanted all of the limelight. And perhaps Gladys was ambivalent about being little more than her brother's sidekick.

It was soon clear to them both that Gladys was vital to the Jesters' success. At Sydney's Lyric Wintergarden Theatre she was the star of the show, despite which one reviewer failed to name her at all:

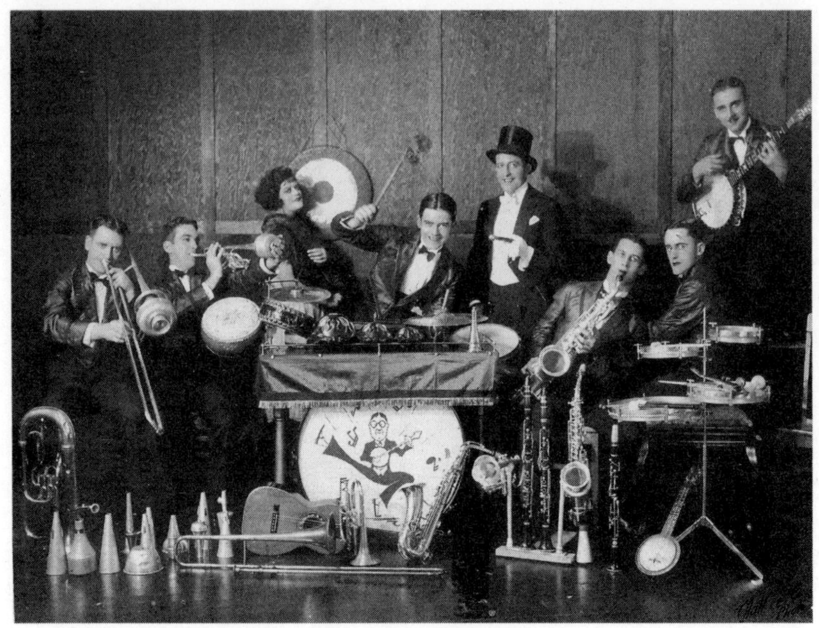

'Spirited jazz', Keith Connolly's Syncopating Jesters, 1926

> GIRL WHISTLER
>
> A particularly clever girl whistler is appearing at the Lyric Wintergarden this week with Keith Connolly and his Syncopated Jesters. The Jesters form a dance band combination of six, backed up by dancing, singing and whistling, by Connolly and the young lady referred to.
>
> They provide really a fine entertainment – one of the best of its kind seen in Sydney.[3]

I'd heard of Keith Connolly's Syncopating Jesters even before finding those band photographs in the old zither case. Dad once told me his father had led a well-known jazz ensemble. 'How well known?' I asked him. 'About as big as Midnight Oil', he replied. Dad was an opera buff and classical music aficionado, but he had more than a

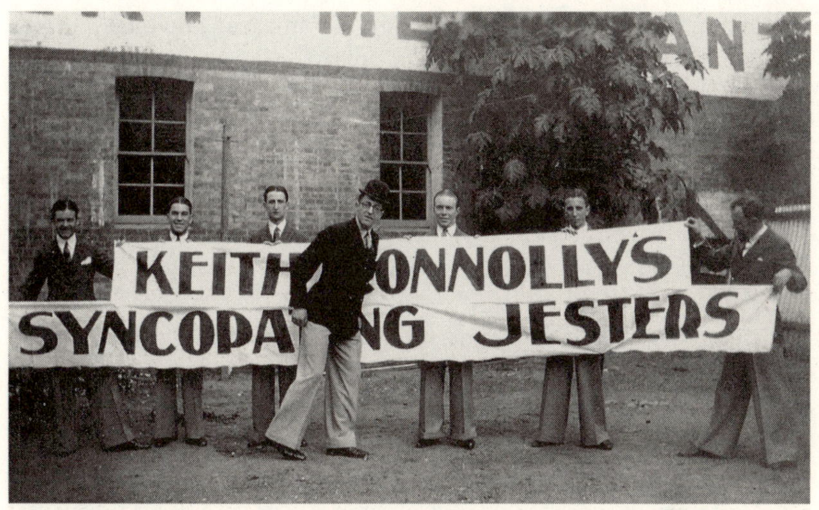

The Jesters without their 'clever girl whistler', 1926

passing acquaintance with the popular music of my generation. My brother Steve was a musician admired for his work with Paul Kelly and the Messengers, Archie Roach and Kev Carmody among others, so I understood how Dad came to know a little about the big acts of our time. But Keith's Syncopating Jesters were popular before Dad was born. I guess he'd heard stories from his parents of a big band led by his father, starring his Aunt Gladys and Uncle Gerry and later joined by his mother.

The Jesters may have impressed him more than some other of his parents' acts, because they played jazz. When Dad was a young man, jazz had undertones and connections that gave the music a greater sense of political purpose than other imported popular entertainments, like musical comedy and variety theatre. Dad's old friend Harry Stein, co-convenor of Australia's first jazz festival, maintained that he 'never heard anybody in Australia talk about jazz as a cause of the proletariat', yet he conceded that jazz was radical 'in the sense of musicians going against the commercial mainstream to play it, and in the new way they see musical language'.[4] Keith Connolly's Syncopating Jesters didn't play the kind of jazz Dad heard decades later in the Communist Party's youth league, yet in their own way they *were* as radical as Dad's music-making comrades.

In his book *The Inaudible Music*, Bruce Johnson describes how visiting American bands brought a new 'Dada-esque' or 'anarchistic' quality to add to the jazz played in Australia in the early 1920s:

> Contemporary reviews describe animal impressions, the banging of kitchenware, revolver shots, drums thrown around the stage – a genial twenties form of the high-energy, in-your-face iconoclasm that announced several phases of popular music. The earliest supporters and opponents of jazz agreed on this: this twentieth-century music was part of a larger post-war interrogation of moral and cultural traditions. It became an anthem for a new age of emancipation that expressed itself in such breaches of Edwardian decorum as short dresses, American slang and immodest energetic dancing. It was meaningfully noted that 'syncopation' began with 'sin'.[5]

Keith's Syncopating Jesters were certainly anarchic and high energy. 'Speed and more speed' was their motto:

> There are eight members in the company and their jazz music is quite a revelation. While making their performance a veritable riot of fun, they gave extraordinary evidence of musical talent in the skilful manipulation of various instruments, which enabled them to present a comedy-in-music with the dialogue understood if not actually articulate. The instrumentalists themselves indulged in a riot of perpetual motion while playing, which added a decided zest to their undoubted skill. The young lady of the company is one of the most accomplished whistlers to visit Brisbane, and is also a most graceful dancer, and her contributions to the programme were deservedly most enthusiastically applauded. Her partner was also a fine acrobatic dancer, and infused plenty of energy into his

> work, both in dancing and jazz songs. Anyone seeking a correct idea of what jazz really is should make a point of visiting the Tivoli and listening to Keith's Syncopating Jesters.[6]

Given the band's newness, and significant competition posed by hundreds of other jazz bands playing around Australia, the *Daily Standard*'s claim that the Jesters played a 'correct' form of jazz was a big one. Especially as jazz was already a term that embraced many styles of music – 'every category of expressive form, from art to trash, from highbrow to lowbrow'.[7]

Their playlist was eclectic and the band's members multi-skilled, but what most distinguished Keith's Jesters from hundreds of other Australian jazz bands was its comic element, and Gladys and her whistling. It was unusual to have women in a band, let alone women as unrepressed as Gladys with her remarkable talent.

In Newcastle, Gladys showed she could do so much more. She used her comedic talents in song, she danced and even yodelled:

> Comedy was infused into the scintillating jazz melodies, the players changing from one instrument to another. Miss Gladys Shaw and Mr. Keith Connolly introduced their act in a topical song, How Do You Do, Everyone, in which smart illusions [sic] were made to current topics, and people of the moment. A whistling interpretation of Carissima was given by Miss Gladys Shaw. Mr. Connolly and Miss Shaw were also associated in syncopated dancing and in a singing comedy sketch My Swiss.[8]

Late in February 1926 the Jesters embarked on a journey across the continent, a trip that would take more than five days and as many changes of train. For Keith in particular their destination had great appeal. In Perth, he would be reunited with his fiancée, Elsie.

The length of the voyage, soaring temperatures and more than 300 miles of dead-straight track across the Nullarbor Plain soon tested the enthusiasm of other band members. One night Keith suggested it would be a good idea to get out of the carriage at the next stop, to relieve the tedium and play 'a little tune just for the natives if any...' Years later Gerry recalled this musical stopover:

> So out we got, instruments and all, when the train stopped for refuelling. There was no station, no anything except a little railway office in view, and we commenced our concert. Within a minute lanterns started bobbing up all around us – the inhabitants had arrived to make up the audience. Where they came from out of the seeming desert was a mystery to all of us. However word was flashed down the line and every time the train stopped at a station we repeated our performance, but next time the audience was ready and waiting. Needless to say the word flashed through to Perth and it was some of the best advertising that the band ever had.[9]

When the band reached the coast, Keith did some additional promotion. In a Perth interview he described the Jesters as different from ordinary jazz bands:

> My partner and I do dances, songs, and whistling before the band, and there is a big element of comedy, notably in burlesques in which the band figures. That is where the variety comes in...This is the only band that has an act before it, and in that respect it is distinctive...I do not think that Australians, now they are taking it up seriously, have anything to learn from the imported musicians when it comes to jazz music. As proof of this, it is worth noting the number of Australians who are going away to take positions in bands in England and elsewhere.[10]

The women's pages of Perth's evening newspaper helped with publicity too, detailing Gladys's costumes if not her performance. She was described as 'an amazing quick change artist' who 'appears in some lovely frocks'. The first was a 'shimmery, shaded, beaded gown that commences almost a nondescript color, but which eventually deepens into the richest violet'. Her second outfit was 'a little pale mauve frock, flimsy, sweet, and feminine in every outline'. Then, 'Aquamarine is the color of a sheeny short frock she dances in. It is simple, but very effective. She finally appears in a grey frock...and has bright cerise pompoms attached to each piquante little point that floats about below the hem'.[11]

Gladys's frocks were often admired, but no one commented when she dressed in men's clothes. Perhaps she was just a flapper having a bit of fun. The flapper image was not straightforward. Male impersonators could be flappers too, and sometimes were. And the slim, boyish physique emphasised by flapper fashion raised questions about gender in more subtle ways. Girlishness and boyishness were both qualities a flapper might have.

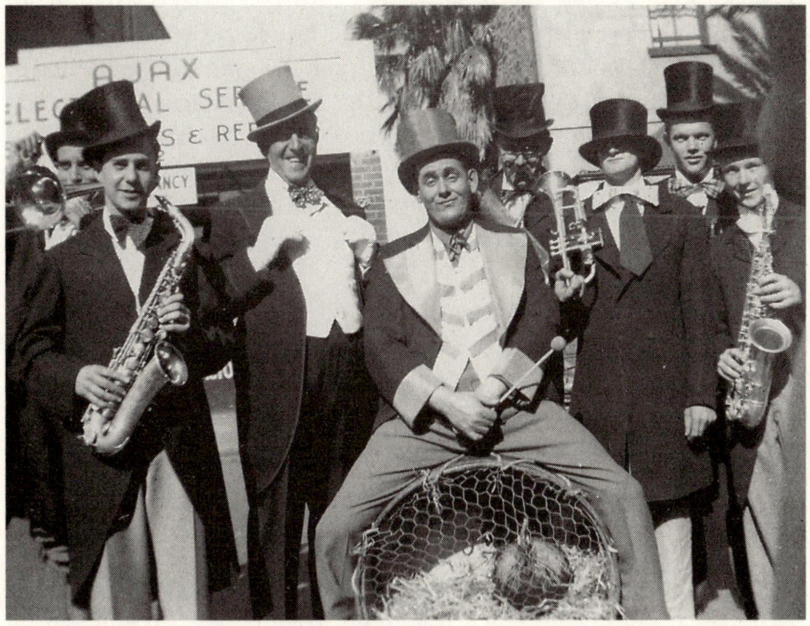

A flapper in a top hat, Gladys (third from right), 1926

Thousands of patrons enjoyed the Jesters during their fortnight at Perth's Prince of Wales Theatre. The season might have been extended had it not been for Keith's ambition to make his name overseas. He decided to take his band from Fremantle to Capetown, where he'd organised the Jesters' first international engagements. Success in South Africa would, he hoped, propel them on to fame and fortune in England.

All that was left was to say farewell to his fiancée Elsie. Which he did on sunny days spent with her at home. Photographs show Elsie there, happy to be with Keith in her own backyard.

Keith dallied too long. Some of his band members accepted dance hall jobs in Perth. The Jesters never did set sail for Africa, and Keith was forced to break the contracts he'd arranged.

Disappointed, Gladys, Keith and Gerry returned to Sydney to begin assembling and rehearsing a new band. The second version of Keith Connolly's Syncopating Jesters didn't have the onstage experience of its predecessor and failed to impress the Tivoli management. But the Fullers' company agreed to give the new line-up a chance, engaging the band for three months of appearances at Melbourne's Bijou Theatre, the Empire Theatre in Brisbane, Fullers' Theatre in Sydney and at the Majestic in Adelaide.

Though hastily pulled together, this band clearly had chemistry. On a day off in Melbourne, the new personnel took their high spirits to the park. Among the rare offstage photographs in the old zither case, those taken in Melbourne's Exhibition Gardens in April 1926 suggest the Jesters' high jinks were not confined to the stage. They cavorted and cartwheeled and formed a human pyramid, with Gladys sharing the top tier.

She was the only woman travelling with a troupe that shared her desire for a life of 'lights and laughter'. Gladys was surrounded by

At home in East Perth,
Elsie, 1926

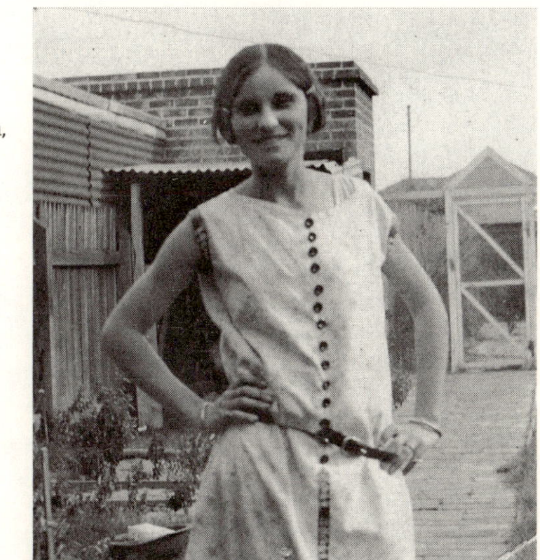

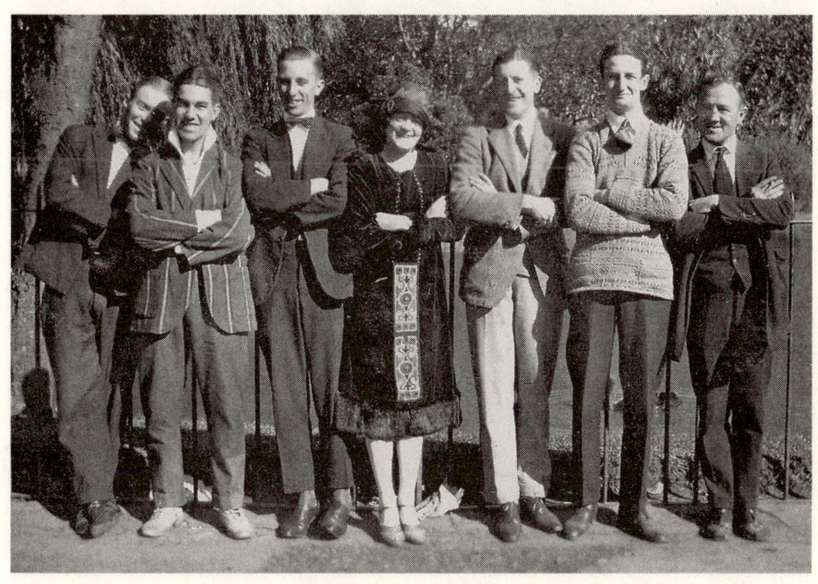

A new line up for the Syncopating Jesters, 1926

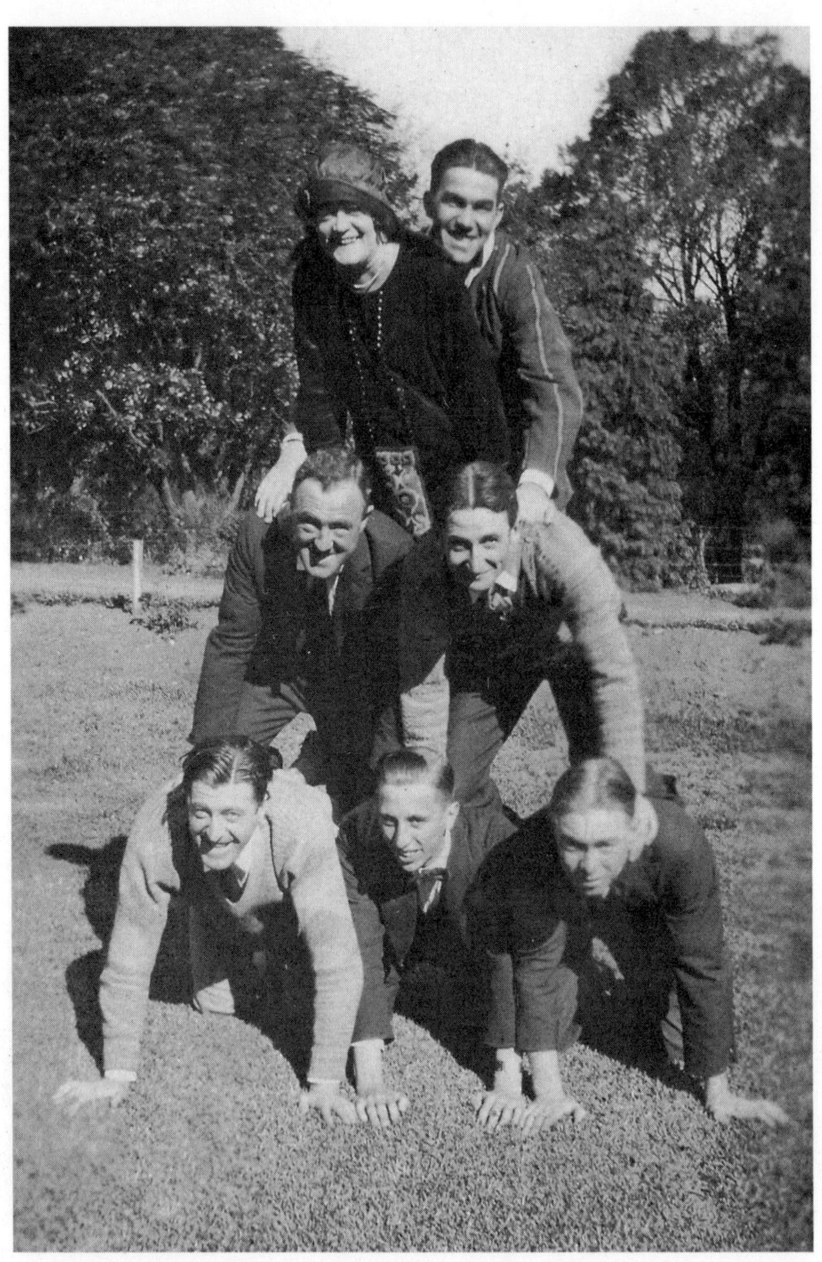

A pyramid of jesters, 1926

young men making the most of their survival only eight years after the end of the First World War:

> The attitude of twentieth century youth towards life is epitomised in the age of Jazz...At the Empire Theatre this week is a jazz band par excellence in Keith Connolly's Syncopating Jesters. The young men of the orchestra, in Oxford bags and sky-blue coats, have been beguiled by the spell of the Lady Jazz, and, swaying to her command, provoke from the diverse instruments which expound jazz the fascinating rhythm and unexpected melodies which set the feet tapping to the beat of the fox-trot.[12]

When their Fullers contract ended, the band was quickly signed by Maurice Chenoweth, a popular tenor and composer who managed Harry Clay's circuit of theatres in suburban and regional New South Wales. For the next eight months Keith's Syncopating Jesters would be based in Sydney.

On the other side of the country young Elsie Hosking was restless. Shortly after Keith, Gladys and Gerry left Perth, tails between their legs and bandless, Nat Phillips – otherwise known as Stiffy – had arrived with his Whirligigs. Nat's wife Daisy Merritt joined them in May and soon so did Jack Kellaway, who became 'Erb, replacing Mo as Stiffy's opposite number. In Perth this illustrious company recruited a new member – Elsie Hosking. Only eighteen years old, she performed with the Whirligigs for the remainder of their twenty-six-week Luxor season and when they left town in October, Elsie went with them.

In Brisbane Elsie appeared at the Empire, in routines and songs that Nat created for her in some of his well-loved revusicals. Daisy Merritt was back in roles that she (and Gladys) had played many times. She was more than holding her own at the side of her husband and Jack Kellaway. According to the *Brisbane Courier*'s review of a revusical titled *Oh, Auntie*, Daisy made:

> ...a very likeable character of Miss Amelia, the perplexed aunt, worried at her soldier nephew's supposed misalliance. She is particularly convincing in several scenes with the inimitable 'Stiffy' and 'Erb', who visit her home as 'soldiers of sort' on leave...[13]

Elsie rated the merest of mentions, though she was noticed; 'Miss Hosking's numbers, with the attractively-gowned ballet, are, No Foolin' and Row, Row, Rosie'. But all the press attention in the world couldn't curb Elsie's enthusiasm for being with Keith. By December she had made her way to Sydney where she and Keith married, a week before Elsie turned nineteen. Her parents, thousands of miles away in Perth, couldn't attend the ceremony. Indeed the sole parent present was Mary Agnes, who by then was the only one that Keith, Gladys and Gerry had.

Edward (Ted) Connolly, the father named on Keith's marriage certificate, was dead. And Keith's biological father, Harry Thomson, also known as Gerald Shaw, was buried four months before his oldest

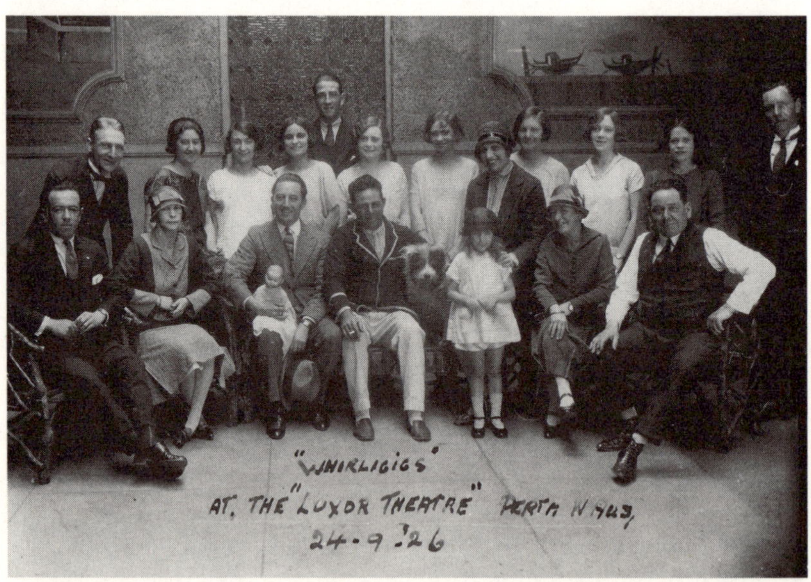

Nat Phillips and the Whirligigs, 1926 (Elsie standing, fourth from left)

son's wedding. He had been living in Melbourne, with his wife Cecilia and their children, when he fell ill. In that city he must have had many opportunities to see his older children when they appeared at the Bijou. He might even have been secretly proud of their theatrical achievements. But the only offspring named on his death certificate were his three youngest, then aged eight, six and three. Mendacious to the end, even Gerald's grave in Box Hill Cemetery concealed the truth. Harry Morewood Thomson, also known as Gerald Shaw, was survived by six children – not only the three named on his headstone – and by many deceits.

When she married, Elsie became both a wife and a Jester. 'Australia's Own and Greatest Jazz Band' now had three female members: Gladys, Elsie and Phyllis Baker, recruited to partner Gerry in the latest dance routines.

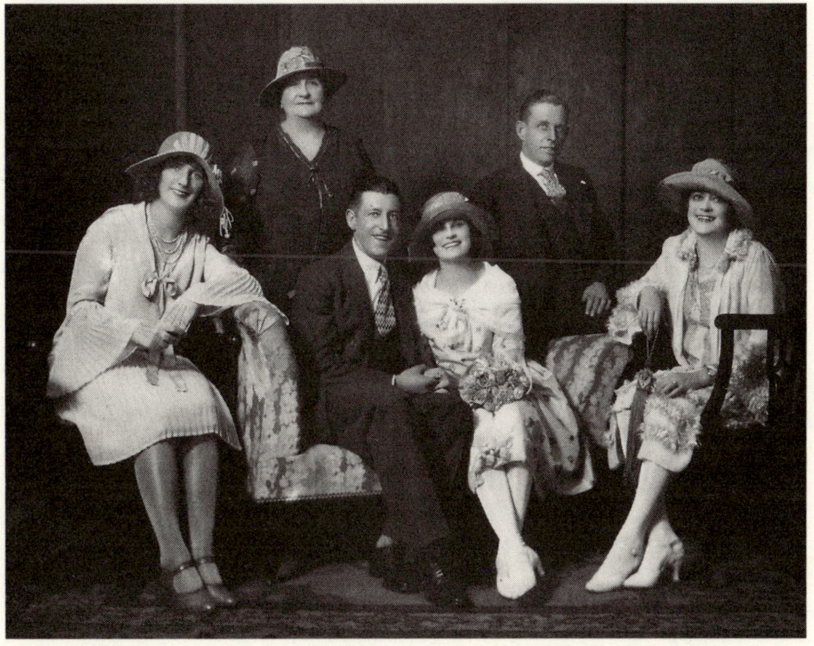

The wedding party, including Mary Agnes (standing), Gladys (r), Keith and Elsie (centre), 1926

Brisbane's John N McCallum signed them for his Cremorne Follies in April 1927, and there they joined old friends Mike Connors and Queenie Paul for the time of their lives. It was the perfect gig. Not only could they see out the winter in the balmy north, but they were among friends, using their multiple talents to the full. There was scope for singing, dancing, instrumental virtuosity, whistling, skylarking, comedy and invention once Mike Connors took over as producer of the Follies show.

It typically featured numerous musical and dancing items by soloists, duos and more, punctuated with comic sketches and a set by the band. Finally a farce – or revusical – included many artists seen earlier in the program. These were friends and colleagues enjoying themselves hugely and their delight was not lost on the spectators:

> …the players do not worry very much about their respective lines, but harangue and harass one another cheerfully. Not infrequently their humour is manifested on the stage before it strikes the audience.[14]

Gladys found room to use all her skills in one show. She sang, danced, whistled, and played a variety of instruments and character parts. The women of the company almost always portrayed scorned female archetypes; from patronised ingenues played by Elsie, to maiden aunts and matrons caricatured by thirty-one-year-old Gladys. The *Sunday Mail* noted that 'as the old maid, Gladys Shaw weathered the handicap of some out-of-date humour'.[15]

It might have been just this kind of typecasting that led Gladys, somewhat provocatively, to take up the saxophone. Somewhere – maybe out on the Nullarbor Plain, or on her rare days off in Sydney – Gladys had acquired yet another musical skill: 'An accomplished siffleur is Miss Gladys Shaw, who also plays the saxophone with marked ability. Her numbers were among the most popular submitted'.[16]

Saxophones hadn't been around all that long. Since their invention in the mid-nineteenth century, they'd mostly been played in military bands, but in the twentieth they were associated with jazz. Sex and sax, sin and syncopation, jazz and licentiousness were linked in the popular imagination. They were uneasily related to African-Americans, the dark of night, the demon drink, the primitive and the modern all at once. For a woman to be whistling and shimmying in public was shocking enough. Gladys only added to her transgressions by picking up the saxophone.

Initially booked for just six weeks, the Jesters entertained Brisbane for more than three months. Packed houses and press attention suggested the city had embraced a new kind of entertainment, one that emerged from the alliance of Follies and Jesters. Yet there was an occasional criticism:

> Keith's Syncopating Jesters set the feet tingling with their jazz. The dances by Gerald Connelly [sic] and Miss Phyllis Baker were, perhaps, the outstanding features of the revue. They danced the Blackbottom to the accompaniment of riotous blares of music from their fellow syncopators. It is a pity that, being Australian, they effect the American style of dress and speech.[17]

It wasn't only American costumes and accents that offended. When Gerry and Phyllis performed their 'Evolution of the Dance' routine, one journalist described how:

> The measured cadence of stately minuet, gave place to the romp of the polka, and the latter to the more sedate waltz. Then came the fox trot, and finally the grotesque Charleston and Blackbottom, copied, as Mr. Connors observed, from the American negro who had so danced for the last 100 years.[18]

Not a lot had changed since the days of minstrelsy and 'coon' singers, when artists in blackface amused audiences with crass caricatures of black people that ridiculed them for a lack of sophistication. Maybe Mike Connors – an American himself – wasn't encouraging the audience to laugh at parodies of African American dances, but rather to admire the artists' skilfully disinhibited movements; stamping and swinging and knees all over the place. And, to give him the benefit of the doubt, perhaps he was hoping to educate the crowd. But despite having some similar steps to earlier African-American dance moves, neither the Charleston nor the Blackbottom was a dance born of plantation slavery. They were entertainments designed for the modern world, in which audio recording, radio and film rapidly spread the latest entertainment fashions.

Both dance crazes had reached Australian cities quickly. Phyllis, Gerry and the Jesters were making the most of them before the next dance fad came along. They played and performed the Charleston and the Blackbottom – despite those who thought them grotesque – to eager audiences all over Queensland and New South Wales.

The Jesters act included 'a number of novel features. The saxophone quintette for instance introduces the largest saxophone seen in the north and it is played by the smallest member of the company'.[19]

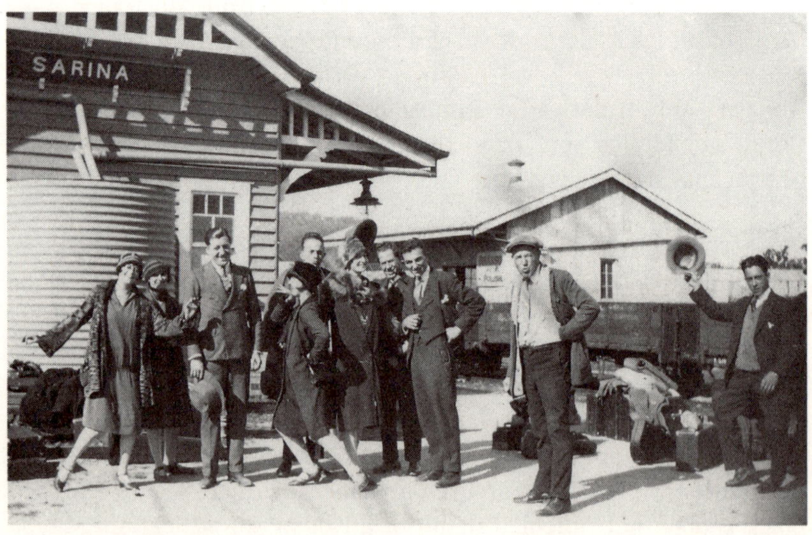

Dance moves at Sarina railway station, 1927

Gladys, always willing to cross the lines of respectability, knew something about the drawing power of novelty. 'The smallest member of the company', she played no mere alto or tenor saxophone, but a baritone or even a bass – the biggest saxophone Rockhampton had seen.

In Townsville:

> …the band then wept (this is not a random statement but a literal truth), the saxophone wailed, the trombone howled, and the drummer wept copiously into a handkerchief, but the atmosphere brightened considerably when Gladys Shaw came into the limelight and whistled. This artiste is rightly called 'the world's foremost lady whistler', and her whistling, though possessed of wonderful strength and volume, is of exquisite sweetness.[20]

Maurice Chenoweth joined them as a performer for the Queensland leg of the tour. Well known and well-liked, he was no mere manager, but also a conservatorium-trained pianist, tenor and actor. After playing in Rockhampton, Mount Morgan, Mackay, and Townsville, Maurice booked the band to work for the remainder of the year on Clay's regional circuit, in the New South Wales towns of Dungog, Lismore, Casino, Grafton, Kempsey, Gloucester, Wingham, Maitland, Cessnock and Bathurst. The band, said its promoter, had something to teach audiences about the latest entertainment craze:

> Syncopation originally came from the Darkies in South Carolina and was handed out to the world as a new form of music, and at the present time, there is not a function or an entertainment that does not include jazz in their programme. To really understand what jazz means the public of Dungog should go along and see and hear Keith's Jazz Band on Saturday next in conjunction with 12 star vaudeville acts who keep the audience entertained from the rise to the fall of the curtain with comedy sketches, songs, dances, whistlers, acrobatics, and laughable interludes.[21]

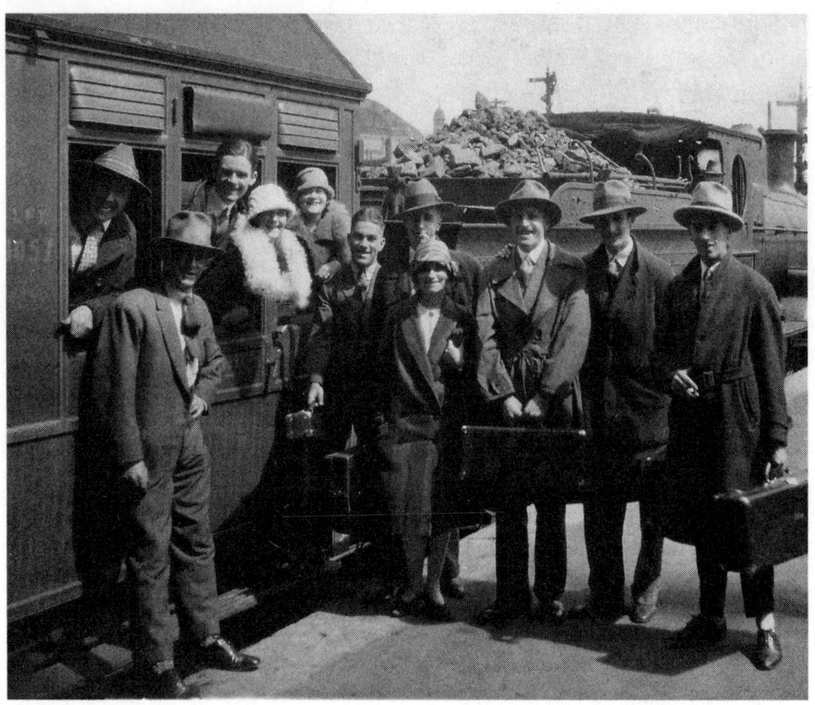

Jesters on tour, 1927

Eventually Maurice steered the Jesters back to Sydney, to play in suburban theatres and cinemas, and in towns closer to home. There, in the harbour city, Keith was offered the kind of role he'd aspired to since returning from war. He would appear in a 'straight' musical comedy, singing and dancing opposite Gwen Matthews in a lavishly cast and costumed 'movie romance of Hollywood and Cuba'.[22] *The Film Girl* opened in the Christmas of 1927, in the newly built Empire Theatre, near Central Station.

Keith's Syncopating Jesters were no more. Following a few new year shows at Lithgow's Theatre Royal, Keith and Elsie left the band when Keith's commitments at the Empire prevented him travelling too far from Sydney.

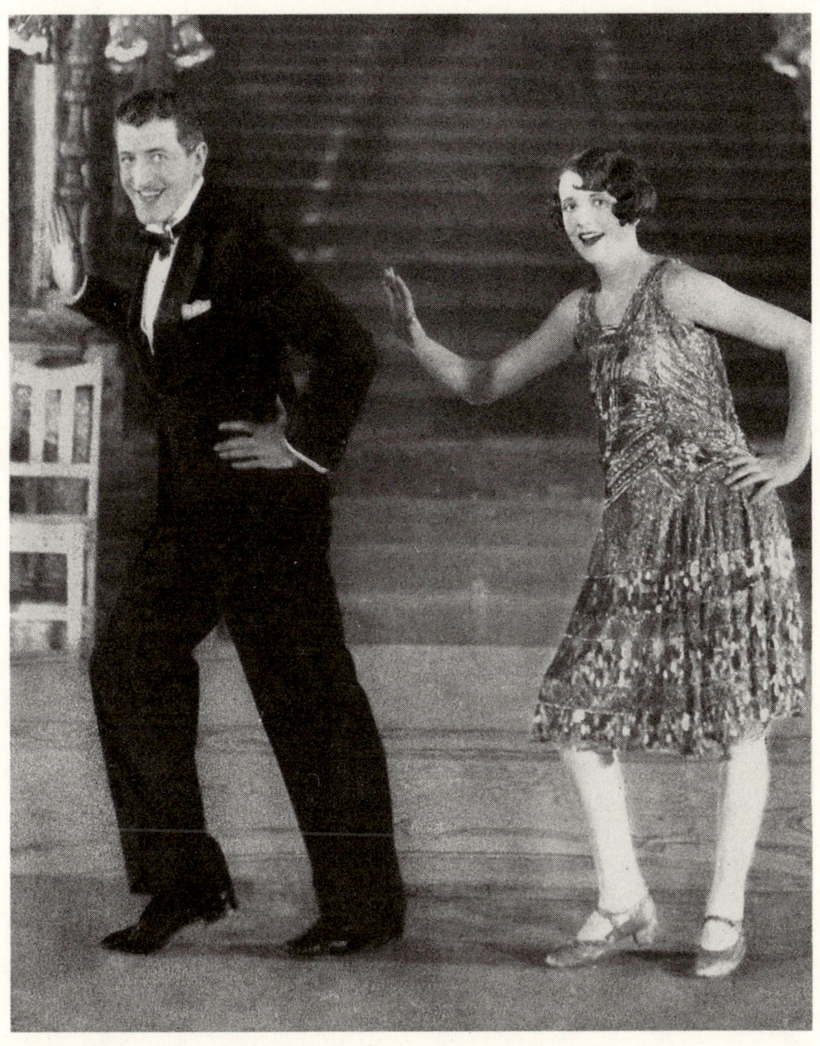

The Film Girl, Keith Connolly and Gwen Matthews, 1928

10
1928

'Gladys Shaw's Syncopating Jesters' soon made an appearance on the program of Elton Black's New Follies at Brisbane's Cremorne Theatre:

> The Syncopating Jesters are a treat in themselves. Their turn alone would have made a success of the New Follies. They are led now by Gladys Shaw, the electric spark, who whistles and keeps the turn bright and interesting from beginning to end. Phyllis Baker, a dainty little lady with winsome smile and twinkling feet; Jack Wright, pianist; Gerald Connolly, drums; Walter Cannon, saxophone, clarinet, and violin; Stan Coltman, solo trumpeter and saxophone; Fred David, violin and saxophone, and George McGrath, banjo, comprise this versatile band.[1]

Gladys hadn't only changed the name of the band, she'd also refreshed its membership. Gladys, Gerry, Phyllis and Fred were remnants of the Syncopating Jesters who played in Queensland and New South Wales in the last months of 1927. Pianist Jack Wright was newly recruited and George McGrath and Stan Coltman were from the original ensemble that entertained desert audiences out on the Nullarbor Plain, but failed to return from the west intact. Now once again they were Jesters, under Gladys's musical direction. At thirty-three she was no second fiddle; she was in charge.

The *Brisbane Courier* described the new Jesters' half-hour act as 'an entertainment that would fill an evening by itself'.[2] The *Daily*

Standard also reported that Gladys now led the band, and praised her 'skilful direction'.[3] When their time at the Cremorne ended, it regretted that Gladys Shaw's Syncopating Jesters appeared for such a short, albeit 'immensely successful season'.[4] But Elton Black's stint as producer of the Cremorne Follies had ended, and with it so did Gladys Shaw's Syncopating Jesters.

Gladys didn't whistle up further work for her band. Considering the enthusiasm with which it was greeted in Brisbane, it's surprising that it didn't go on to entertain audiences elsewhere. The musicians might have had other plans. Or perhaps Gladys lacked the entrepreneurial experience of her crooked father and ambitious brother, despite being a talented siffleur, saxophonist, comedienne and musical director. In the business of popular theatre, women were typically performers managed by men – offstage and on. It wasn't unheard-of for women to become musical directors, but rare indeed was the female theatrical mogul or manager. Elton Black's former wife Kate Howarde was an exception, but to one observer she was 'a conundrum'. Acknowledging that 'she may be a good business-woman, and have stage experience that is of the greatest service to her in the producing line', the same commentator was less impressed by Howarde's revusical appearances. He wrote that they were 'a class of work for which, in my opinion, she has absolutely no qualifications whatsoever. Miss Howarde should put some other girl in her place'.[5] Men like Elton Black, Nat Phillips and scores of others managed, directed and played many parts in their own productions, but a woman could not, it seemed, be both a businesswoman and a 'girl'. And girlishness was a vital prerequisite for women hoping to succeed as performers in the popular entertainment industries of the twentieth century.

In Sydney *The Film Girl* reached its end too, after a well-patronised eleven-week run. Between productions at the Empire, Keith put together a program that reunited Gladys and her brothers. It featured Keith's Jazz Band and The Ginger Girls Revue Company; 'a bevy of beauty and brains direct from the Empire Theatre'. According to the advertising this was 'Not an ordinary show, but a real Theatrical Company. Nothing in it to offend the most fastidious, but a wealth of

MUSIC, DANCING, and NOVELTY ACTS and COMEDIANS'. [6] For two 'rollicking nights', this company entertained Kiama on the New South Wales South Coast, where, thirty-three years before, Claire Delmar's Comedy Company had advertised for pianists and skirt dancers.

Gladys wasn't back with Keith's band for long. She'd committed to another and was less available for musical ventures squeezed in around her brother's engagements at the Empire. But she did appear with Keith's Jazz Band when it played between boxing matches at Leichardt Stadium. Apparently, they 'got the bird', or so my father said at his mother's funeral when he recalled Elsie's story about appearing at the stadium. According to *Everyone's Magazine* in 1926:

> Every Australian vaudeville patron understands the meaning of the term 'getting the bird'. For the benefit of those whose education must have been sadly neglected, it is here explained that 'giving the bird' is the audience's polite (?) way of intimating to a performer that his services are no longer required, and that they have no further desire to hear evidence regarding his skill as an entertainer. The bird is given in various ways – by the count out, by throwing pennies on the stage, and by the more vulgar method of heaving at the unfortunate artists vegetables long past their prime.[7]

The stadium crowd was a very different audience to the one Gladys had entertained a few days earlier, when she appeared in all-female company before acrobats and movies at the Haymarket Theatre.

Gladys had become one of 'seven sirens of syncopation' in a musical act known as 'Lynette and Her Six Redheads'. 'Lynette' was Muriel Errington, who'd taken over leadership of the band after its founder, Jock Thompson, left to concentrate on his work with another musical ensemble, Tom Katz and His Bellboys.

Looking to emulate successful American groups, Jock had tried to form an all-female saxophone band, but struggled to find enough women who could actually play the instrument. Muriel and her sister Clarice were from a family of entertainers, and were already accomplished musicians when Jock taught them to play the sax. Jock had seen Gladys perform in Brisbane and knew she was experienced as an all-round entertainer and saxophonist. She must have seemed a godsend.

She joined Muriel and Clarice, their saxophones and four other women who played trumpet, trombone, piano and drums. Not being a redhead was no impediment to joining 'Lynette's' band. With the exception of Clarice, who dyed her hair, the women wore red wigs: 'terrible things. They were hot and you'd perspire…'[8] On the other hand there was barely enough fabric in their costumes to keep them warm. Glittering with gold and silver lamé, their outfits were sufficiently revealing that some theatre managers required them to wear net skirts in a gesture to modesty.

After playing at the Haymarket, Lynette and Her Six Redheads appeared at the Lyceum, where *Get Your Man* was screening. It was a Hollywood film notable for having been written by a woman (Hope Loring) and directed by another (Dorothy Arzner) – and for starring Clara Bow.

Clara Bow was the most famous redhead of them all. It was said that when her fans learned she used henna to redden her locks, sales of the dye tripled. She was seen as the quintessential flapper, imitated and reviled in equal measure.

Bow found fame as the 'It Girl' after starring in the film *It*, adapted from a novel of the same name by Elinor Glyn, prolific novelist and screenwriter. When asked to describe what an 'it girl' was, Clara Bow is said to have replied in her perfect Brooklyn accent, 'I ain't real sure'. In 1928, Bow starred in another Glyn screenplay: *Red Hair*.

At the pictures, watching Clara Bow, Gladys might have imagined herself in the movie business. As in Hollywood, Australian women sought roles both in front of – and behind – the cameras. Louise Lovely, actress and former Tivoli star, had returned from the United States to make *Jewelled Nights* – co-directing with her then husband,

Wilton Welch, and playing the lead. Adapted from a novel by Marie Bjelke-Petersen, it told the tale of a socialite who dresses as a man to escape to Tasmania's north-west. Fleeing a promise to enter into a loveless match, she finds a handsome miner who sees through her cross-dressing. Reader, she marries him.

Lovely's picture was expensive to make by Australian standards and didn't recoup its budget. She told a Royal Commission on the Moving Picture Industry that large cuts taken by the distributor and the exhibitor were at least partly to blame.

Australian filmmakers, pioneers of world cinema, were doing it tough. Access to their own country's cinema screens was restricted by booking systems under which cinemas signed up to exhibit the catalogues of American-controlled distributors. Meagre budgets available for local productions already put them at a significant disadvantage when competing with the lavish extravaganzas of Hollywood. By comparison Australian production values and promotional budgets were at best modest, at worst poor.

Isabel McDonagh also gave evidence to the Royal Commission. She and her sisters, Phyllis and Paulette, made *Those Who Love* in 1926. It earned more money at the Australian box office than Charlie Chaplin's *The Gold Rush*. Initially able to finance their films with their doctor father's money, the McDonaghs shot many scenes in their Drummoyne family home. Friends and acquaintances were conscripted to appear in party scenes. Dr McDonagh was the official medical man for JC Williamsons Theatre company, and in the small world of Sydney entertainers it's possible that Gladys and these filmmaking sisters crossed paths, though I've never found her name on their credits nor her face in their crowd scenes.

Despite reporting that 'the cinema occupies a lasting place in the life of the people, and is becoming increasingly important in its activities in the social, cultural and moral development of the community', the Royal Commission offered little help to Australian filmmakers. On 26 April 1928 it delivered its findings, largely supporting the arguments of powerful interest groups – exhibitors and distributors – at the expense of performers and creators.[9]

Opportunities for filmmakers, and for actors like Gladys, were narrowing. Their prospects weren't improved by the government's failure to introduce measures to protect Australia's entertainment industries from an overwhelming amount of imported production. By 1928 Australians were cinematically literate and attending the cinema in record numbers. Increasingly sophisticated American and English movies competed for their attention not only with homemade films, but also with serious theatre, musical comedies, vaudeville and radio. Local entrepreneurs imported stars, filled programs to bursting point with movies and live acts, and built lavish theatres as the contest intensified.

Gladys played with Lynette and Her Six Redheads at Union theatres in and around Sydney and Brisbane. They played half-hour sets between two feature films each afternoon and evening, mingling popular tunes with singing, dancing and comedy. Every week they came up with a different routine, arranging the latest music, devising new dance and comic numbers, and rehearsing them each morning.

Meanwhile, Keith returned to the Empire, where he worked for much of the year, in a company making strenuous efforts to find a winning format. Built and opened only a year earlier by Rufe Naylor, sports promoter and punter, the theatre was huge. It seated 2500 people in a city of just over a million, all of them potential patrons relentlessly wooed by entertainment entrepreneurs. The Empire's spectacular balletic tableaux distinguished its shows from many other productions, but were not without significant costs.

After *The Film Girl*, Keith was cast in *Top Hole*, a golfing musical comedy. Given the sporting interests of the theatre's proprietors, its theme was not so surprising. An earlier production, *Take the Air*, sought to capitalise on the contemporary obsession with aviation, a subject then of as much interest to Australians as sport. Indeed pioneer aviator Bert Hinkler appeared onstage on *Take the Air*'s last

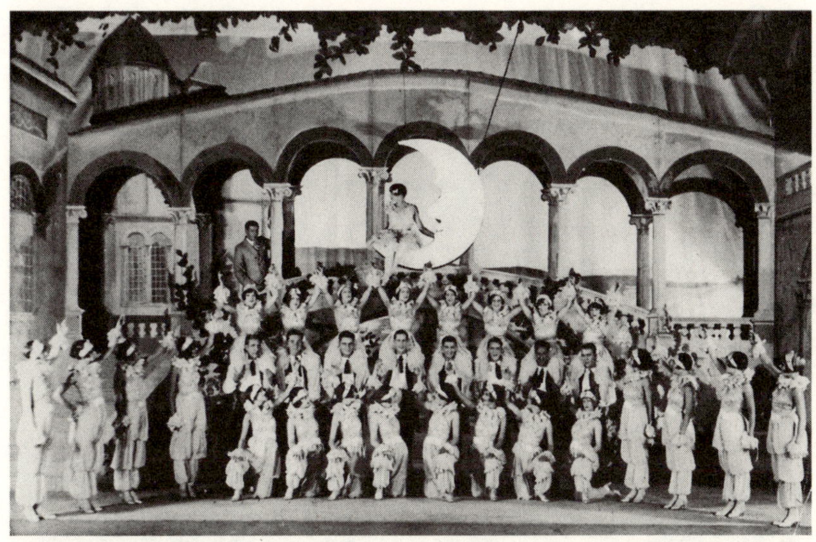

A lavish Empire Theatre show, ca. 1928

night, less than two months after making the first solo flight from England to Australia. No great golfer graced the Empire stage during the season of *Top Hole*, but Keith was said to be 'outstanding' as the villain.[10]

For all their efforts, Lynette and Her Six Redheads attracted far less press attention. Where male ensembles usually rated at least a few lines in reviews – even when the commentary concentrated on a program's cinematic offerings – the all-female band attracted little comment. Perhaps words failed the newspaper men of the day.

In Elsie's case of keepsakes my favourite photograph turned out to be the most difficult to identify.

Nothing was pencilled on the back to say who these women were, where they were or when it was taken. At first I thought they belonged to a revusical ballet or chorus, but those usually came in even numbers, like the 'Exquisite Eight' and the 'Radio Six'. Here were seven young

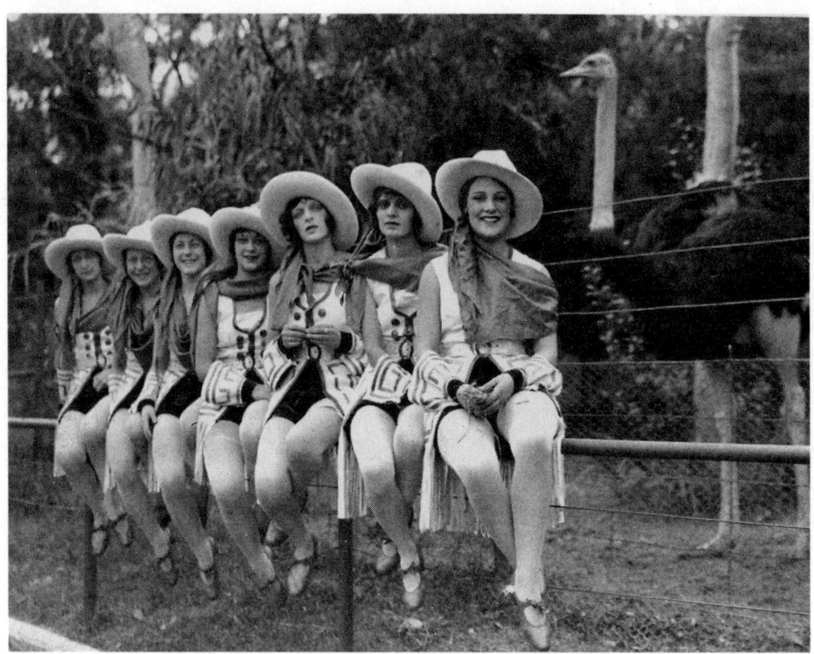

Lynette and her Six Redheads, 1928

women, cheerfully meeting the camera's gaze, nothing coy about them. In the very centre of this happy row perches Gladys. When I discovered that Gladys had been a 'Redhead' it all fell into place. The photograph is a rare shot of Lynette and Her Six Redheads, possibly taken at Brisbane's Botanic Gardens, where once there was a zoo. An ostrich looks fixedly over the women's heads, seeming to ignore them every bit as much as did the entertainment writers of the day.

In describing the ensemble in her book about Australian all-girl jazz bands and orchestras between the wars, historian Kay Dreyfus quoted from her interview with 'Lynette', whose real name was Muriel Pearce (nee Errington). Interviewed when she was ninety-four years old, Muriel recalled that the women 'took care of one another, did not drink much, and in any case were all "petrified of getting pregnant"'.[11]

Was it the company of women, moderation of her drinking habits, or the playful costumes that made Gladys look so well? She appears younger than her thirty-two years, fresher than she did in those photographs of Jesters on tour.

Muriel also remembered that Gladys taught her to play the banjo and that the pair had performed a double banjo act. She said she'd loaned Gladys her banjo and never got it back.[12]

When we were children, Grandma Elsie gave us an old banjo uke. We thought she must once have played it on the stage. Certainly she knew how to strum a simple tune. Nowadays that instrument lives in a dusty case shoved behind a bedroom door at my mother's house. I fished it out when I learned that Muriel's banjo was never returned to her, but there was nothing to suggest the identity of its original owner. It may have belonged to Elsie, or Gladys, or even Muriel. Popular with vaudeville performers in the 1920s, it was also called a banjolele and might have been the very same instrument Gladys taught Muriel to play. It had the four-stringed body of a banjo and the fretted neck of a ukulele and was as easy to learn as the latter, though considerably louder – a quality that would have appealed to my brother Steve when he took it up as his first instrument.

Playing banjos, saxophones, a trombone, a trumpet, percussion instruments and a piano, 'Lynette' and her band performed in Sydney and Brisbane. Muriel said later that membership of the band remained pretty constant, but she was wrong about that. Shortly before they were to play in Newcastle, Gladys was offered a place alongside her younger brother Gerry and old friends Mike and Queenie in their newly formed revue company. Gladys deserted her redheaded sisters to join the 'League of Notions', a classic vaudeville troupe, featuring individual acts, singing, dancing, whistling and comic sketches in a program lasting up to three and a half hours.

By late May the new company was touring Fullers' theatres in New Zealand, and Gladys was back to using a greater range of her talents than Lynette's Redheads could ever have accommodated. At the end of July the company appeared before a large crowd at the Opera House in Palmerston North.

> There was a wealth of amusing comedy judiciously intermingled with effective ballet ensembles, catchy and tuneful syncopation with last but far from least some unusual numbers provided by the girl whistler, Miss Gladys Shaw.[13]

She'd been noticed in the town of her birth, the place where her mother, Mary Agnes, first promised to raise her intelligent baby daughter for a life on the stage.

If only Mary Agnes could have seen Gladys all grown-up and entertaining the people of Palmerston North. Instead she was in Sydney dealing with an inheritance of her own. After forty-three pitiless years in the asylums of New South Wales, her mother had died. Eighty-nine years old, senile, physically frail, 'but no trouble',[14] Mary Gertrude slipped quietly away.

As so often happens, a departure was followed by an arrival. Three months after Mary Gertrude's death, my father was born. Keith and Elsie gave their son an impressive list of names. 'Keith' was handed on by his father. His second name, Andrew, was inherited from his mother's father. The third, Warrington, was that of his great-grandfather. But Dad's surname – by which both he and I would be known for the rest of our days – was that of a man to whom he was not related.

It is some kind of proof that Dad was largely ignorant about his origins that he took the name Connolly so seriously. Well read in Irish history, he was quietly pleased to share it with the heroic James Connolly, executed in Dublin after the 1916 Easter uprising. Indeed my brother Steve was given 'James' as his middle name. Once, during the Troubles, Dad took us to a meeting of the Connolly Association in Melbourne. After that, we wore our label with even more pride. We children liked to fantasise that we had a familial connection with a rebel, a hero who fought against the imperial oppressor. Years later Steve and some friends would even form a band they named 'The Troubles'.

In its own way my father's family *was* engaged in some kind of war against imperialism, albeit of a cultural kind. It was a war that, as 1928 drew to a close, Australian artists were clearly losing. The Royal Commission hadn't prevented United States distributors from exercising their considerable muscle and increasingly the movies shown in Australian cinemas were imported. The money they earned at the box office largely left the country.

Live entertainment had once employed thousands of workers on and offstage. Even the Tivoli, which imported so many overseas artists, ploughed significant money back into the Australian and New Zealand industries. Fullers, Clays and lesser theatrical empires were great contributors to the structures that underpinned the enjoyment and employment of many Australians. Now those companies, as well as movie producers, were being challenged by Hollywood film studios with seemingly infinite capacity to seduce audiences. Their movies had the appeal of stars, sophisticated production techniques and all the publicity money could buy.

The greatest blow in the contest for Australian audiences came in the last days of the year. On Saturday 29 December 1928 *The Jazz Singer* premiered at Sydney's Lyceum Theatre. For the first time Australians heard the movies talk. Despite the novelty of sound, critics were underwhelmed by the film. It would be some time before talking pictures reached all corners of the land, but *The Jazz Singer* screened for forty-six weeks in Sydney. It broke box office records and ushered in a new era for Australian audiences, dramatically changing the lives of those who had earlier entertained them.

11
Auld Lang Syne

Gladys and Gerry were in New Zealand with the League of Notions for more than nine months. While they were away their mother, now sixty-four, finally found a place to call her own in Sydney. Mary Agnes and her sister Maud had at last inherited what remained of their mother's assets. The Master in Lunacy had not, as threatened almost twenty years earlier, sold all of Mary Gertrude's properties to pay for her keep in the asylum. Three of them remained and so, with a loan secured against her share of the estate, Mary Agnes bought herself a small bungalow. She could at last retire to the kind of quiet cottage she was never able to provide for her own mother. Not since leaving Ted and her sons in Manly more than thirty years ago had Mary Agnes had a home to call her own.

'Indiana' was in recently developed Rosebery, a short distance from the centre of Sydney. Mary Agnes was proud of her cottage, of its newness and location, close to tram and train lines. She referred to it as 'our house', possibly hoping it would be a home that her children, and their children, might come to regard as the hub of family life. In the old zither case I found a happy photograph of Elsie visiting Indiana with her son, Mary Agnes's first grandchild, my father Keith. He was just five months old.

But Mary Agnes would have the house to herself for most of the year. Her children were even more often away from Sydney now there were new challenges to earning a livelihood in the entertainment business.

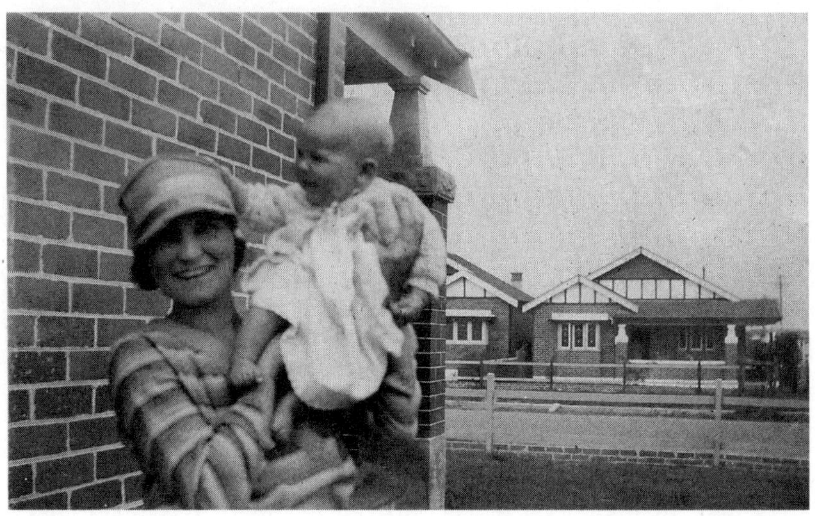

At 'Indiana', Elsie and baby Keith, 1929

Elsie and baby Keith left in March 1929, soon after having their photograph taken at 'Indiana'. Elsie would return to Perth's Luxor stage while her own parents cared for their grandson. His father stayed behind to wind up a season with Fullers' 'Novelettes', the company's latest revue troupe. Then Keith senior also left Sydney to dance in Broken Hill and Adelaide and back to Broken Hill again.

Returning to Australia, Gladys, Gerry and the League of Notions went straight to Melbourne, convinced that live shows still had the upper hand. In one skit the company even mocked the pictures that talked:

> Talkie competition has little or no effect on the drawing power of the League of Notions Revue Company at the Bijou Theatre, and capacity houses greeted the complete change of programme on Saturday. The big audience was kept in a state of laughter from the opening chorus to the final curtain. A novelty was a clever burlesque of the 'first Australian-made talkies', featuring 'Orrie', 'Orb', Gladys Shaw and Queenie Paul.[1]

This lampooning of the 'first Australian made talkies' satirised only a few productions that, in 1930 and 1931, claimed to be the first Australian sound films. They were hampered by inadequate recording and reproduction technologies. Not until Efftee productions used expensive imported equipment to record sound for *The Diggers* – released two years after the League of Notions' parody of local talkies – did an Australian sound film make an impression on the cinema-going public.

Initially dismissive of competition posed by talkies, theatrical entrepreneurs were about to encounter some new difficulties they hadn't anticipated. In August 1929 the Bruce Government brought down a budget which proposed to increase taxes to deal with a growing deficit. Among those to be raised was the Amusements Tax.

Impresario Sir Benjamin Fuller spoke against the measure at a protest meeting in Perth:

> I should like to see the public aroused…Mr. Bruce seems to think that we are making a lot of money in this business, but if he has access to the Taxation Department he can easily find that he is mistaken.[2]

Among those who agreed with Sir Benjamin were members of the government, including the Member for Wentworth, Walter Marks, chair of the recent Royal Commission on the Moving Picture Industry. Frustrated by his own government's failure to implement the commission's modest recommendations, he showed his support for the Australian movie industry by joining six other Nationalist members of Parliament to cross the floor during a vote on an industrial relations matter. As a result, the Maritime Industries Bill failed, an election was called and on 12 October the Nationalist–Country coalition lost government. Prime Minister Bruce lost his seat and Labor won a huge majority in the House of Representatives.

Less than a fortnight later Wall Street crashed, marking the beginnings of an economic catastrophe that would play out over more than a decade, stealing the livelihoods of many Australians, including some of the nation's entertainers.

It's often said that the Depression and the advent of talkies spelled the end for vaudeville theatre, but the reality wasn't so simple. Well-established artists like Gladys, Elsie, Keith and Gerry had experience, talent, reputations and an extensive theatrical network to keep them in work. And accustomed as they were to a nomadic existence, they were willing to traipse the continent for it, despite the effects of their constant travel on family life.

My father accompanied his parents and Fullers' Novelettes to Broken Hill late in 1929. Still young enough to be easily transported, baby Keith had his first birthday in the mining town, where his father and the Novelettes occupied the Crystal Theatre stage for thirteen weeks. After a hundred performances they left Broken Hill, days before Gladys and Gerry arrived with the League of Notions Revue Company.

They were lucky to get there, travelling 300 miles from Adelaide in the November of 1929, shortly before the breaking of a six-month drought. A few days later and the road to town would have been impassable. When the storm came, said the *Barrier Miner*:

> Hearts were lightened and the patter of rain on the roofs heightened the pleasure of those who were at entertainments. Connors and Paul were on the stage in the Crystal Theatre when there were several heavy rolls of thunder and a sharp shower was falling. They happened to be singing something then about sunshine, but Mr. Connors, evidently sensing what the sounds meant to those in the theatre, stopped for a moment and said 'That's better than the sunshine, isn't it?'!
>
> When people came out of the amusement places the street gutters were carrying wide streams, and pools of water were everywhere, but even women and girls, when they splashed into the water with frail shoes and delicate stockings, only laughed light-heartedly,

because the rain meant that although damage might be done to their finery, there would be money to buy more.[3]

The rain also brought better box-office receipts. Broken Hill's population was estimated at only 27 500 at the end of 1929, but thousands more people lived in surrounding settlements. Once the waters subsided, many of them would travel into town to catch entertainments on offer in the lead-up to Christmas – no longer worried about spending on a few pleasures instead of saving for hard times.

The League of Notions season extended into early January, when the company departed Broken Hill for Sydney. Its arrival was eagerly awaited by Mary Agnes, keen to show off her new house, and more than a little annoyed about her children's lack of attentiveness. She wrote to Gerry in Broken Hill, as the League of Notions was about to finish its run:

Indiana,
Morley and Primrose Avenues,
Rosebery,
Sydney

Sunday 5/1/30

My darling Gerald,

Thank you dear for £2 in your letter last Monday. Glad has not written to me so regularly as you do and even Keith has not sent me wires since he left…I fancy Fuller is going to put off a lot of his people. Williamsons is also putting off a great number of performers and lowering the salaries of those he is keeping on. It seems it is through the Amusements Taxation...Let me know dear if you still think you will be here by Thursday by the ten past nine train at night. I will be there to meet you…

Despite her retirement, Mary Agnes kept a close eye on the entertainment industry, following its ups and downs as they affected her children's theatrical careers.

After the dismissal of Prime Minister Bruce and the election of the Scullin Labor Government, the new Australian treasurer, Ted Theodore, refused to increase the Amusements Tax. But the New South Wales State Government approved its own, introducing it on the first day of 1930.

On 15 February the League of Notions opened at Fullers' Castlereagh Street theatre in Sydney, with both Gladys and Gerry among its featured artists. Mary Agnes might have taken a tram into the city to see her children perform. For Gladys, appearing at Sydney's Fullers' Theatre was a kind of homecoming. Looking out at an audience seated in the theatre's ornate two tiers, she'd whistled and danced and sung and bantered with Freddie Webber, then with her brother Keith. In that same Fullers' Theatre she'd worked long and hard to earn praise as a new comedienne with Stiffy and Mo. It was a venue almost as familiar as were her friends and associates in the League of Notions. With Mike Connors and Queenie Paul, brother Gerald and other longtime colleagues, Gladys was back in the comfortable embrace of family, friends and the Sydney theatre she knew best.

Queenie had been onstage when Fullers' Sydney home reopened ten years earlier, after Henry White's extensive redesign:

> The new theatre may be said to have received its vocal baptism while Queenie Paul was singing with appealing charm 'My Australian Rose', and 'That Soothing Serenade'.[4]

Now the *Sydney Morning Herald* again reported Queenie's success on the Fullers' stage, with talented performers she and her husband Mike had themselves recruited and rehearsed:

> Mike Connors and Queenie Paul and their League of Notions Revue Company presented an entertaining programme at Fullers' Theatre

> on Saturday night. Amusing sketches, new songs, the playing of a jazz band, and dancing by a sprightly ballet provided an enjoyable variety of short scenes...Among the musical numbers most applause was earned by a series of duets sung by Queenie Paul and Mike Connors harmoniously and attractively...Gerald Connelly's [sic] buoyant personality made him popular whether he was singing, dancing, or performing as a jazz drummer. Song and dance numbers were given by Phyllis Baker, and sentimental songs by William Beresford, while Gladys Shaw contributed to the success of the comic scenes.[5]

With the arrival of talkies things had changed – cinema now dominated storytelling. Vaudeville relied on variety, and revusicals were largely abandoned in favour of the old revue format of loosely linked acts and sketches. But just like revusicals, revues were expensive to stage. It was far cheaper to exhibit mostly imported movies. New taxes had added to the costs of live theatre, and audiences were shrinking in tough economic times.

Only two days after the League of Notions opened its Sydney show, John and Ben Fuller announced they would close their Castlereagh Street theatre for live performance. They would convert it, and most of their Australian theatres, to screen motion pictures:

> Sir Benjamin said that it was with infinite regret that he had to bow to public demand for talkie pictures and 'canned' music. It appeared to him to be only a temporary fascination, and when the time became opportune he would revert to 'flesh and blood' performances with the utmost pleasure.[6]

The Fullers had delayed closing their vaudeville operations for a little longer than some of their competitors, but hopes that Gladys and her League of Notions colleagues held for the survival of Fullers' vaudeville were dashed. They would, it seemed, have the dubious privilege of being the last to perform in this most beloved of vaudeville houses. Queenie, whose singing reopened the theatre in 1919, would sing *Auld Lang Syne* to close it, joined by her fellow artists:

> The ringing down of the curtain at Fullers' Theatre on Saturday night marked the passing of vaudeville in Sydney. Whether the exit will be temporary or permanent remains to be seen, but the fact is that the popularity of the talkies has made impossible the successful and profitable running of vaudeville entertainments.
>
> Fullers' Theatre was no less famous than the old Tivoli, which shut its doors to vaudeville last September. Both theatres fought bravely against the onslaught of the new entertainment, but succumbed.
>
> ...Neither the discomfort of the evening nor the consciousness that perhaps they were appearing for the last time on a stage having many years of vaudeville history affected the spirit of the League of Notions Revue Company on Saturday night.[7]

At the final curtain there were speeches and optimistic words about the return of vaudeville from Mike Connors, who declared that 'Sydney has shown a preference for canned art, but it will want vaudeville again before too long'.[8] He announced that the theatre would reopen shortly as 'The Roxy', named like many picture houses around the world for the greatest American showman of his age, Samuel L. Rothapfel, otherwise known as 'Roxy'.

The doors to the new picture house opened within a week, and the Roxy's first cinematic offering only added insult to injury. *The Hollywood Revue* was a variety show on film. Produced by Metro Goldwyn Mayer to introduce the voices of that studio's leading players, the picture had little story but plenty of formerly silent movie stars. Laurel and Hardy, Norma Shearer, Joan Crawford and Jack Benny were among those whose voices were heard for the first time by audiences already familiar with their faces. Canned variety had replaced the real thing, and American entertainers their Australian counterparts. It was a painfully anxious time for local performers like Gladys, out of work after the League of Notions Sydney season was so abruptly curtailed.

But the company soon resurfaced in Brisbane, singing the chorus 'Don't Worry' to open a new show. Six weeks after closing Fullers' Theatre in Sydney, the League of Notions was the first company engaged when Fullers opened a new vaudeville house in Brisbane on Easter Saturday. The old Empire Theatre had been converted for movies and the Theatre Royal temporarily leased for variety:

> It has been many weeks since a vaudeville troupe has been heard in Brisbane, and on Saturday night the League of Notions Revue Company, starring Queenie Paul, Mike Connors, and Syd Beck, which commenced a season at the Theatre Royal, was accorded a hearty welcome. People look for variety in entertainment, and the surest way of getting it is in vaudeville revue. Judging by the opening production, the company, which is under the direction of Sir Benjamin and Mr. John Fuller, is to be congratulated on its determined efforts to make vaudeville live. Several months ago a prominent theatrical director stated that 'vaudeville is as dead as a wooden battleship'. Had he been at the Theatre Royal on Saturday, and seen the way in which the huge crowd enjoyed itself and roared with laughter, he would have had cause to doubt the wisdom of his words.[9]

Perth too remained enthusiastic about vaudeville. Returning to the west early in 1930, Elsie and Keith appeared at the new Ambassadors theatre, in a show called 'Jazz a la Carte', a live entertainment in a packed program that included short and feature-length films.

When Nat Phillips, Daisy Merritt and the still spinning Whirligigs turned up in Perth, Nat declared his faith in programming like that of the Ambassadors, bills that mingled movies and live acts. A newspaper article headed 'Stiffy Looks In – Says Vaudeville Isn't Dead' noted:

> Nat ISN'T DOWNHEARTED about the future of the flesh-and-blood artist. 'Talkies with vaudeville acts are the next development in stage entertainment as far as I can see,' he states 'and there's no need for good performers to lose hope.'[10]

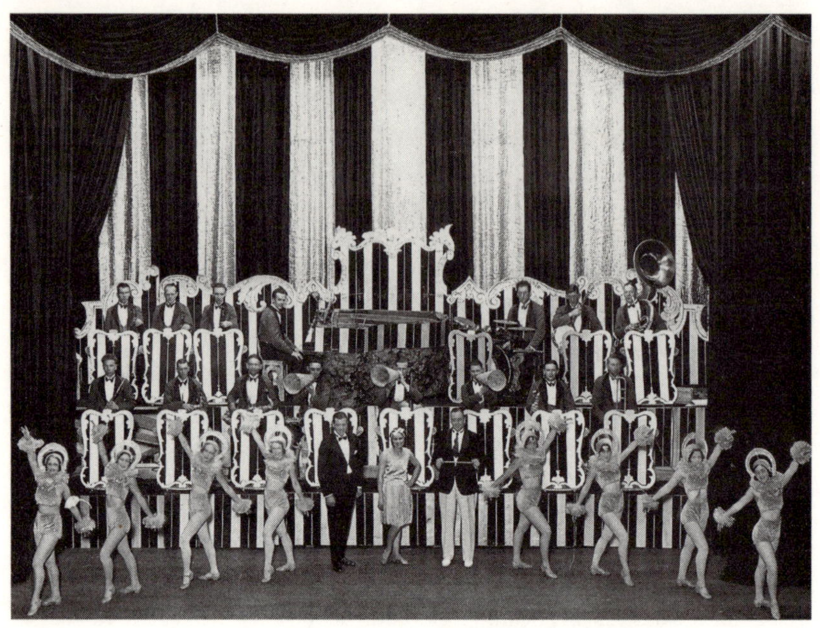

'Jazz a la carte,' with Keith, Elsie, Bert Howell and his band, Ambassadors, Perth, 1930

Keith joined Nat and Daisy's company in May, for a season of more than three months at the Luxor and a few nights in Kalgoorlie, part of a cast that included Daisy Merritt, Stella Lamond and Stan Foley – Nat's latest stage partner. Their comedy duo was known as Stiffy and Stud.

Elsie's name did not appear on the bill, though she did rate a mention in Perth's *Weekly Judge*:

> It is not generally known the chic little wife of Keith Connolly, now at the Luxor, is none other than Elsie Hosking. The little lady will be well remembered as a child performer and later as a soubrette. It would not be surprising to hear that Keith and family have decided to build their nest in Perth at the conclusion of the present contract.[11]

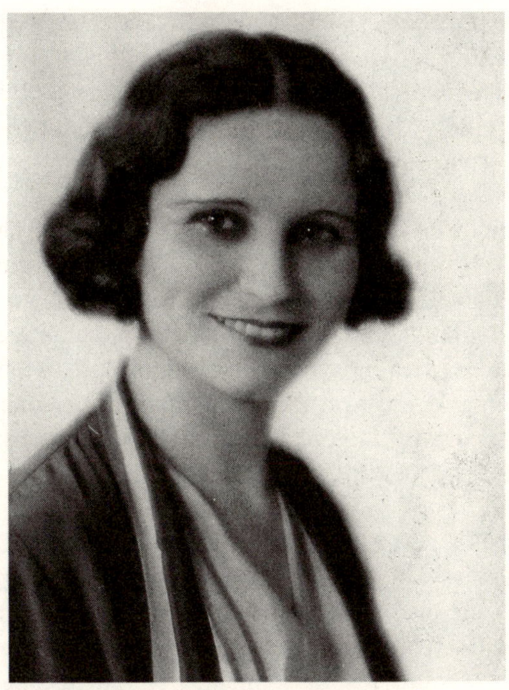

'A chic little wife,' Elsie ca. 1930

In Queensland, at the Theatre Royal, Gladys might have been forgiven for being more pessimistic than Nat Phillips. After barely surviving the closure of Fullers' Sydney home, the League of Notions disbanded at the close of its Brisbane season:

> 'People favour the "talkies", so we have to go,' declared Mike Connors when acknowledging, at the final performance of Connors and Paul's League of Notions Revue Company at the Theatre Royal on Saturday night, the excellent reception which the large audience gave the company. Mr. Connors expressed regret that the company was disbanding after two and a half years of happy associations. They were more like a big family, he said, and they had stored up many happy memories.[12]

The League's members went separate ways. Gerry moved on to Rockhampton to find whatever work he could as a sign painter and dancing teacher. Gladys, her theatrical family and brothers scattered, returned to Sydney. There she soon discovered that even her mother could no longer be relied upon.

Alone at home in Rosebery, Mary Agnes had become depressed and agitated. She'd lost a great deal of weight and was no longer able to take care of herself. Gladys organised for her mother to leave her much-loved 'Indiana', and be admitted as a voluntary patient to Bayview House, a private psychiatric hospital close to the Cooks River in nearby Tempe. It was said to be a 'facility for persons of means to obtain privacy during mental troubles, something ordinary public institutions failed to provide'.[13]

Hospital records report no evidence of previous mental illness, nor of any circumstances which might have triggered Mary Agnes's sudden breakdown at the age of sixty-six. But they do record that her late mother, Mary Gertrude, was 'insane' and had once been an inmate of Gladesville Mental Hospital. 'Melancholia, delusional, heredity',[14] say the notes on Mary Agnes's file. Her condition was thought to be a terrible maternal legacy.

In fact mother and daughter suffered quite different illnesses. Mary Gertrude had some kind of chronic psychosis and, later, dementia. Her daughter, Mary Agnes, had a severe depressive illness. What their conditions had in common was a dearth of effective treatments.

For the next six months, while her mother remained in hospital, Gladys did little work. There may not have been much on offer in Sydney. And with Keith and Gerry both away, Gladys might have declined out-of-town engagements which meant leaving her mother unvisited in hospital.

Gladys didn't move in to Indiana. Instead she took a modern furnished apartment in the White House Flats, just near the busy corner of

Crown and Oxford streets in Darlinghurst. She needed more company than the suburban streets of Rosebery offered, companionship her mother too might have missed when she settled there after so many years in crowded but sociable boarding houses and hotels.

In just three months Gladys had lost her family of fellow artists, the company of her brothers and the constancy of her mother. Perhaps she was also burdened by daughterly guilt, suspecting that Mary Agnes had been lonely and regretting being too busy with her own career to share her mother's pleasure in at last having a home of her own. She might have wondered whether, had she been closer, she could have prevented Mary Agnes's deterioration.

Keith and Elsie didn't 'build their nest in Perth' as the local press had speculated. They returned to Sydney in November 1930. By then Mary Agnes had been in Bayview House Hospital for six months. As she could no longer care for herself, let alone a child, two-year-old Keith stayed with family friends in Waterloo when his parents went to work. They were appearing with the Snapshots, a newly named Nat Phillips ensemble. As if to prove Nat's earlier optimistic predictions about the future of vaudeville correct, the Snapshots would go on to enjoy an unbroken eight-month season at Sydney's Grand Opera House.

In that time Mary Agnes's condition changed little. At the end of 1930, Gladys signed papers requesting that her mother be committed to the Licensed House at Cooks River, Bayview Hospital for the Insane. Accompanying doctors' certificates reported that Mary Agnes was apathetic and depressed, constantly muttering incoherently and very contrary. 'When being fed', noted a Dr Stiles, 'she sometimes states that she must not eat as she has no money to pay for it'.[15]

After seven months of private hospitalisation, the cost of her care had indeed become concerning. Early in the new year Gladys wrote to Grace Wilson, superintendent at Bayview House.

White House Flats,
Darlinghurst
Wed Jan 14th 1931

Dear Miss Wilson,
I am writing to ask you if you would see to the transfer of my mother, Mrs M.A. Connolly from your hospital to Gladesville.

Owing to financial difficulties we are unable to keep up the payment of a private hospital.

Hoping you will see to this urgently as I am going to the country and would like to see everything fixed before leaving town.

Yours faithfully,
Gladys Connolly[16]

Penned in a florid hand, this letter is the only one from Gladys I have found – a brief request, its consequences horrific. Mary Agnes would be sent to the very same hospital to which her own mother was first admitted, in a committal that began her forty-three years of asylum life. Though Keith and Gladys may have made the awful decision together, it was Gladys, not her brother, who had the harrowing task of seeing it through.

12
Every Day's a Rainbow Day

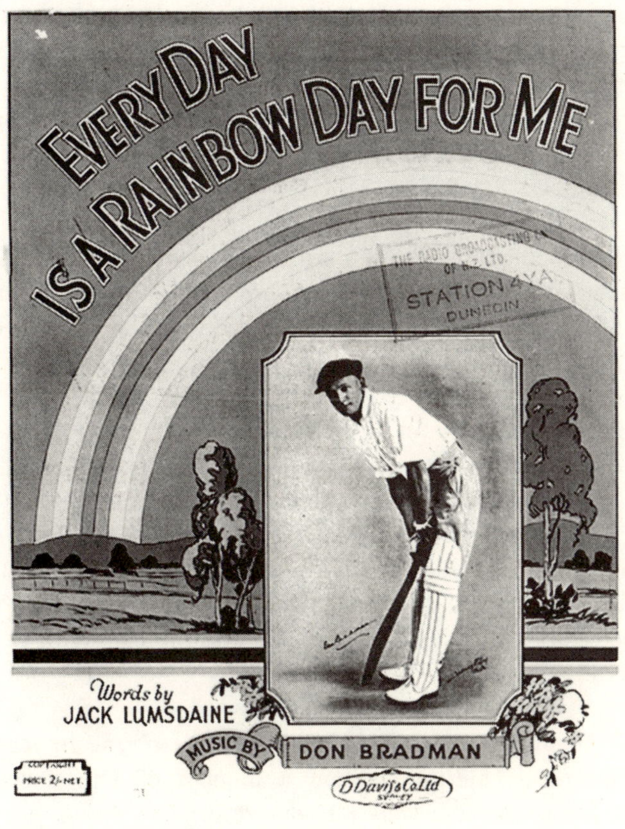

A happy song for hard times, 1930

Meanwhile at the Grand Opera House Elsie was being applauded for her performances of a new song, 'Every Day is a Rainbow Day for Me', composed by none other than cricket legend Don Bradman:

> The song, composed by Mr. Bradman to words by Mr. Jack Lumsdaine, was sung by Miss Elsie Hosking, and proved pleasantly melodious and sentimental, with a refrain in which saxophones and brasses vigorously supported the vocal theme, ere it was taken up smartly by a well trained ballet.[1]

On the occasion of the song's first public performance, the audience, including the first West Indian cricket team to visit Australia, was said to have cheered.[2] Then Bradman appeared onstage and said he'd 'enjoyed very much the experience of hearing for the first time this composition sung in public. "I hope", he added, amid renewed applause, "that we shall be able to apply the title of this song to our experiences in Australia in the year now opening, and that every day will be a rainbow day for us" '.[3]

Bradman presented Elsie with a box of chocolates and complimented her on her performance. ' "It's a very great pleasure and a very great honour to sing this song," replied Elsie sweetly. And the house cheered again.'[4]

'Melodious and sentimental' songs such as Bradman and Lumsdaine's had been Elsie's specialty since her childhood as Perth's Little Idol, though they weren't her only contribution to the success of Nat Phillips's revue company at the Grand Opera House. She appeared with Nat in comic skits, sang duets with Keith and danced with Stella Lamond, Hilda Waring and other women. And she played 'Boy Blue' in *Beauty and the Beast*, the 'up to date pantomime'[5] with which Nat ushered in the new year:

> All the fabled characters of the fairy tale again made their appearance, but in addition a number of topical songs and humorous sketches were introduced. Bright quips on present-day politics brought forth great applause. The depression, the shilling

in the pound tax, currency inflation, Mr. Lang's proposed loan, and a host of other topics were touched upon. One can hardly imagine Baron Bounty in the original fairy tale saying, 'If the depression doesn't get you, the bob in the pound must.'[6]

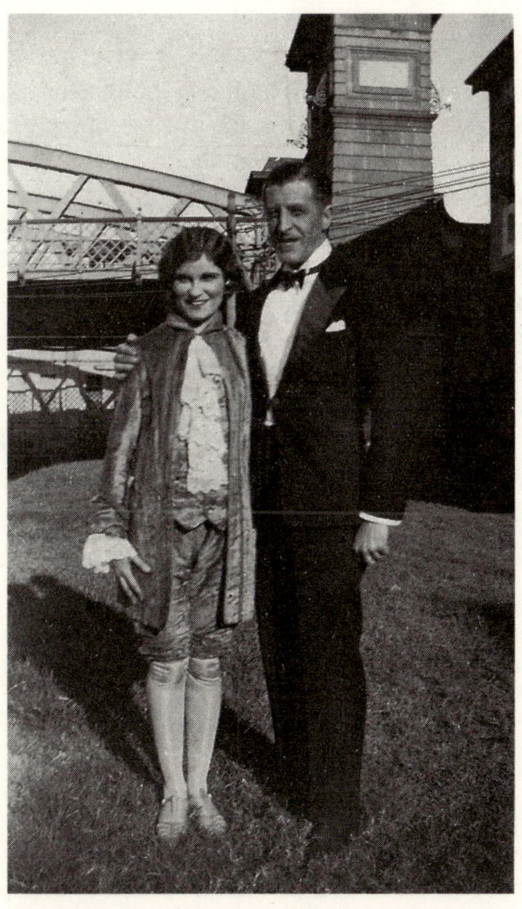

'Boy Blue', and 'Baron Bounty', Elsie and Keith in costume for 'Beauty and the Beast', 1931

Don Bradman's hope that there would be rainbow days aplenty for Australians in 1931 was echoed, perhaps less colourfully, by Prime Minister Scullin. The same day that Elsie's performance of Bradman's song was reported in the *Sydney Morning Herald*, the newspaper also published remarks made by the prime minister, just returned from an Imperial Conference in London. He said there was 'a disposition to view Australia's future pessimistically, both at home and abroad. He did not want to minimise the seriousness of the situation, but he did not think the future was as black as it was painted'.[7]

There was much disagreement, especially from an increasing number of unemployed Australians, and among politicians arguing about how to tackle the economic crisis. The prime minister said that 'in the past Australia had leaned too heavily on overseas money markets (applause)...He mentioned it because he did not want anyone to think that there would be permanently continued a policy of borrowing overseas and bringing overseas loans into Australia in the form of imported goods to the detriment of Australian industry'.[8]

But nothing would stop the continued importation of British and American movies. On the same page as the prime minister's comments, the *Sydney Morning Herald* told of business developments that would certainly be to the detriment of the Australian entertainment industry:

> PICTURE THEATRES
>
> ———
>
> American Control.
>
> ———
>
> WARNER BROTHERS AND FULLERS.
>
> A merger between Fuller's Theatres, Ltd., and Warner Brothers' First National Pictures, Ltd., which is in course of negotiation, will be the third instance within the last 12 months of an American company obtaining an interest in Australian picture theatres...

> This new merging of interests is of some importance, for the Fuller's Theatres in Australasia number over 50, of which two are in Sydney—the Roxy and the Newtown Majestic, both of them devoted to talking films...
>
> In America Warner Brothers control well over a thousand theatres, which give them an assured outlet for their productions.[9]

In fact there would be no merger between Fullers and Warner Brothers. But there was an agreement under which Fullers would release Warners movies in their newly converted cinemas. American companies continued to take control of exhibition all around the country. Australian filmmakers would increasingly be locked out and surviving vaudeville companies would have to find alternative venues.

Like many Australians in pursuit of work Gladys took to the road, not as a swaggie but as a member of Coles Comedy Players. Advance publicity said 'she was bound to make a host of friends with her bright personality songs and feature whistling'.[10] Under a giant marquee, one of several now touring regional Australia, she lightened life in Nowra, Crookwell, Goulburn, Wellington and Dubbo.

The Coles tour paused for Easter and Gladys spent a fortnight in Sydney, where she briefly joined Mike Connors and Queenie Paul onstage at the New Haymarket Theatre. On Easter Saturday they launched their 'Two-a-day and Vaudeville Revue'.

Roy Rene recalled:

> ...Queenie Paul decided that the theatre wasn't finished at all. The only thing was that working men couldn't afford the prices in depression times, so she planned to charge 1/- throughout the house on matinees, and 3/-, 2/- and 1/- at night – the old vaudeville prices. No matter how broke a man is he can raise a bob to see a good show...
>
> The Connors and Paul opening was one of the most important things ever to happen in the history of Australian vaudeville...

> Theatres were closing everywhere, not just flesh and blood theatres, but even picture shows. We were in the thick of the depression... Hundreds of trained theatricals were leaving the profession...[11]

Almost as importantly, the Connors-Paul initiative marked a major leap in Queenie Paul's entrepreneurial career. She would continue to perform, but with (and later without) Mike, she became a rare creature indeed – a female impresario.

Gladys played a number of characters for Queenie and Mike that April, including a militant woman in *At the Domain*, a sketch which introduced 'popular (and unpopular) politicians in ludicrous situations, and called forth generous mirth and applause'.[12] Then, having seen Mike and Queenie's venture launched she was off to Queensland with the Coles Company again – to play under canvas in Rockhampton, MacKay, Townsville, Charters Towers and Bowen. Her contract with Coles might have prevented a longer stay in Sydney, but life on the road had its advantages.

She was with friends – a musical crony in pianist Fay Gordon, and a diverting young companion in twenty-two-year-old Frank McGrath, a minor member of the Coles cast and Gladys's junior by fourteen years. It wasn't the first time Gladys had found a much younger companion; a decade earlier she'd toured with Freddie Webber. The age gap between Gladys and Frank was wider than that which had divided Gladys and Freddie, but Gladys's relationship with Frank McGrath would last longer. Yet there was surprisingly little to show for it. Neither the zither case nor newspaper archives revealed anything about Frank. Official records held little more information, though I did find a rather grim photograph taken ten years after Frank's Coles Company career, at the start of a period of war service which lasted only three months. When photographed he was already suffering from the heart disease which saw him discharged from the army on medical grounds. I can only imagine that a decade before that photograph Frank was a happier and healthier young man when he travelled with Gladys in the Coles tent show.

They were fortunate to have regular work at a time when, as Mo wrote, 'the general picture was as black as a thunderstorm, with just about the whole profession wringing its hands and saying the end had come'.[13]

Away from Sydney and far from Mary Agnes in the asylum, Gladys was also spared some distress at seeing her mother so diminished. Perhaps, on the road, she reproached herself less for failing at what was widely considered an unmarried daughter's duty, that of caring for an ailing parent.

Despite the general gloom that Mo described, Elsie and Keith remained in work at Sydney's Grand Opera House. Their little free time was spent with their son and each week Keith visited his mother in Gladesville Hospital. After months of this routine Keith and Elsie moved on to Melbourne with the Snapshots. Days later they received word that Mary Agnes was gravely ill with pneumonia. She died on 26 July, shortly before her sixty-seventh birthday. An audience of only one, a nurse, saw Mary Agnes take her final bow.

She had called herself Claire Delmar – light of the sea – as the limitations of life for women in late nineteenth-century Australia threatened to smother her. Yet having once escaped the aimlessness that Louisa Lawson so powerfully described, it revisited her toward the end of her life. Mary Agnes had made herself a peaceful home when the hard years of work and child-rearing were over, but in the end perhaps it was too quiet a retirement. She was lonely and became depressed. A few miles away and a few years earlier Louisa Lawson endured a similar isolation until she too was taken to Gladesville Hospital for the Insane. Like Mary Agnes, she died there.

In notices after her death Mary Agnes's children were restored to her. All five were named: Gladys, Keith, Gerry, as well as Reg and Leslie, the boys she'd left in Sydney almost forty years before. But nothing was said about 'Claire Delmar', burlesque actress and gifted songstress, nor about 'Madam Marie', the music teacher who trained her only daughter for the stage.

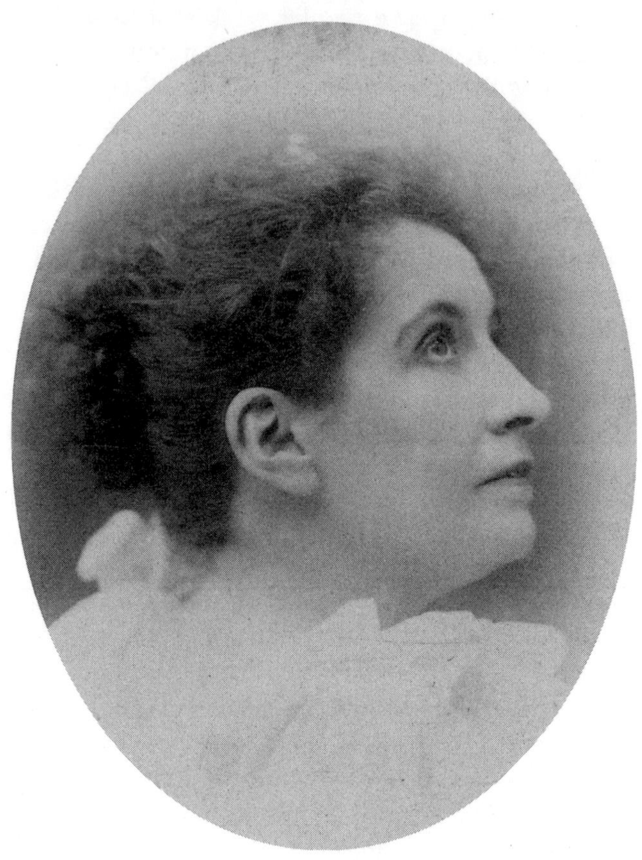

Mary Agnes, ca. 1894

13
Ladies and Gentlemen, That's Love

Mary Agnes had given all her talented children an education that would see them through tough times. After her funeral, Gladys, Keith and Gerry scattered once more – parted by the demanding business of earning their livings as entertainers in the 1930s.

In Brisbane, Gladys and Fay Gordon, soubrette and musician, were 'Two Girls and a Piano', performing at movie houses between the cartoons and the main feature. Then they rejoined Coles Comedy Company on the road:

> ...good vaudeville offerings were contributed by Fay Gordon at the piano, well aided by Gladys Shaw, a vivacious comedienne in songs (Over the Garden Wall in particular), whistling with two fingers and comedy items...[1]

Once talkies arrived in Australia the Coles company began presenting more vaudeville programs and musical comedies to its country audiences. But it maintained a reputation for drama and Gladys, a valuable all-rounder, acted in many plays after first singing and whistling in the opening section of the program and at intermission too.

In Horsham, Victoria, the troupe was eagerly awaited:

> Since their last appearance, the company has returned to the ever popular spoken drama, and the management has secured

> many of the old favourites and a host of new stars...The opening production will be Mrs. Todd-Stewart's latest comedy drama Ten to One, a thrilling and novel mystery play of great interest.[2]

Todd-Stewart's plays dealt with some unlikely subjects. *Ten to One* was 'a mystery story dealing with the evils of the drug traffic'. In Rockhampton, Gladys was star of the show:

> ...the hit of the night in the play proper was again scored by Miss Shaw who appeared as Babe Cassilless, a chorus girl.[3]

The title of Todd-Stewart's play *Lady of the Night* promised an equally dangerous subject. In the end however:

> The lady in question proved to be an orphan girl adopted by three pals, for whom she keeps house...Gladys Shaw and Roy Grennete appeared as Tiny and Benny Duggy, a vaudeville couple always in trouble over their act. The scene in which they introduced their singing and dancing numbers was productive of loud and hearty applause.[4]

Another play, *Her Unborn Child*, touched on abortion and birth control, in a plot ultimately resolved by marriage. Prospective patrons were warned that owing to its subject matter, unaccompanied children would not be admitted to the marquee during its performance.

On Coles Company programs, Todd-Stewart's plays were not the only works written by a woman. At first glance Kate Howarde's romantic bush comedies, *Gum Tree Gully* and the earlier *Possum Paddock* seemed less controversial than those penned by Todd-Stewart. Howarde was an actor, manager, writer, journalist and the first woman to be credited as a director of an Australian feature film. She produced, co-directed and acted in the movie version of *Possum Paddock* in 1921. Like the play, the film was a success, despite the censors removing scenes of an unmarried mother imagining herself despairingly casting her child into a river. But *Possum Paddock* would be Howarde's only cinematic venture.

More than ten years after her film's release, Howarde's plays were still drawing crowds in regional towns, but some thought them too old-fashioned for big-city audiences. Amid intense jockeying for a place on Sydney stages in the weeks leading up to the opening of its Harbour Bridge, Grand Opera House proprietor George Marlow thought better of having booked Kate Howarde's latest production of *Possum Paddock*. He decided there might be a fresher show to mark celebrations of Sydney's status as a modern city.

Howarde didn't vacate the stage without a fight. She took legal action against Marlow, who reported in court that 'when he told Miss Howarde that the show was a bad one she retorted: "Possum Paddock is good for five or six weeks!" He replied, "I do not think it's good enough for five or six minutes."'[5] Marlow won the fight and wasted no time in replacing *Possum Paddock* with George Sorlie's revue, *Quit Yer Kiddin'*.

By then Gerry had joined Sorlie's company. And so he was the only one of Mary Agnes's performing children to be in Sydney when the Harbour Bridge was finally opened in March 1932. When the ribbon was cut, he was appearing in a matinee show of *Quit Yer Kiddin'* at the Grand Opera House. For years Gladys and her brothers had returned to Sydney again and again, watching the bridge take shape as pillars were constructed, girders riveted and arches joined. But none saw the final act in the drama of the bridge, in which an unhinged ideologue on horseback brandished a sword to slash the ceremonial ribbon ahead of the state's premier, Jack Lang. Undeterred, hundreds of thousands of citizens then walked across the bridge in the largest public event the city had hosted.

Meanwhile Gladys was entertaining a far smaller crowd in the New South Wales town of Crookwell, where it was show week. Further away in Melbourne, Keith was appearing on a Tivoli bill of mixed quality and more mixed reviews. Not that being in another city prevented him using the opening of the bridge as material for a subsequent comic routine. 'Stan Foley and Keith Connolly, in topicalities, caused a furore by their references to the ribbon-cutting incident at the opening of the Harbor Bridge.'[6]

Keith's and Stan's jokes caused a commotion in tumultuous times. De Groot, the man who'd upstaged Jack Lang, was a member of the New Guard, a militarist, monarchist movement vehemently opposed to the New South Wales Premier's socialist policies. Deteriorating economic conditions intensified political ruptures born of disputes about wartime conscription. A new coalition of conservative parties led by Joe Lyons won government federally, and in New South Wales Jack Lang would soon be dismissed as premier, for defaulting on British bank loans.

By mid-1932 almost a third of Australian workers were unemployed, and there was little help for them beyond food handouts. Sixty people jumped to their deaths from Sydney's Harbour Bridge in the seven months after it opened.[7]

As she whistled her way up and down the east coast, Gladys watched the swagmen endlessly on the move in search of work. She saw despair in capital cities and country towns alike, so it might have been a relief to reach Rockhampton for the carnival of 1932. North and Central Queensland's dairy and sugar industries spared the region the worst of the Depression, the weather was glorious and her brother Gerry was in town too, with George Sorlie's company and a young dancer named Hilda Waring.

Hilda's true name was Hildegard Wong Hing. Her father George was a Brisbane vegetable merchant, market gardener and sometime caretaker of the joss house at Breakfast Creek. Hilda was among nine children born to George and his wife Ann Smales, and she'd been winning admirers since childhood. At a Brisbane dinner dance one society hostess:

> ...had a huge bandbox arranged on the table and, at a signal, out danced the most delectable little siren imaginable. The lassie, Hilda Wong...was dressed as a fairy, and flitted like one over the table, scattering rose petals over the delighted guests.

> Every man there laid his heart at her small brown feet, and there was a rush of enthusiastic cavaliers to lift the miniature Circe from the table.[8]

By the age of sixteen Hilda was working with Stiffy and Mo. At twenty she was ballet mistress for Nat Phillips's 'Snapshots' show that featured Elsie and Keith.

So they may have been responsible for introducing Hilda to Gerry. She must have had quite an effect on him. Later that year, looking for theatrical work and for Hilda, he sent a telegram to band leader Tiny Douglas, who'd recently joined George Sorlie's travelling show. So had Hilda Waring:

> CAN YOU PLACE ME IN YOUR BAND CAN START IMMEDIATELY IF NECESSARY DOUBLE DRUMS SOUSAPHONE AND VIBRAHARP WORK AS JUVENILE IN SHOW ALSO DO ANY POSTER WORK NEEDED DESIRE TO KNOW IMMEDIATELY KINDEST REGARDS GERRY CONNOLLY.

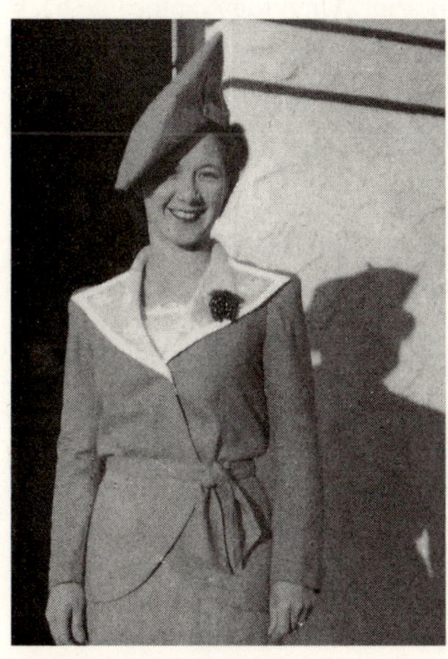

Hilda Waring, dancer

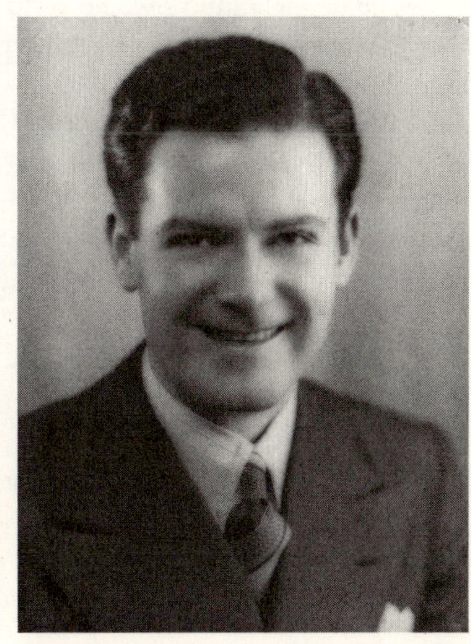

Gerry Connolly

Frugally punctuated, the telegram succeeded in winning him both a place with Tiny Douglas and his Varsity Boys and work beside Hilda, in the country's best-known travelling show.

Against the odds, a number of travelling companies continued to do well in the Depression years. According to actor and entertainer Ron Shand:

> ...these shows were well established, they all knew the name of George Sorlie, they all knew the name of Coles, they all knew the name of Humphrey Bishop, they were known just like J.C. Williamson in the cities. The shows that went broke were the less well established ones...[9]

Rockhampton's four-day racing carnival and annual show brought graziers and families to town, along with scores of entertainers. Ron Shand described the way the circuit worked:

> All these shows would merge in on Rockhampton for the Show and then they'd break up and they'd do the smaller towns, five would go to one and five would go to another. Then they'd all come back to Townsville which is a bigger town. Then some would play other towns in and out of Ingham and Innisfail but they'd all merge again in Cairns...[10]

In Rockhampton in 1932 there were not as many visitors as usual and 'there was perhaps a quieter tone in all the entertainments... nevertheless the carnival spirit of spending was well in evidence...'[11]

> THERE are some good shows in town, Williamson's Gilbert and Sullivan Company is playing at The Wintergarden. George Sorlie has switched over from drama to revue and has brought along a crackerjack show, Warton and McKay are at the School of Arts, and Coles are on the School of Arts vacant block. Last year the talkies were comparatively new and attracted the country visitors. This year the visiting shows are all doing well.[12]

On a revamped Sorlie bill, Gerry appeared with Tiny Douglas's band and in a revue titled *The New Recruit*. Hilda danced as one of 'The Two Hildas', while further along the street Gladys had roles in half a dozen three-act dramas that Coles continued to produce. In *The Whole Damn Family*, 'a bright and amusing play of domestic trials and squabble...the greater part of the comedy was supplied by Gladys Shaw'.[13] She also appeared in *The Tie That Binds, Turned Up, Glass Houses, Ten to One* and *Lady of the Night* – all in the space of one week. And during intermissions she and Fay Gordon entertained with musical numbers, whistling and comedy.

Despite the gaiety and though their audiences would not have known it, Gladys, Gerry and Hilda were not feeling especially cheerful. Shortly after arriving in Rockhampton, they'd received terrible news. Nat Phillips was dead:

> News was received in Brisbane yesterday afternoon by Connors and Paul Theatres Ltd, that one of their artists, Mr. Nat. Phillips, who was well known to theatregoers as 'Stiffy', had died suddenly about midday. From the information available it appears that Mr. Phillips was in the Sydney office of the company making arrangements to travel to Melbourne, where he was to appear with the company controlled by Connors and Paul, playing at the Melbourne Tivoli. He complained of a slight dizziness, and was given a glass of water. His condition did not improve, however, and he was taken to a private hospital, where he died about half an hour later. 'Stiffy' was to have appeared with his old partner, Roy Rene ('Mo'), at the re-opening of the Grand Opera House in Sydney at the end of July, and it was chiefly for the purpose of rehearsal that he was going to Melbourne. The two, who had been together for several years, separated about three years ago, and although many attempts had been made to get them to come together again it was only recently that negotiations had been successful.[14]

Only fifty when he died, Nat was one of the greatest theatrical talents in Australia's history and his death was keenly felt by younger entertainers like Gladys, Elsie, Keith and Hilda, artists he'd supported and encouraged. They grieved for a friend and mentor, a whirligig whose time ran out too soon.

Nat's death came while Gladys was negotiating her return to Sydney to appear with Stiffy and Mo at the Grand Opera House, newly leased by Mike and Queenie and renamed the New Tivoli. Despite the attractions of the travelling show, Gladys couldn't pass up an opportunity to appear again in a Sydney city theatre, with the country's most popular performers and old friends Mike and Queenie.

Despite losing Nat, the New Tivoli opened a month later.

> 'MO' (Roy Rene) is back in Sydney again. The new Tivoli (late Grand Opera House, plus Neon lighting equipment) has greater seating capacity than any other theatre in Australia but at Saturday night's showing of this Connors and Paul revue, the 'house full' sign had to be hung out for the first time on record. Even the aisles in the circle and 'gods' were used for extra seating space. 'Mo' repeats all his old tricks, and manages to squeeze in a few new ones as well...The return of 'Mo' signifies the return of the popular priced theatre.[15]

Gladys joined Mo and the Connors Paul troupe at the New Tivoli. With its rich red carpet, new furniture and neon lights, it was a very different venue to the Coles marquee. Amid the splendour, New Tivoli patrons enjoyed a familiar style of entertainment; vaudeville acts in the first half of the program and a revue – a fresh one each week – in the second. The artists who featured were well known, the ballet ran to sixteen members, and female artists included 'giddy' Gladys Shaw,[16] Queenie Paul, Sadie Gale and male impersonator Nellie Kolle.

Nellie Kolle, like her colleague Effie Fellowes, had been a cross-dressing star on Australian and New Zealand variety stages for almost two decades. A gifted mimic, singer and pianist, she survived a public and scandalous divorce in her early twenties. Her husband wanted her to give up the stage to raise their two children, but Kolle said 'she would not give up the stage to live a domestic life, and would not live with him any longer'.[17]

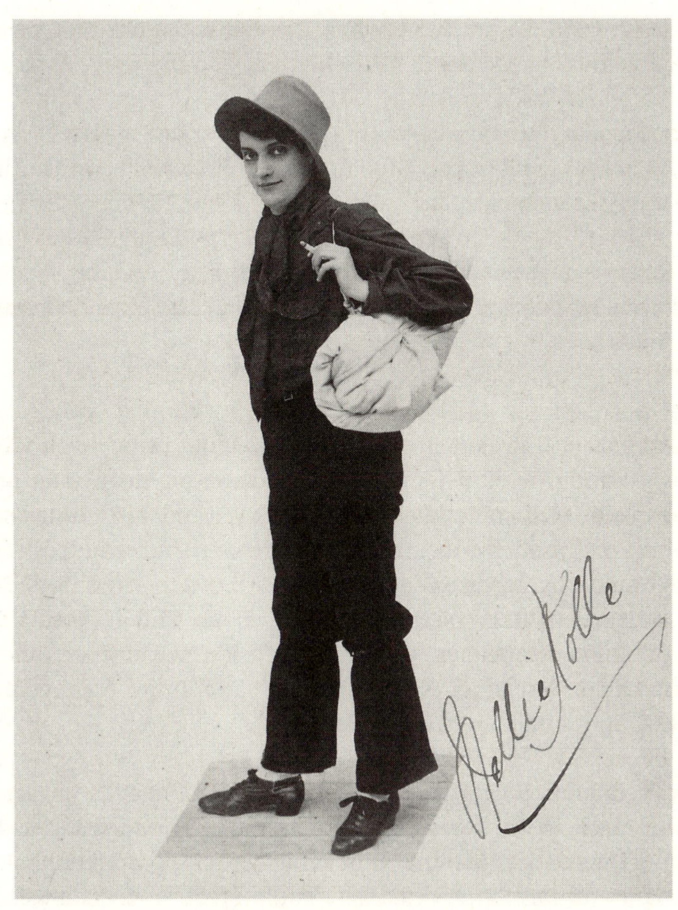

Nellie Kolle as a swaggie

Despite her divorce – or because of it – Nellie Kolle's career thrived, and she became one of the most celebrated artists on Australian vaudeville stages.

Sadie Gale, comedienne and soubrette, was the daughter of vaudeville artists, and Mo's second wife. By 1933 she and her husband had two children. As well as playing her own parts, Gladys was sometimes called upon to fill in for Sadie when the demands of a toddler and a small baby meant she couldn't take her place on the New Tivoli stage:

> With only four more nights of the season to go, the New Tivoli was on Saturday night packed to the doors to see and hear 'Mo and his Merry Monarchs'.
>
> Sadie Gale was absent, but her place in the various items was taken by Gladys Shaw, who again sang, Ladies and Gentlemen, that's Love.[18]

Gladys had neither husband nor children, though young Frank McGrath was still in her life. But she was doing rather well without the responsibilities of a family. For the next eighteen months she worked beside and sometimes opposite Roy Rene, her contributions not totally eclipsed by the illustrious Mo and his male colleagues: 'In the humorous scenes Gladys Shaw, Alec Carr, and Will Miller acted as excellent foils for the wit of Roy Rene, and assisted to keep the production moving at a fast rate'.[19] She won press mentions in Melbourne, Adelaide, Newcastle and Sydney – for her acting, whistling, and 'some hilarious makeups'.[20]

Suddenly, late in 1933, Mike Connors and Queenie Paul's six-year-old daughter died. With her went Mike and Queenie's enthusiasm for managing Australia's leading vaudeville circuit, a project that may have required more hope than they could spare in their grief. They took on a new business partner, a showman and entrepreneur named Frank Neil, and took a break from making comedy.

Gladys was out of work again, though she wasn't too concerned. It was Christmas, summertime in Sydney, and she could afford to take a holiday. She'd been earning steadily for some time, which was fortunate because unemployed single women were not eligible for government relief during the Depression.

Theatrically and economically times were still tough. Australia's recovery from the Depression was slow and unemployment remained high throughout the 1930s. But Gladys was confident she could still whistle impressively enough to earn her living and maintain a little faith in a life of lights and laughter. When summer was almost over she signed on with old family friend and impresario Les Shipp to play the theatres of the Hunter and Illawarra regions, not too far from Sydney. Later in 1934 she ventured further afield, again with the Coles Company, now renamed Coles Varieties. The return of Gladys Shaw, 'Cole favorite of former years',[21] was welcomed.

In Queensland during carnival season she met up with Gerry and Hilda, still touring with Sorlie's travelling show. Tiny Douglas had left the company, but 'Gerry Connolly's Varsity Boys', an eight-piece musical outfit, now accompanied Sorlie throughout Queensland and New South Wales. In 1933 their touring schedule paused just long enough – between engagements in Charters Towers and Wagga Wagga – for Gerry and Hilda to marry.

While Gerry led his Varsity Boys in Rockhampton during the winter of 1934, Hilda was a soloist in Sorlie's ballet, playing a 'human offering sacrificed to the "Spirit of the Flame"'.[22] Performing under the nearby Coles marquee, Gladys was said to be 'the original "it" girl.'[23] Of course that claim wasn't true, though by now her career had outlasted that of the first 'it girl', Clara Bow.

While playing the flapper of the Coles Show, Gladys may have had her own uncertainties about what it meant to be an 'it girl', especially one approaching the age of forty in the Depression years. Despite her billing Gladys knew these were more sober times than those of the roaring twenties.

She was no longer a girl of any kind. Her parents were dead and her brothers wed. She had no family to call her own. And while she had her many talents, the characters she portrayed had taught her something about attitudes to women like herself. 'It girls' were not the only single women Gladys played. She'd also caricatured enough 'old maids' to know that mature unmarried women were figures of derision.

On 12 July 1934, Gladys married Frank McGrath at St Johns Presbyterian Church in Paddington, Sydney. No wedding photographs found their way into the zither case. No member of Gladys's family signed the marriage register.

Almost thirty-nine and Frank's senior by fourteen years, Gladys declared herself to be just twenty-seven on her marriage certificate. Her husband was twenty-five and described as an actor, but he might have been stretching the truth almost as much as Gladys. There's little evidence of Frank's acting career in newspapers of the day. After a few small mentions in advertisements for Coles Comedy Company in the early 1930s, his name did not appear again.

Marriages were often happy endings in popular dramas of the era and the careers of many female performers mirrored those finales. They retired, happily or unhappily, when they married. Australia's own Jane King, who once hurled grenades when playing Emilienne Moreau, disappeared from stage and screen after she wed. Muriel Pearce, otherwise known as Lynette, didn't make music professionally after her marriage. But a wedding wouldn't lower the curtain on Gladys's performing life.

Though the old zither case offered up nothing about Frank and her relationship with him, newspapers told me that after becoming a wife Gladys was soon back on the stage, even if she didn't venture as far or as often from Sydney as she once had. With Les Shipp's troupe she whistled, sang and made fun in the suburbs and in nearby towns. But she was no longer known as the 'it girl'.

Within months of her wedding Gladys was instead described as 'a Mae Westian comedienne. Built on Mae West lines'[24] she whistled and was 'diverting in burlesque dances'.[25]

Such comments suggest she cut a voluptuous figure, but Gladys may also have been evoking something of the wantonness and wit of Mae West, an American star well known for sexual innuendo and for her independence.

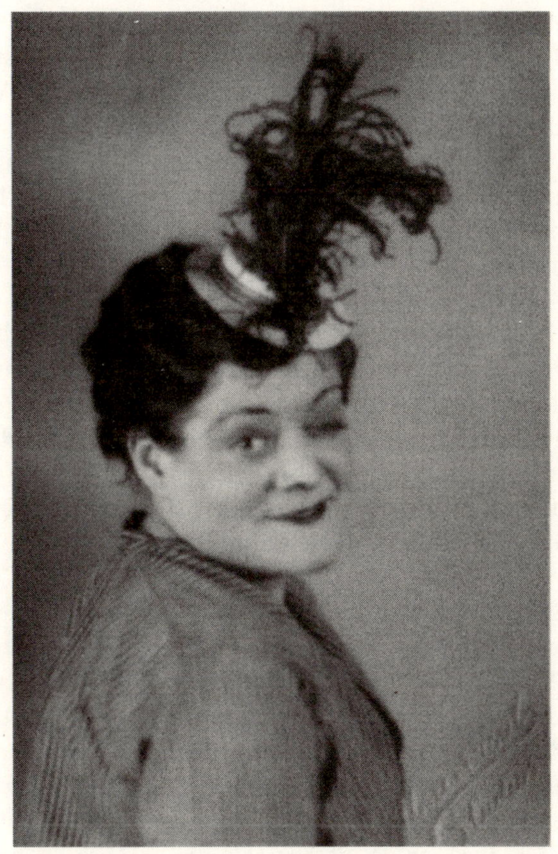

Gladys Shaw, ca. 1935

West's movie career did not begin until 1932, when she was thirty-nine, the same age that Gladys was when first described as 'Mae Westian'. She knew West's work from only three movies: *Night after Night*, *She Done him Wrong* and *I'm No Angel*, all produced before a tightening of censorship began to water down some of the star's lewder lines. By then Mae West was one of the best known and best paid actresses in Hollywood.

Gladys sent her own photograph and details to Australia's Cinesound, the most significant of a few film production companies still making movies locally in the 1930s. The Moving Pictures Royal Commission hadn't resulted in measures to support a struggling industry and so, as tidal waves of Hollywood production crashed on Australia's shores, the McDonagh sisters made their last feature film. A handful of other filmmakers battled on, but Cinesound was the only Australian company in continuous production throughout the decade.

Strike Me Lucky was one of the company's films, a vehicle for Mo that called for a Mae West impersonator. 'Kate' was a gangster who called her Mae West persona 'June East' and her partner 'Al Baloney'. But if Gladys hoped to win the role of Kate in Ken Hall's film she was disappointed; it went instead to Yvonne (Fifi) Banvard, a musical comedy actress with a reputation for playing the vamp. The film failed at the box office and Mo never made another:

> An experienced director of Hollywood farce could perhaps have reshaped the comedian's style to fit the new medium; but Mr. Ken Hall has made only an amateurish job of things...all the actors have the air of novices in a suburban repertory show. As for the plot and the dialogue, one had best relapse into a resigned silence...Brings in kangaroos and emus and incredible burlesque aborigines for the mere sake of showing them. A good deal of American influence comes in too. For no discoverable reason Miss Yvonne Banvard goes through her part in exact and avowed impersonation of Mae West. The gangsters all talk American slang.[26]

By the end of the decade Australia's movie output had greatly reduced. Though Ken Hall made more successful comedies than *Strike Me Lucky*, Hollywood productions and their exhibitors were outstripping and out-marketing the Australian competition. There would be no more local film opportunities for a mature 'Mae Westian' comedienne.

Radio, however, was booming. Transmission arrangements improved during the 1930s, and a new array of stations emerged. Australians tuned to their wireless sets in ever larger numbers. Gladys had occasionally been heard on radio as early as 1925, when Keith's Syncopating Jesters were broadcast live from the Haymarket Theatre. It was only later, when technology in Australia advanced, that items were recorded before being put to air.

Then Gladys could be heard in community singing events. More popular than ever during the Depression and throughout the 1930s, they were often presented and programmed by radio stations that would stage and record the shows for broadcast. More than sing-along but less than vaudeville, community singing shows were held in theatres, cinemas and local halls. Morale-boosting and cheap entertainments in wartime and depression, they featured 'turns' from well-known artists, vaudevillians who knew how to encourage an audience to participate.

Gladys appeared in comedy routines and musical numbers, even sometimes whistling at these events, though radio might not have been the best medium for a siffleuse. Whistling, especially a woman's whistle, might have been thought shrill, as women's voices sometimes were. Nor was radio the most suitable medium for a comedienne whose exaggerated wink in her Cinesound file picture suggests she relied on gesture, facial expression and 'hilarious make ups' as much as on her voice and her gags. Too broad and maybe too piercing for radio, too old for roles in the few movies being made in Australia, it seemed that Gladys belonged on the stage.

14
Happy Go Lucky Lane

Elsie was struggling to care for her small son while touring the country's remaining theatres. She often had to leave him in Sydney, and so he grew close to the family that cared for him in Waterloo during his parents' many absences.

In 1933, four-year-old Keith went to Perth with his mother and father. There his grandparents looked after him while Elsie and Keith senior appeared at the Luxor with comedians Elton Black and Stan Foley, known as 'Stud' Foley since he'd played opposite Nat Phillips in a duo known as 'Stiffy and Stud'.

Elsie's contributions to comic sketches at the Luxor with Keith and Stud mostly passed without mention. When she was acknowledged, she seemed barely more significant than the scenery:

> ...Stud Foley and Keith Connolly were also seen to advantage in a humorous sketch *The Will*, in which Elsie Hosking played the wife.[1]

But Elsie was also dancing and singing the sweet and cheerful songs that had been her forte since she was Perth's little idol. In her hometown she would always win the most recognition as 'Western Australian girl Elsie Hosking, who tripped sweetly in during the week with more dainty work'.[2] Back in Perth with her husband and her son, and reunited with her parents, Elsie sang 'Ain't It Nice' and 'Happy Go Lucky Lane', songs that became audience favourites.

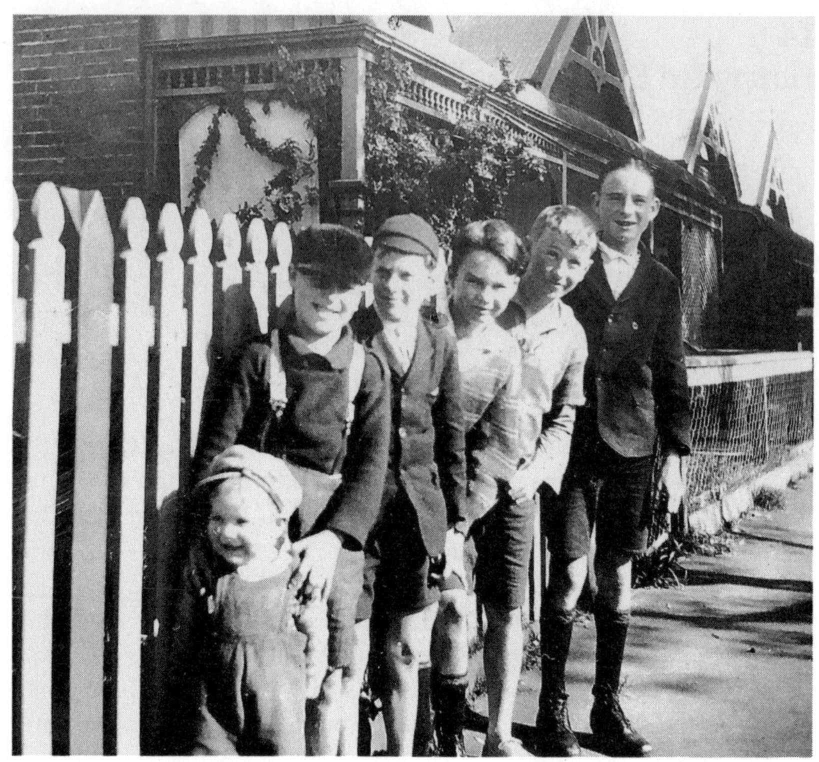

Keith (the smallest boy), with friends in Waterloo ca. 1931

She sang the kind of optimistic lyrics that were popular in difficult times. Unemployment remained high and Elsie's sister Lydia had been forced to move her five children into a one-room shack in a camp close to the heart of Perth after her husband lost his job. They were there for two years before their fortunes improved.

By contrast Elsie did seem to be living in 'happy go lucky lane'. She had just one child, a working husband and a career of her own. Yet when her son turned five in October, she had difficult decisions to make. Young Keith was due to start at school and Elsie would have to choose between parenting and stage work, son and husband.

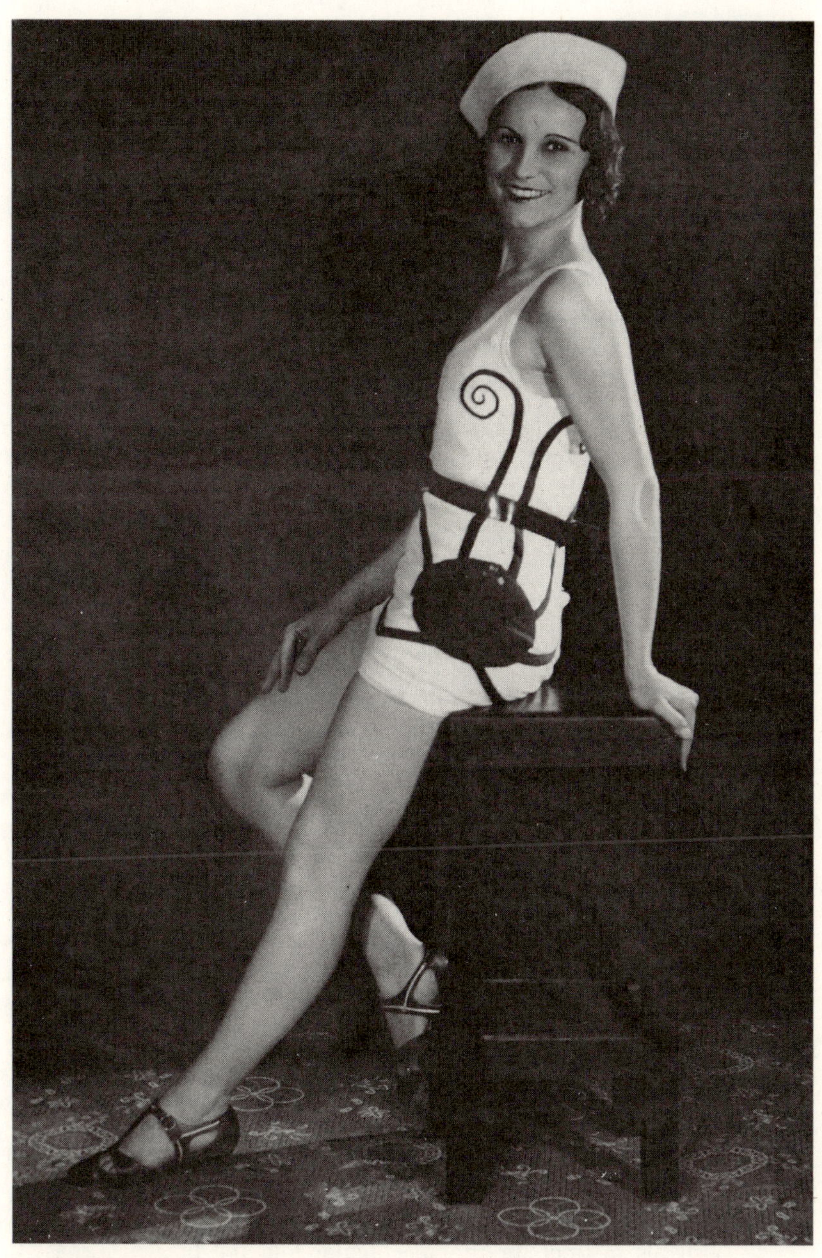

'Dainty work,' Elsie, ca. 1933

She'd married a man who wasn't about to sacrifice his own ambitions for his family. Settling in Perth, or indeed staying in any one place so that his son might attend school, would require his father Keith to abandon hope of further theatrical success. And that he would not surrender. Even if Elsie was not herself driven by any need for greater celebrity, she couldn't choose to stay with her son unless she was prepared to give up life with her husband.

In any event, those close to her might have thought it best that Elsie was not solely responsible for her son's day-to-day care. It was reported that when he was a baby and being breast fed, she would suddenly put him down and go off for long walks. Today we might call it 'forgotten-baby syndrome', an absent-mindedness in new parents now understood to be an effect of stress and sleep deprivation. But many years ago, Elsie's behaviour as a young mother was considered most peculiar. She was branded an 'anxious type'.

Keith was engaged by Frank Neil for a 'vaudeville end of the programme', at Sydney's Tivoli in 1934.[3] Elsie's name was not mentioned in publicity, though she could have been among the 'girls and gaiety' promised in advertisements.[4] Or perhaps she had decided to stay with young Keith in Perth a little longer.

Nor was she among the cast members of *The Merry Malones* when, later that year, Keith won the kind of musical comedy role he preferred. In a show written by George M Cohan, 'the man who owned Broadway', the main parts were filled by actors from the United States. Keith played a supporting role until the American leading man fell out with the show's producer, Ernest C Rolls, after a dispute over money. Keith then won the lead. He danced and sang as 'John Malone' in a role taken by George M Cohan himself in the original Broadway version.

Next Keith was cast in a sprawling revue featuring Roy Rene, among too many others:

> With his instinct for the spectacular and the bizarre, Ernest C. Rolls piles scene upon scene until he gropes about exhausted amid

> the confusion. Rhapsodies of 1935, a revue which was presented before a gay house at the Apollo Theatre on Saturday, is just one heap of entertainment. The opening night, beginning twenty minutes late and lasting for four hours, was thus in the nature of a full-dress rehearsal, and no doubt would be fit subject for effective criticism as a whole after the process of selection and rejection takes place. In England a revue is usually tried out in the provinces. The idea of Mr. Rolls seems to be that in Australia it should be tried out in Melbourne.[5]

Despite an enormous Rhapsodies cast, Elsie was not among its members. It seems likely that she was still in Perth, struggling to decide between being mother to young Keith or wife to his father, or simply being Elsie Hosking, soubrette.

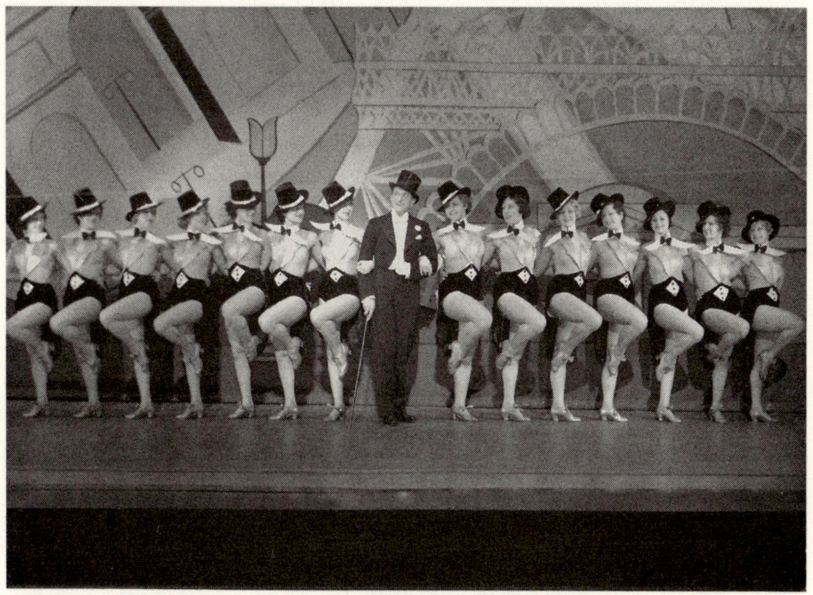

Keith Connolly, centre stage at the Tivoli, 1935

It was the middle of 1935 before she returned to the stage, with Keith and old friends Joe Lawman and Stella Lamond. They were engaged by Les Shipp, from whose company Gladys had only recently departed. As a 'singing soubrette', Elsie appeared in towns and suburbs around Sydney, even after Keith left to rejoin Frank Neil's Tivoli revue. Studded with imported talent, Neil's big-city productions gave Keith greater opportunity to be noticed:

> KEITH CONNELLY (sic), *sound Digger trouper, gives another capital contribution to revue programme at Tiv. Our private opinion is that he ranks with many major stars for general ability.*[6]

Encouraged by the attention paid to his Tivoli appearances, Keith decided once again to try his luck overseas. Elsie trailed him as far as Perth where, while Keith waited for his ship to sail, the couple again appeared at the Luxor:

> Another change of programme was made by the Serenaders at the Luxor Theatre last night when Keith Connolly and Elsie Hoskings [sic] began their season with the company. They are no strangers to Perth audiences and are a Perth couple, but are always the recipients of a big welcome and last night was no exception. Their topical duet was extremely clever, also their dancing, and they did well in the sketches. Elsie has a pleasing voice.[7]

Keith and Elsie were among many married couples working together in popular entertainment in the 1930s. They included Mike Connors and Queenie Paul, Roy Rene and Sadie Gale, Stella Lamond and Joe Lawman, Ron Shand and Letty Craydon. Queenie had already become something of a theatrical mogul in her own right and Stella would go on to eclipse both her first and second husbands on stage and screen.[8] In a long career Letty Craydon, soubrette and comedienne, would work in popular entertainment, film, comedy and serious drama. But at the Luxor in 1936 she was trying her hand at writing and producing. Though her husband Ron was the headlined comedian on the program, Letty was in charge of the whole show:

> The production of the show has now passed into the hands of Letty Craydon who has had lengthy experience in show business, and who has a lot of new material to offer. She has infused pep and snap into the show and the gags and sketches are packed with laughs and surprises.[9]

In Letty's production:

> Keith Connolly and Elsie Hoskins [sic] are two who at all times pull their weight in the boat. Keith, it is understood, is to leave for London later in the year and he should be well received. One of the boys who saw service with the Aussies in the big scrap, he is a
>
> POLISHED PERFORMER
>
> and his long career on the Australian stage has found him called upon to play all manner of parts. One of the hardest workers in the business, Keith does not spare the enthusiasm which he introduces into every part he has to play.[10]

When Keith finally boarded the SS *Narkunda* and headed for England in search of international success, Elsie took a rest from the stage and spent more time with her son. She sang a little on radio, but it was another two months before Stud Foley lured her back to the Luxor Theatre. Then she won praise both for her singing and her comic acting in sketches and revues featuring Stud.

> The best of the sketches were perhaps "The Diver Cabaret" and "A Scene in a Hollywood Apartment." In the latter of these Elsie Hoskings [sic] appeared as Greta Garbo, ...Stud Foley, the producer.[11]

Having once been managed by her father, then by her husband, in his absence she was managed by his male colleague. The men typically arranged things to suit themselves and so, when Keith returned from London after four months away, he resumed his role as Stan's foil and

Elsie once again found herself playing wife to Keith in more ways than one:

> One of the evening's most amusing sketches was THE WEDDING BREAKFAST, in which Keith Connolly and Elsie Hosking, as the husband and wife respectively, were outstanding...[12]

But Keith had come home with little to show for his journey; no British engagements, not even an agent. Instead, he and Stud committed their 'Mirthmakers' to appearances in Broken Hill and Adelaide. Having spent a precious year close to her boy, Elsie left him again a few days after his eighth birthday.

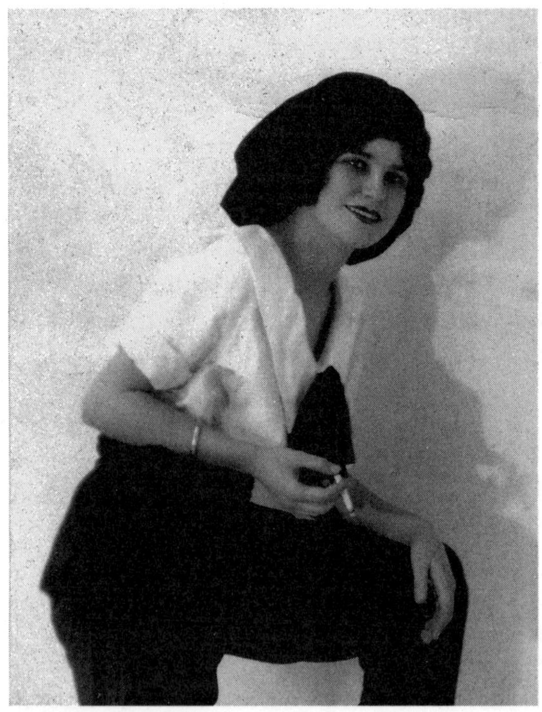

Elsie Hosking, 1936

Later Elsie maintained she was happy travelling Australia and New Zealand with her husband, happy with her occupation and happy for her parents to look after young Keith. But it's hard to believe that these repeated separations were not sometimes distressing for mother and son. Even if she wished it otherwise, Elsie couldn't have said so. She was in a difficult business in especially tough times. And she'd married a man driven by a ferocious need for success. For her final Perth appearances in 1936 Elsie sang 'I Believe in Miracles'. To reconcile her roles as performer, wife and mother, she was in need of one herself.

In Adelaide, Elsie worked with Keith and Stud in a program that included Tex Morton, an artist fresh from the recording studio where he'd recently made a disc that marked the beginnings of Australian country music. *Wrap me up with my stockwhip and blanket*, sang Tex, in an Australianised version of an old song. Then Elsie was off to Brisbane, with her husband and Stud. They made a popular trio, all three contributing to the success of their act.

> HEADED by Keith Connolly and Stan Foley the Jesters kept a ripple of laughter running through the audience from beginning to end. The appearance of Foley, the comedian, and Connolly, his foil, was always the signal for shrieks of laughter. Foley is undoubtedly a clever comedian, but much of his success last night was due to the excellent performances of Connolly.
>
> With his serious face Connolly never allowed a flicker of a smile to spoil his efforts, a direction in which several other players offended when Foley was going through his antics. Connolly was outstanding in The Haunted House, although here again Foley gained most of the laughs. Assisting these two male performers in their comedy was Elsie Hoskings [sic], the personality girl of the show. Always a dainty and attractive figure, she was a favourite of last night's audience. Coupled with Foley she achieved great success in the comedy sketch, Eat and Grumble.[13]

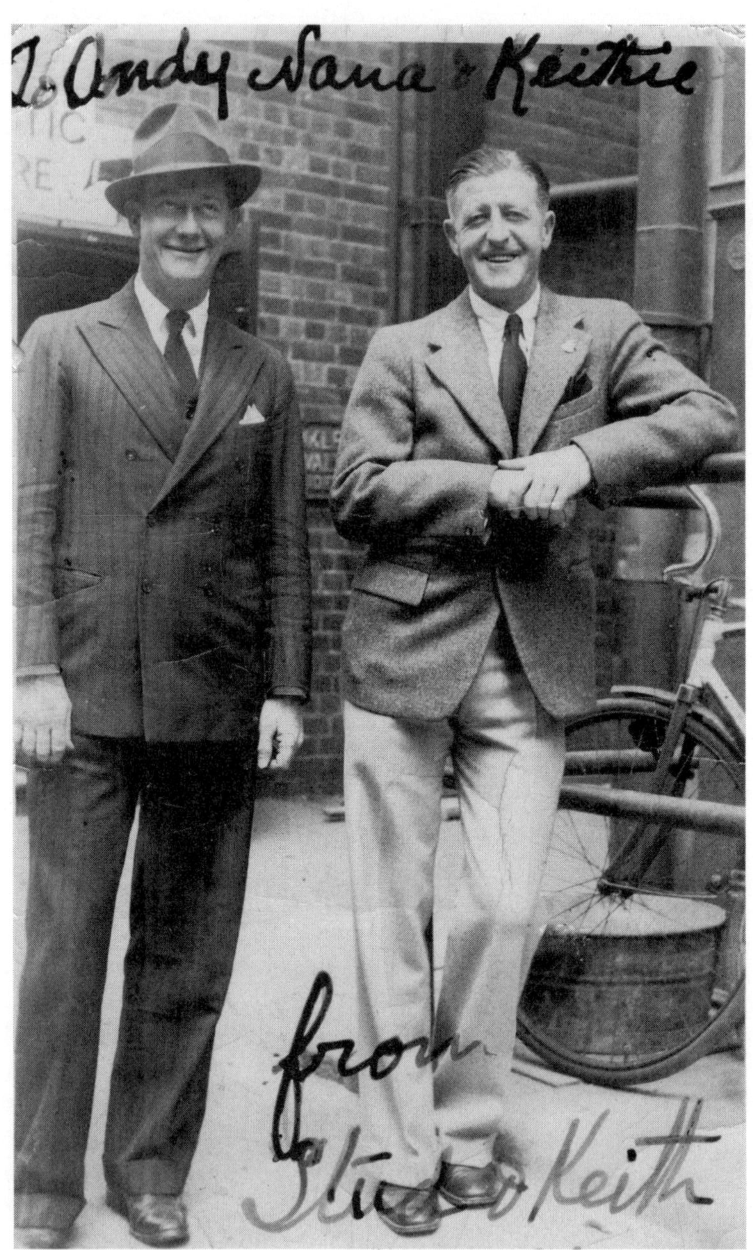

Stud Foley (l) and Keith, 1937

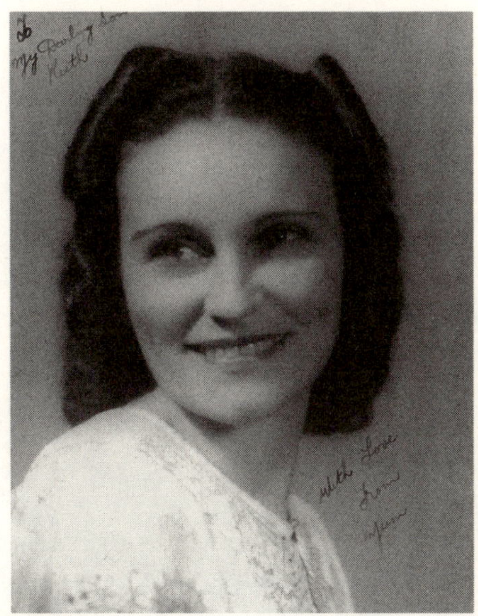

Elsie, 1937

'Dainty and attractive', 'assisting' the men, was exactly what was required. Elsie pitched her own performance carefully. It wouldn't have done to let her fellow comedians down – nor to outshine them.

At Brisbane's Rex, the only woman to take a larger share of the limelight than the men was one who wore trousers. Nellie Small, male impersonator, dressed as a man on and offstage. The Sydney-born daughter of West Indian parents, she was often incorrectly described as an American:

> Although the numbers of the orchestra are enjoyable in themselves, the one entitled 'The Blue Prelude' was made even more so by the appearance of Nellie Small; the American negress. This performer is the outstanding soloist on the programme at present, and the manner in which the audience welcomed her was a tribute to her popularity.[14]

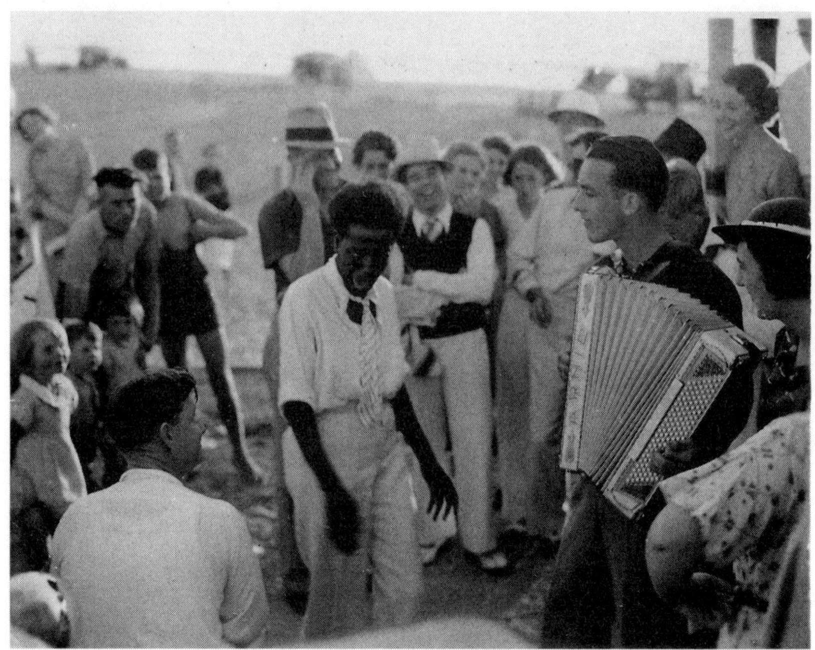

Nellie Small among friends, including Keith (behind Nellie), 1937

Nellie didn't always find Brisbane so welcoming. Some years later she told a reporter that when visiting Queensland she invariably stayed with friends, having been refused accommodation by many hotels. 'When she tried to book in at one in Anne Street in 1948, the proprietress snapped: "We don't allow blacks in here" '.[15]

In June 1937 Elsie and Keith joined a new company put together by Frank Neil. Having bought Connors and Paul out of the Tivoli circuit, Neil was determined to make it pay. He'd reintroduced the schedule of two shows a day and vigorously promoted 'stars from overseas and the best of local ones'.[16]

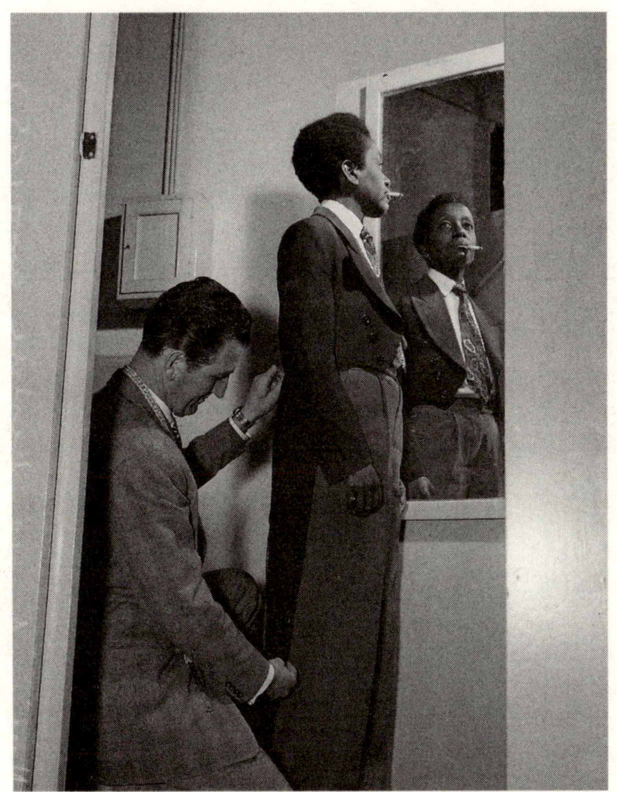

Nellie Small, 1952

Elsie and Keith worked on the Tivoli circuit for most of the next three years, always given lesser billing than imported 'stars'. The effects of the Depression and the rise of talking pictures might not have meant the end of vaudeville, but they'd made life difficult for entertainers everywhere. Many artists from the United States and United Kingdom were happy to make the long journey to Australia to work:

> On an average, Frank Neil brings out from America and England 265 persons (110 acts) a year, paying £27,000 in fares. Each company plays five weeks in each of the big cities, the round trip

being Melbourne, Sydney, Brisbane, New Zealand, and Adelaide. Some acts are also sent to Perth.[17]

Keith, who hadn't succeeded in exporting his own talents to Britain, instead found himself partnering British artists here:

> HAVE you played 'Headlines'? It's the new craze, according to George Bolton and Keith Connolly, who introduced it to Brisbane with a series of gags when the new Frank Neil opened on Saturday night at His Majesty's Theatre. The idea is that one player reads a piquant headline from a newspaper, and the other endeavours to cap it with a second. The result is usually most amusing and the thing has possibilities.
>
> The show is a Tivoli production, and is entitled 'The World Looks Up'. George Bolton, the London comedian, provides the main thread of fun...[18]

Despite not even being named in much of the advertising for these Tivoli shows, Keith and Elsie were more than pulling their weight. In Brisbane, while Keith partnered the leading comedian, Elsie opened the entertainment:

> There was a stormy opening to the show on Saturday; it was a storm ballet led by Elsie Hosking, and featured damsels in oilskins and carrying umbrellas stepping high in the rain, a very successful presentation. This was followed by a rainbow ballet.[19]

They worked with United States-born male impersonator, Ella Shields, who sang her hit song 'Burlington Bertie from Bow'. In 1938 another of their Tivoli programs was headed by American actor, Billy Costello – the voice of cartoon character 'Popeye the Sailor Man'.

Even an Australian artist as famous as Mo received lesser billing than imported acts when he was on the same program as one-legged New York tap-dancing man, Peg Leg Bates, and Chang the Mysterious Magician:

NEW TIVOLI SHOW

> CHANG (the mysterious?) is the advertised star attraction of the new show at the Sydney Tivoli. Alas! Chang isn't exceptionally good – or let's say the mystery is familiar rather than novel. Some of his numbers go off well. More entertaining is our old friend ROY (MO) RENE...he is the brightest of bright spots in this quite colorful show.[20]

A few of the artists Neil imported, notably Americans Will Mahoney and Evie Hayes, eventually settled in Australia. Mahoney, reputed to have been the highest paid variety artist in the United States, arrived in Australia with his third wife Evie in 1938 and it wasn't long before Keith was appearing at his side.

> Will Mahoney, a remarkable comedian, is chief man in the show. But the cast does not feed him with laughs. They all do their part and get their own applause and very often Keith Connolly, a firm Tivoli favourite, is swapping laughs with Mahoney.[21]

Elsie and Keith were holding their own with talented British and American colleagues, though it wasn't doing much to bring Keith the celebrity and travel he craved. Nor a huge income. In the zither case I found a notebook in which he'd recorded the couple's combined income for 1938 as £12 a week – for twenty-eight weeks' work by two performers working six days a week. It was hardly a princely sum. The minimum wage that year was almost £4 for a man working five days a week, all year long. Keith might have left Australia to seek his fortune elsewhere, had he not had an increasingly fragile wife to consider.

Though Elsie knew her son to be well cared for, she was far from him and not so content. In Perth, young Keith seemed happy living with his grandparents. He was enrolled at Highgate School, where his mother had once been a pupil. His grandfather Andy took him to the football every winter weekend and Keith became an enthusiastic cricket fan and Bradman worshipper. He saw movies at the local open-air cinema, and listened to *Dad and Dave* on the radio.

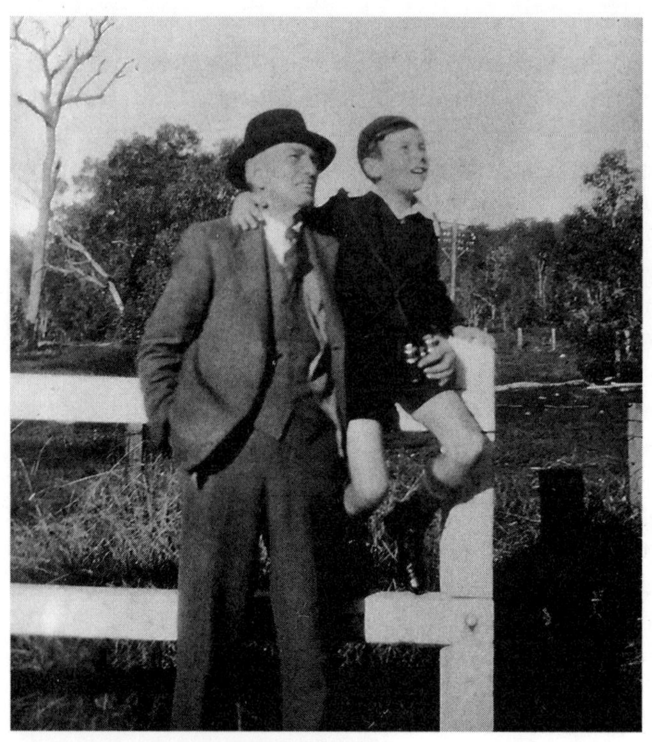

Watching magpies, Keith jnr and grandfather Andy, 1938

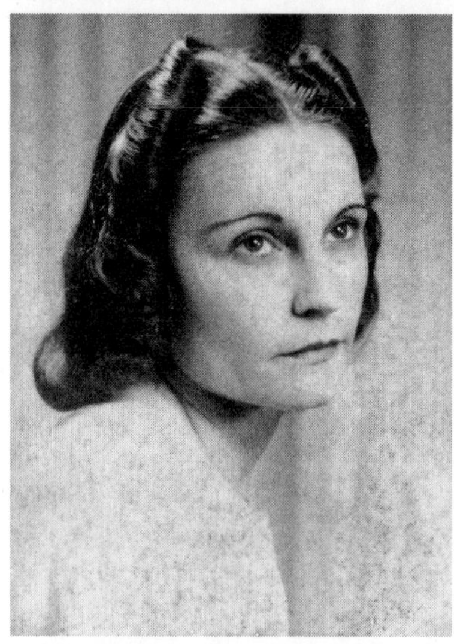

Elsie Hosking, ca. 1939

On the other side of the country, Elsie began to suffer stomach trouble for which no cause could be found. It was an illness accompanied by attacks of acute anxiety for which she required sedation. Only after being sent to Perth to rest for some months was she well enough to rejoin her husband onstage.

In June 1939 they travelled to New Zealand with *Funz a Poppin*, promoted as 'an all American variety show'. According to one Dunedin reviewer:

> One of the surprising things about this 'All American' show, by the way, is the almost complete absence of the American accent from the speech of the artists. This, need it be said, was not altogether a disappointing feature.[22]

In New Zealand they were also featured in a show titled *International Varieties*, in which they appeared before the Great North China troupe of acrobats, singers and dancers. Reviewers were impressed by the physical contortions of *big Chinamen and their natty little women.*[23]

> Some of the acts were one woman shows, and the performers proved to be as attractive as they were skilful. Literally hair-raising stunts were performed, the sensation of them all being the little Chinese who swung by her own long hair from a sturdy rope and whose impassivity was broken by a flashing smile as she completed a difficult feat at the end of her act...[24]

When it came to commenting on the performances of less acrobatic female entertainers on the program, most words were devoted to their costumes:

> ...A crisp frock of starched white organdie was worn, by Elsa Hoskins [sic] in her act with Keith Connolly, black appliques and small black buttons at the waistline giving the gown an unusual finish...the first part of the programme being completed by the male impersonations of Effie Fellows, debonair in a full-dress suit.[25]

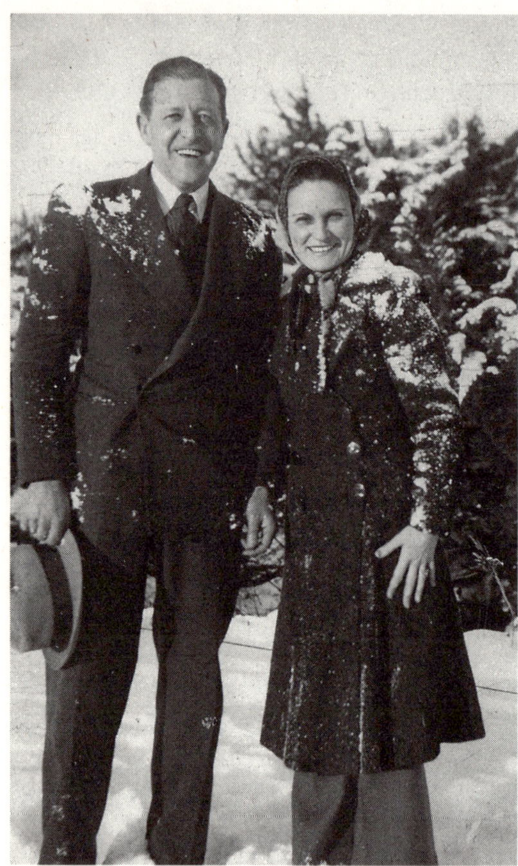

In New Zealand, Elsie and Keith, 1939

Advertised as a 'patter artist', and sometimes called 'The Different Girl', Elsie's outfits typically received more press attention than the content or quality of her performances. That besuited Effie Fellows received similar treatment suggests that some observers simply didn't know what to say about women's stage work – even when they dressed as men.

In Wellington, Keith played British prime minister, Neville Chamberlain, in *The Peace Conference*, a sketch 'putting international politics in a happier light indeed'.[26]

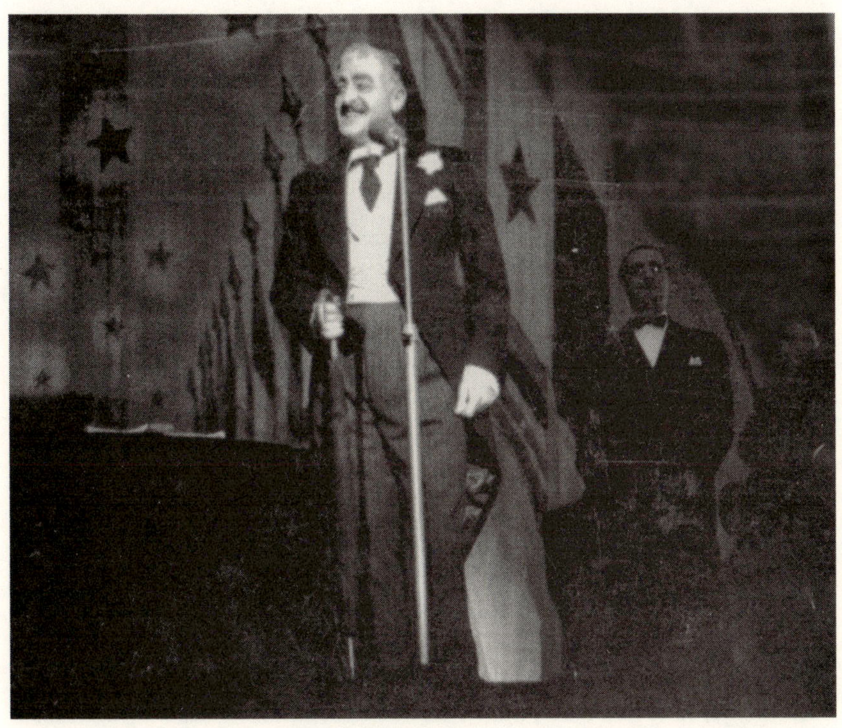

As British PM Chamberlain, Keith Connolly, 1939

When the show moved south, Dunedin audiences were, predictably, not so easily amused:

> The free use of topicalities was a novelty for visiting vaudeville. A really clever burlesque—marred, however, by a lapse into coarse vulgarity—was The Peace Conference, in which appeared Chamberlain and his umbrella, Hitler and his unruly lock of hair. Mussolini who was all for 'Piece'—a piece of Rumania, a piece of Poland—and Stalin with his modest request for a world revolution. The one character out of focus was Mahatma Gandhi, who was as unlike that Easterner as it was possible to make it, being more in line with a robust, hairy-chested Chinese coolie.[27]

There were few roles for women when the theatrical stage parodied the world stage, though international affairs soon ceased to be the stuff of comedy. A month after Elsie stood in the wings to watch her husband play the British prime minister, Chamberlain declared war on Germany. Within days Australia was also at war.

Vaudevillians who had survived the arrival of silent cinema, radio and talkies now faced the challenges of wartime. But for the first eight months or so after the declaration of war life went on much as before. Elsie and Keith continued playing to live audiences and to those at home tuned into their wireless sets. It was the period sometimes called the 'Phoney War'.

Indeed war even created some opportunities. After spoofing Chamberlain in New Zealand, in 1940 Keith won his first and only film role – as a Nazi agent in *The Power and the Glory*. It was a local film production and the first Australian movie to be distributed by Metro Goldwyn Mayer. Peter Finch was in the cast, along with film director Raymond Longford. The Nazi roles were played as 'stock characters of evil incarnate'.[28]

Film acting was a change from the punishing schedule of the Tivoli circuit. For most of 1940 Keith and Elsie took a break from the exhausting two-shows-a-day routine and stayed closer to Sydney. Together they were a popular act at community concerts staged by radio stations in towns not too far from the city, where Elsie again sang the cheerful songs for which she was known:

> Elsie Hosking, a soubrette and novelty player, sang Ain't It Nice, Chestnut Tree, and Make the Best of Each Day. Keith Connolly, the versatile Sydney radio comedian, very soon had the audience in fits of laughter and was voted a general favourite by everyone...this pair also presented a dual turn of song and dance and by the time they had concluded this item they had won the admiration and

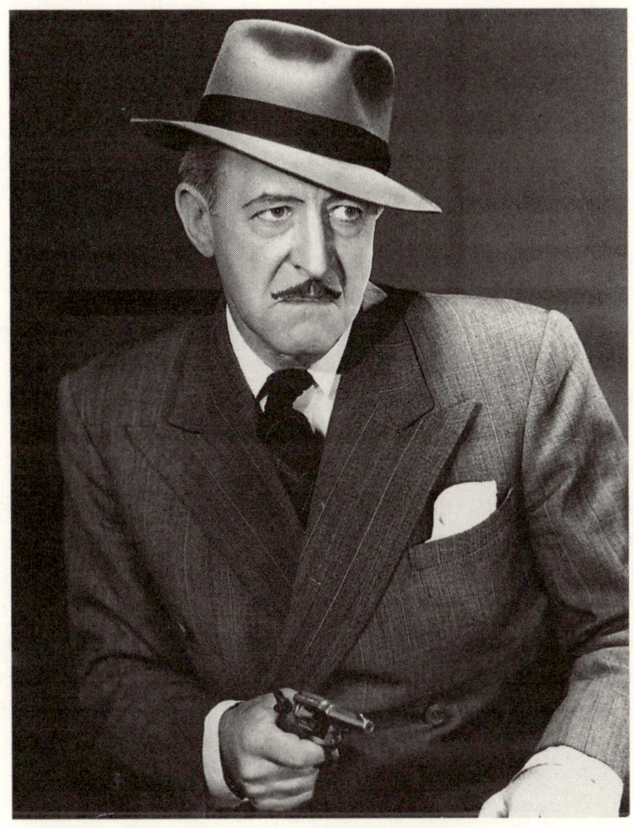

Playing a stock character of evil incarnate, Keith Connolly, 1941

> respect of the audience if the prolonged applause which followed is any criterion.[29]

But by November they were back on the road, with Mo in *Black Velvet*, a London wartime show staged in Tivoli theatres around the country in the early part of 1941. After seasons in Adelaide, Melbourne, Sydney and Brisbane, Elsie again became unwell. Later she told a doctor that she was at the piano, playing an Al Jolson hit, 'A Quarter to Nine', when she began to feel terribly afraid:

I know I won't be late
Cause at half past eight
I'm going to hurry there.
I'll be waiting where the lane begins
Waiting for you on needles and pins.
And then the world is going to be mine
Mine all mine!
This evening about a quarter to nine.[30]

She was overcome by the numbers in the song. They made her so nervous and anxious that she had to stop playing. She worried about the number nine for weeks and spent time under sedation in a Sydney hospital. Then she was sent to recuperate in Perth with her son and her parents, while Keith went to work in Adelaide. Months passed before Elsie was recovered enough to rejoin her husband onstage at the Cremorne Theatre in Brisbane.

It was a family reunion of sorts. Keith's brother Gerry and his wife Hilda were living in Brisbane, where Gerry had given up theatre to join radio station 4BC. And their sister Gladys was on the Cremorne program too, with a new stage partner and a whole new act.

15
The Whistling Cowgirl

In my search for information about my great-aunt Gladys, I found only two people who remembered her. One was her nephew Bruce, son of Mary Agnes's firstborn, Reg. In Sydney I called him and we arranged to meet, but he fell ill and our appointment was cancelled. Bruce died before we could speak face-to-face, though our one and only telephone conversation was memorable. Gladys had made quite an impression on him when he was a child.

'Oh Gladys', he chuckled, 'she was great, she was a rebel'. He was excited to talk about her and recalled that when he and his brother Barry were boys, Gladys would give them 'amazing' Christmas presents – novelty neckties and the like. He said that his mother, Dorothy (Reg's second wife), was not keen on her sister-in-law, Gladys, though the women would occasionally meet for afternoon tea in the city. Dorothy would return full of disapproving observations about Gladys and her manners. Apparently she was in the habit of stubbing out her cigarettes in any available saucer. Bruce remembered that Gladys wore a large ring in the shape of a question mark, but his sharpest memory was of her extraordinary whistle.

He said that Gladys once had a whip-cracking act. I had my doubts – I hadn't found any photos in the zither case that showed Gladys with whips, nor had I read mention of any such thing in my research into Gladys's career. But though Bruce was elderly when we spoke, his memory hadn't failed him.

It seems Tex Morton was not the only one to have seen possibilities in giving American folk traditions an Australian flavour. While Tex yodelled and sang 'Wrap Me Up with My Stockwhip and Blanket', Gladys restyled herself as 'the whistling cowgirl', adept at 'a-ropin' and a-tyin''.[1]

In 1939 she teamed up with Jeanne Cracknell, a former circus performer, vaudeville artist and sharpshooter known as the 'Bulls Eye Girl'. Jeanne was a great shot. With the aid of a mirror she could shoot her rifle backwards. She could hit a target whilst standing on her head, and extinguish lighted candles with rifle fire. Gladys updated her own skills. To her well-established whistling, comic, singing and yodelling talents she added whip-cracking, rope-twirling, shooting, and a performing Pomeranian. Gladys and Jeanne were known as the Arizona Girls. Their dog was called Goldie.

Making their first appearance together in Brisbane late in 1939, they showed audiences at the Theatre Royal 'that sharpshooting and rope spinning are tricks not exclusive to the he-man of the American West':[2]

> The Arizona Girls twirled ropes and handled their six-shooters as dexterously as any cowboy in a fast-moving act...[3]

The kind of wild west show tricks that made the Arizona Girls popular in Brisbane had been around for many years. Before teaming up with Gladys, Jeanne was one of an earlier pair of sharpshooting women, also known as the Arizona Girls. And before that Jeanne and her husband Leo were well known on vaudeville circuits for an act that included shooting, whip-cracking and trained dogs, cats and monkeys:

> The Cracknells are an attractive pair handsomely dressed in white. The man cracks stockwhips and throws ropes into rings, also using them as lassos. He whips the girl round the neck and body, and she apparently likes being beaten in that fashion. Some very clever shooting is done by both.[4]

Maybe Jeanne didn't like being whipped as much as she appeared to. Her partnership with Leo was over by the early 1930s, at least professionally speaking. Leo went on to train animals for movies and later for television. Jeanne became an Arizona Girl. When Gladys joined her, she brought a new trick to the Arizona Girls act. Whistling, as well as their gender, would make Gladys and Jeanne stand out from the he-men of the crowd.

Though Jeanne was sometimes called Australia's Annie Oakley, the Arizona Girls weren't as militant as the legendary American sharp-shooter. Oakley believed women should be educated and independent, and that learning to use guns made them seem more so. But there were neither weapons nor whips in the Arizona Girls' publicity shots. Even Goldie the wonder dog wasn't in the pictures.

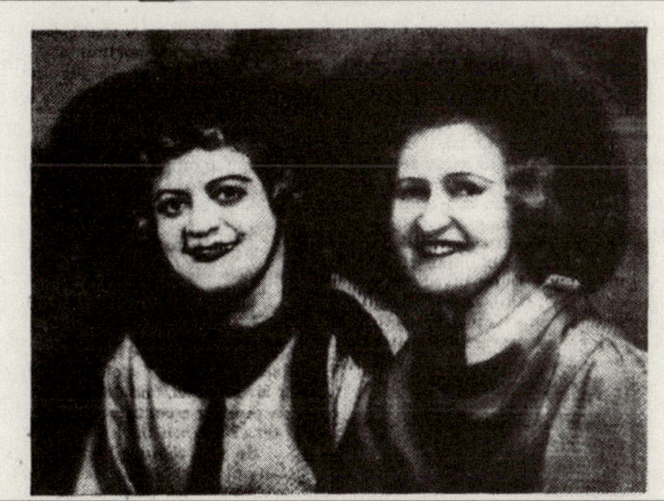

FOR 2LT RADIO CONCERT

The Two Arizona Girls, who will present a Novelty Act at the Theatre Royal on Friday Night.

Lithgow Mercury, 1940

Gladys and Jeanne smiled for the camera of course, but Gladys looks particularly happy as an Arizona Girl; more relaxed than the winking Mae Westian character actress who'd sent her photograph to Cinesound a few years earlier. Maybe female company suited Gladys, just as it had over a decade earlier when she posed with Lynette and Her Six Redheads. Even then she was among women wearing Stetsons.

With Jeanne she led community singing before movies screening in Lithgow and Newcastle. New radio station 2LT programmed *A Night in Arizona*, from Lithgow's Theatre Royal. Fittingly it starred The Arizona Girls, together with Smiling Billy Blinkhorn and The Yodelling Miners. It was declared 'easily the best radio concert held in Lithgow',[5] though its patrons may not have attended too many others.

For some time before she teamed up with Jeanne in the Arizona Girls, Gladys had been venturing further from Sydney to work. Frank stayed in the city, where he managed picture theatres whilst Gladys made more frequent appearances in nearby provincial towns. Early in 1939, she played in Adelaide for more than a month and, after becoming an Arizona Girl, she joined Stanley McKay's famous Gaieties company for a trip around the Queensland show circuit. Gladys and Jeanne cracked their whips under canvas in Rockhampton, Mackay, Townsville, Bowen and Cairns. Their last stop was Broken Hill in New South Wales. By the time Gladys returned to Sydney in September 1940, her husband Frank had found another woman.

After discovering Frank with retired actress, Vera James, Gladys wasted no time in filing for divorce. The next day she visited her lawyer cousin, Warrington Connolly. Marjorie, his daughter and newly articled clerk, completed the necessary paperwork. Maybe Frank and Vera had given Gladys just the excuse she needed to end a marriage that was over in all but the eyes of the law. Enjoying a happy stage partnership with Jeanne, touring with the Arizona Girls and on the road for months at a stretch, Gladys may have been escaping an unhappy marriage.

Yet relationship breakdown alone was insufficient reason for divorce in Australia before no-fault divorce was introduced in the 1970s. Gladys needed a legally acceptable reason to end her marriage, and adultery was one of the grounds upon which it could be dissolved. It took more than a year for the divorce to work its way through the legal system, but eventually Gladys became a free woman again.

She was forty-five and no longer girlish, but was nonetheless described as 'A Charming Soubrette' in publicity for a solo appearance at Lithgow's Theatre Royal early in 1941. Gladys was the only woman named on the bill, and certainly its best-known performer, yet there was no role for her in the revue that concluded the program. *The Mighty Dictator* featured a host of blokes playing parts like 'Adanuff Stinker', 'Marshal Gorging', and 'Beero Vasilini', but there weren't too many openings for women in this kind of playground poke at Australia's enemies.

There were few substantial roles for women in the farces of wartime, though it wasn't a dearth of female parts that most limited engagements for Gladys and Jeanne. Since being displaced from big cities by mass unemployment and talkies, vaudeville artists had come to rely on their patrons in smaller places – especially those in the many towns dotted up and down Australia's eastern coastline. But in wartime petrol was rationed, unnecessary train journeys discouraged and travel permits required. Travelling players found it hard to reach their audiences and gradually regional theatrical and show circuits were destroyed. Even some remaining city theatres closed. For most of the war Gladys would travel no further from Sydney than Newcastle, 100 miles away. After their brief reunion at Brisbane's Cremorne theatre in 1941, she didn't see her brothers again until the fighting was over.

Keith and Elsie moved on from the Cremorne to Brisbane's spruced-up Theatre Royal, where they appeared in a show titled *Black and Blue*, in a cast led by Mo. Halfway through its run all hell broke loose. The Japanese bombed Pearl Harbor. Within a couple of months Singapore and other British colonies fell and Darwin and Broome were bombed too. The Theatre Royal was soon commandeered by the United

States military for the entertainment of troops on leave. On its stage, American and Australian performers combined to present vaudeville shows for United States servicemen, but there were relatively few wartime productions. One local later wrote that when he visited the Royal in 1943, 'the Yanks were boiling their billies in the stalls'.[6]

Many Australian artists enlisted. Gerry joined up in 1942 and was first assigned to the Australian Mobile Broadcasting Unit, then to the 5th Division Concert Party with which he served in New Guinea. Finally, he joined the newly created Australian Entertainment Unit.

Keith became a clerk with the airforce. He and Elsie settled in Adelaide, very occasionally performing on the stage or on radio. Though both were uniformed in publicity shots for a wartime show hosted by radio star Jack Davey, Elsie's garb was mere costume.

She remained a civilian, though she did change her name. Henceforth she called herself 'Sunny Day'. I suppose it was a reference to the song made famous by Vera Lynn, 'We'll Meet Again (…some sunny day)'. It was an appropriate alias for Elsie, a singer of optimistic and sentimentally cheerful songs, especially appealing in wartime. But it was a name that belied her sometimes crippling anxiety.

In Sydney Gladys scraped by through the war years, performing with the Arizona Girls at occasional fundraisers, parties and children's shows. She and Jeanne appeared with their performing Pomeranian and with Gladys's former partner Freddie Webber, at a children's party to celebrate the one hundred and twentieth anniversary of Anthony Hordern and Sons department store. In 1944 the Arizona Girls were back in vaudeville for a brief season in Wollongong with Stanley McKay's Gaieties. Then, as the war entered its sixth year, they visited Canberra, appearing at the Albert Hall for two nights, with American comedian and radio star Wayne Froman, and jazz singer Barbara James.

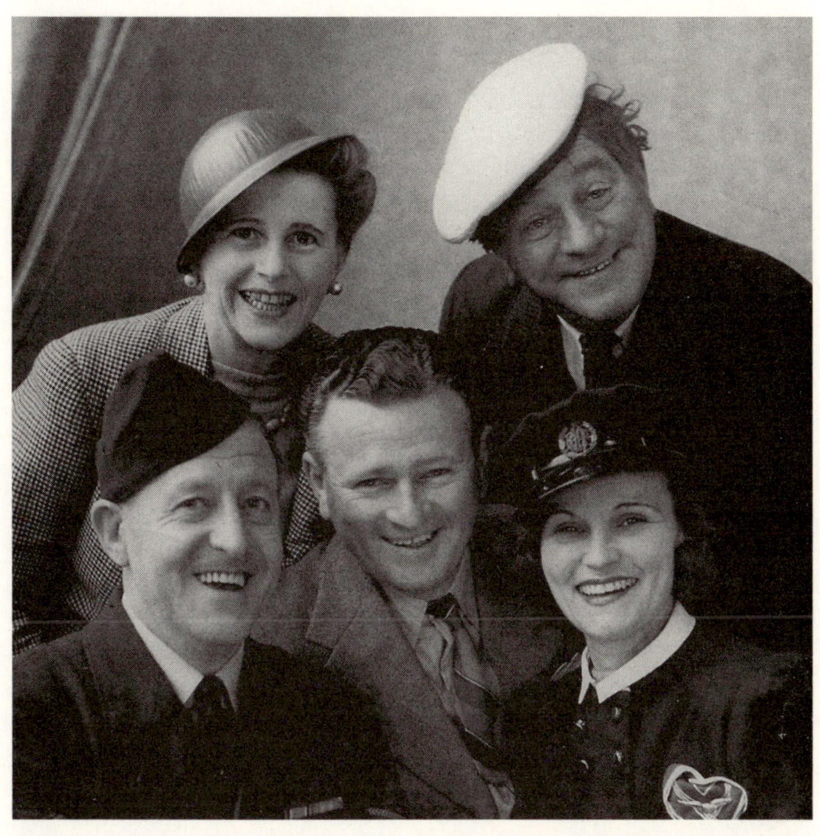

Keith, Jack Davey and 'Sunny Day,' (front) with Ida Newton and Joe Brennan (top), 1943

> Introducing herself with a breezy 'How Do You Do?' Gladys Shaw scored topical hits at the expense of the Commissioner for Railways (Mr. Hartigan), Dr. L. W. Nott and the Royal Canberra Golf Links. Miss Shaw displayed her versatility as one of the Arizona Girls, a feature of which item was the wonder dog, 'Goldie', who delighted with her antics, including a skipping display. Miss Shaw was also partnered in skits with Wayne Froman.[7]

Gladys Shaw was back. She was cracking a whip, writing and performing a stand-up comedy routine and playing opposite Froman, known in Australia (for his work on radio's *Calling the Stars*) as 'the man who makes the nation chuckle'.[8]

Jeanne also showed her versatility:

> A novelty in rag pictures was produced by Jeanne Cracknell in her portrayals of Mr. Churchill, Marshal Stalin, a Christmas scene, an American Red Indian, a cowboy and an Australian soldier. She also displayed her talents with a lassoo [sic] in the Arizona Girls act.[9]

The war was almost at an end, but Jeanne had finally figured out how to deal with the problem of scarce female parts in topical wartime skits. She simply played the men.

16
Sunny Day

The war's end didn't immediately bring relief to entertainers. Petrol rationing continued for years afterward, limiting travel until early in 1950. Keith and Elsie were more mobile than most, moving between capital cities by train for appearances with old friends like George Wallace, Will Mahoney, Stan Foley and Stella Lamond, in Brisbane, Melbourne, Adelaide and Perth. But this flurry of post-war engagements didn't last long. They settled back in Adelaide and by 1947 were working only locally, mostly in radio drama.

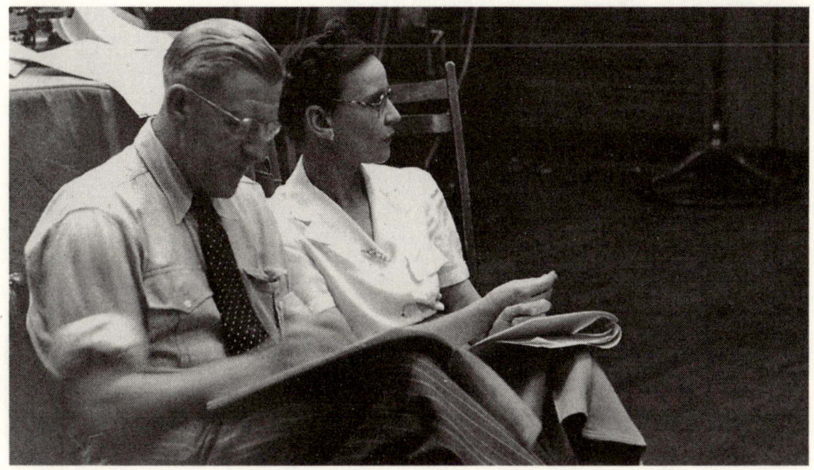

At work in Adelaide, Elsie and Keith at the ABC, ca. 1948

Neither enjoyed good health; Keith had been discharged from his airforce clerical position on medical grounds, and Elsie remained mentally and emotionally fragile. The pair may have decided to slow down, and perhaps Elsie had come to prefer working in radio, where there was less risk of being embarrassed by the kind of anxiety attack that had struck years earlier while she was performing 'A Quarter to Nine'.

In 1948, having just turned fifty, Keith applied for a licence as a 'business salesman'. For him it was a surrender, an end to his campaign to win fame and fortune as a performer. The following year he and Elsie returned to Perth, where their son was about to turn twenty-one.

Elsie at least was happy to be back, and the pair's presence was noted in the social pages:

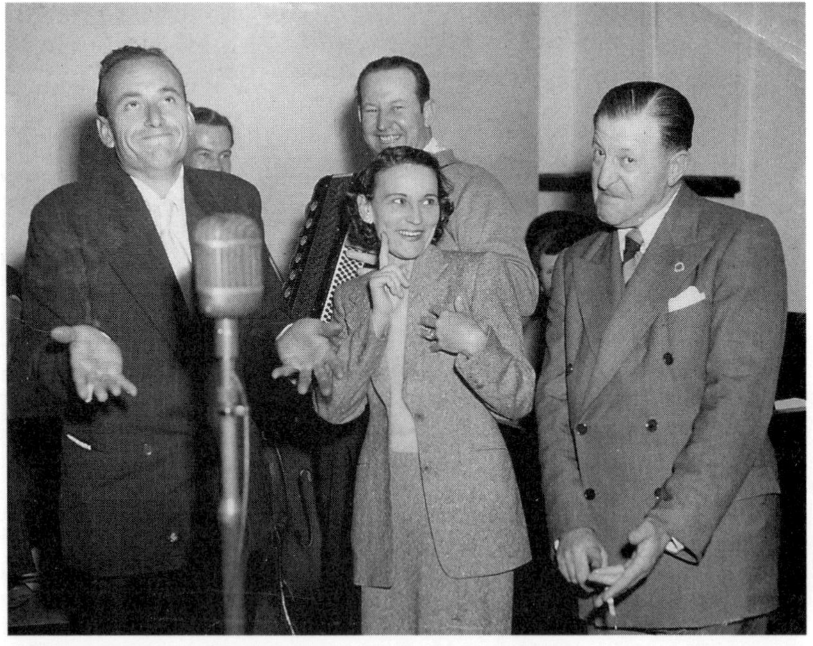

With colleagues at the ABC Perth, Elsie and Keith (r), ca. 1949

> That popular and well-known couple, Elsie and Keith Connolly, celebrated their wedding anniversary last Thursday...On this special occasion Elsie looked very vivacious in navy and white. This clever lass is better known in radio circles as Sunnie [sic] Day.[1]

They settled in Bayswater, a few miles from town, and continued working in radio drama. Keith still appeared on the stage where he could, took brief engagements as a radio announcer and otherwise eked out a living as a salesman. He drank too much and blamed others – mostly Elsie – for ruining his career. Perhaps she had a similar resentment toward a husband whose ambition led her to put his career before her own, and to have her only child raised by others.

But she was happy to be near young Keith, even though it wouldn't be for long. Her son had become a journalist with political ideas and his own career ambitions. He pursued them in Sydney and later in Melbourne, leaving behind a mother and a father struggling with some serious demons. Despite her more settled life, Elsie was ever more anxious, and her husband now added to his disappointments a sense of grievance about his son's departure. Keith senior wanted help to cope with his fragile wife.

Although her mental health was poor, Elsie still took roles in ABC radio plays. In 1953 she was cast in Coral Lansbury's *Mockery Bend*, and she played the lead in *Peaceful Departure*, a drama about an elderly woman waiting to hear she has become a great-grandmother. But Elsie's anxiety made it hard for her to function. When my father and mother married in Perth in 1954, she didn't stay long at the wedding. Mum says Elsie was afraid she'd left a kettle boiling on her stove, and excused herself from the celebrations. Just a few months later she was hospitalised, in an 'obsessional state'.

The admission register records that she was a voluntary patient of Heathcote Psychiatric Hospital. She was treated with electro-convulsive therapy, or shock treatment, and discharged after a month, her condition recorded as 'relieved'.

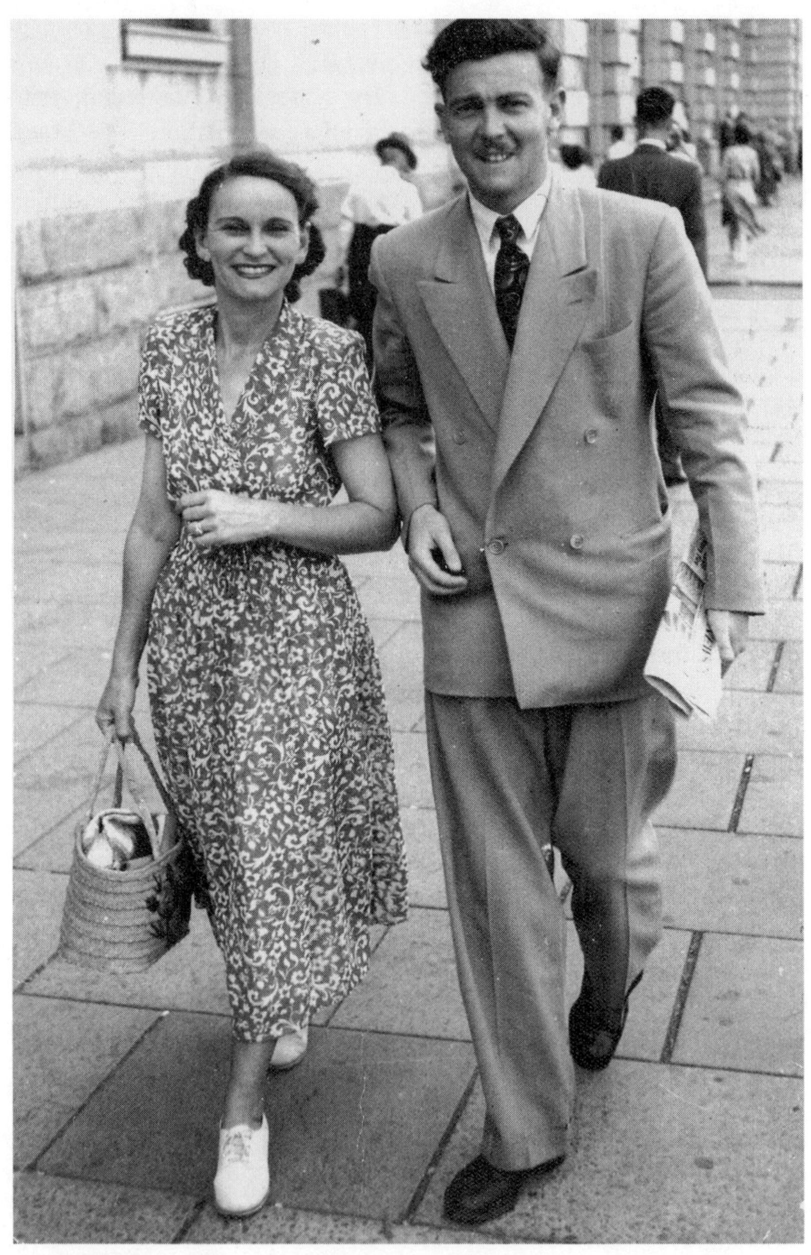

Mother and son – Elsie and Keith jnr, ca. 1949

When my father and I watched the James L Brooks movie, *As Good as It Gets*, Dad told me that his mother's illness, obsessive compulsive disorder, was far more debilitating than the disorder as it was depicted by Jack Nicholson, who won an Oscar for his work as an unwell novelist, Melvin Udall. He avoids stepping on cracks in the pavement, sticks to rigid routines and has a pathological fear of germs, but these behaviours are played for laughs rather than as symptoms of serious illness. Dad was angered by what he saw as the film's trivialisation of obsessive compulsive disorder. He'd seen how it disabled his mother.

Any relief provided by Elsie's stay in hospital didn't last long. She returned to Heathcote less than two months after her first admission. This time she was there for only a week before being sent on to Royal Perth Hospital. She said she thought she was becoming worse. She was tearful, depressed and worried by her obsession with numbers. She associated them with objects. According to hospital notes, the numbers were sometimes those of 'her husband's age, her parents' street number, the numbers of fingers on her hand'. They were conjured up by the sight of certain things – hairpins especially – and they frightened her. Even in hospital she was 'very upset with the number over her bed, vis 47, as this is her age'.[2]

Five months earlier her psychiatrist had recommended psychosurgery, commonly known as lobotomy or leucotomy. It was a suggestion that only made Elsie more distressed and afraid. But after her second spell in Heathcote, its Medical Superintendent, a Dr Gray, referred her for just such an operation. He wrote:

> She is very apprehensive at the prospect of going to Royal Perth Hospital and of having surgery, but then she is so apprehensive of life generally that she is quite incapable of making decisions.[3]

Despite her terrible fear of the operation, hospital admission notes say Elsie realised that she had to 'have it done'.

During the surgery her skull was opened and cuts were made into the lower parts of her brain's frontal lobes. William Scoville, an American neurosurgeon who gave his name to the 'orbital undercutting' technique performed on Elsie, said the procedure caused an 'appreciable lift in mood, lessening of anxiety and a minimum personality blunting'.[4]

Discharged a fortnight after surgery, Elsie's acute anxiety had lessened. She said she still thought of numbers but was no longer worried by them. She was sent from Royal Perth Hospital back to Heathcote Psychiatric Hospital, and soon went home.

Two months later she relapsed and was treated with sedating and antipsychotic drugs. Elsie was now also having occasional seizures and would be in and out of hospital for more than a year, sometimes for months at a stretch. Even when she no longer needed in-patient treatment, her condition was cautiously described by her doctors as only 'fair'. She was, said one report, 'at least maintaining outside the hospital'. It was suggested that 'she might benefit from further surgery'.[5] Elsie was spared a second operation when Heathcote's Dr Gray made a 'private assessment' that she was unable to afford the cost of another procedure.

When New Zealand author Janet Frame was hospitalised in the early 1950s, she narrowly avoided similar surgery. In her autobiography she recalls:

> ...the ward sister, suddenly interested that something was about to be 'done' with and to me, painted her picture of how I would be when it was 'all over'.
>
> 'We had one patient who was here for years until she had a leucotomy. And now she's selling hats in a hat shop. I saw her just the other day, selling hats, as normal as anyone. Wouldn't you like to be normal?'
>
> Everyone felt that it was better for me to be 'normal' and not have fancy intellectual notions about being a writer...[6]

The success or otherwise of Elsie's leucotomy was not measured in terms of her ability to resume the 'radio work' recorded as her usual occupation – along with 'home duties' – on Heathcote's admissions register. Any thoughts of her return to acting may have been regarded as fanciful, just like Janet Frame's ideas about being a writer.

American feminist and writer Elaine Showalter observes that in Britain women were over-represented among leucotomy subjects. One doctor she quotes claimed that the operation was considered 'potentially more effective with women because it is easier for them to assume or resume the role of a housewife'.[7] In Western Australia from the late 1940s until the early 1970s most leucotomy subjects were women, and most of those were married and middle-aged.[8]

Showalter also mentions a psychiatry textbook that recommended the procedure for depressed women 'who may owe [their] illness to a psychopathic husband who cannot change and will not accept treatment'.[9] Lobotomy, it said, would help women unable to leave their marriages for religious reasons or because of their 'financial or emotional dependence' on their husbands.[10]

Elsie was both financially and emotionally dependent on Keith, a husband who'd long had his own problems. His years on the Western Front may have inflicted psychological injuries that no amount of alcohol could relieve. Excessive drinking probably amplified his narcissistic traits, his need for attention and applause. My mother knew him only a little, but remembers Keith senior as vain, grandiose and embittered. Perhaps Elsie's surgery did help her to live with him as he was.

It may also have helped Elsie to live with herself as she was. Her fear of the number forty-seven may not have been completely irrational – it was a perilous age for a woman who relied upon her girlishness.

By now there were precious few roles available to her either on or offstage. It was the 1950s and women were usually defined by their relationships: wife, mother, grandmother. But Elsie had been a largely absent mother and was unlikely to be more than a distant grandmother. And she might even have despaired about continuing to play wife to an unhappy man who'd lost his dreams.

Surgical treatment did however mean that Elsie was not institutionalised long-term, as her in-laws had been; both Mary Agnes and, before her, Mary Gertrude. Leucotomy reduced Elsie's symptoms, but at a cost. Though Scoville claimed that the 'personality blunting' effect of his procedure was minimal, it was enough to ensure that Elsie would never again be described as a 'vivacious, clever lass', nor be billed as the 'Personality Girl'. 'Sunny Day' was a name she never used again.

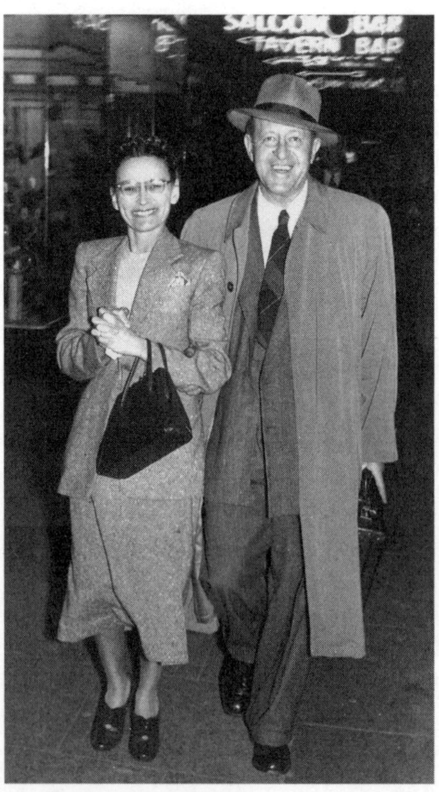

Elsie and Keith, Perth, 1950s

17
Nylons and Nonsense

Gladys was still being advertised as a 'whistling girl' when she turned fifty-five in 1950, the year she joined George Sorlie's newly resurrected travelling show.

She'd survived the lean postwar years with the help of a widow's pension, available at the time to divorcees older than fifty who hadn't remarried. Somewhere toward the end of the 1940s Gladys, perhaps liberated by her pension, separated from her stage partner. Jeanne Cracknell, the other Arizona Girl, began working with a different performer, one who might have been more willing than Gladys to take whatever work was on offer:

> MISS PAULA PRATT, redhead, and Miss Jeanne Cracknell, blonde (both very shy about their ages), are an added attraction this week at the Tatler Theatre.
>
> The main attractions are the two films *The Bride of Frankenstein* and *Dracula's Daughter*.
>
> Adding one horror upon another, the management displays in a glass case a reclining woman who either represents Frankenstein's bride or Dracula's daughter, depending upon the time of day.
>
> That is where Miss Pratt and Miss Cracknell come in. Miss Cracknell as Frankenstein's bride, lies on the case, allegedly mesmerised,

from 11 am to 8.30 pm. Miss Pratt as Dracula's daughter takes over from 8.30 pm and does a 24-hour stretch (she says).

The girls are mesmerised by Theodore, master hypnotist, who will guard them day and night until next Thursday. Theodore says he can't leave the girls unguarded because people throw cigarette butts on them.

The girls like the shift work.

Miss Cracknell said: 'We are good friends. We always let each other know when there is a good job going.

'This is easy money. Lots of people wouldn't like to do it, but it's honest.'[1]

Maybe Gladys didn't need the money as much as Jeanne, or maybe she just couldn't stay still for long enough. A resurrected Sorlie show gave her a chance to hit the road again.

Sorlie had died in 1948, leaving an estate that enabled his widow Grace to restart their canvas theatre once restrictions on fuel were finally lifted. Grace said she wanted to take quality vaudeville to country audiences again, as she and her late husband had done for so many years.

When George was alive Grace had sometimes performed in her husband's productions, but mostly she 'was too busy to play parts because her time was taken up with the front of house management. This entailed looking after the staff, money and general running of the show'.[2]

In partnership with comedian Bobby Le Brun, Grace took Sorlie's show on the road for eleven more years and for the first of those Gladys was with them. They declared it to be 'still the best vaudeville and revue show touring Australia'.[3]

With the Sorlie company Gladys revisited the carnivals and backblocks of Queensland and New South Wales with rising stars like ingenue Gloria Dawn, and an animal circus featuring Peter the Amazing Cockatoo and Mick the Monkey. Toward the end of the year the Sorlie tent was erected in Wollongong, where the *Mercury* reviewed the production:

> Excellent support is given Bobby le Brun, in his frequent appearances: by Tom Richards, Nell O'Brien and Gladys Shaw, and an atmosphere of camaraderie and light-hearted fun amongst these artists certainly, 'gets across' the footlights…tomorrow night a complete change of programme will be featured when the revue Nylons and Nonsense will be staged.[4]

Nylons and Nonsense may have been Gladys's last show. I've found no subsequent reports of her acting, or even whistling. Indeed there are precious few records of her older years. When eventually I unearthed some fragments of her later history, I rather wished I hadn't. It would have made for a happier ending had I left her whistling in Wollongong, under the Sorlie marquee in Burelli Street, near the timber yard.

A woman's place in the 1950s was said to be at home. Unfortunately for Gladys she didn't really have one. Her nephew Bruce told me that when he was a boy she'd lived in Kings Cross, and mingled with the likes of Tilly Devine, notorious sly grog trader and brothel proprietor. In the 1930s and 1940s Gladys did have a number of addresses close to Kings Cross, in nearby Darlinghurst. I wouldn't be surprised if she had encountered the disreputable Tilly, though I never found evidence to back up Bruce's claim that Gladys was a member of Sydney's demimonde.

Sometime in the early 1950s she moved from Darlinghurst to shabby Bondi where, before war and divorce, she'd once lived with Frank. She rented rooms from a friend in the down-at-heel suburb, where accommodation was cheap enough to afford on her pension. From Castlefield Street, a stone's throw from shops and the Royal Hotel, she could ride the tram up Bondi Road into town, or downhill to join the crowds on the sparkling sands of the famous beach.

Her brother Gerry, with his wife Hilda and their five-year old daughter, also set up house in Bondi when they relocated from Brisbane to Sydney at the end of 1953. 'Family reasons' had brought him back, Gerry said,[5] though he had taken a high-profile job on air at radio station 2UW. By 'family reasons' he must have meant Gladys. Someone had sounded the alarm. Perhaps it was Keith who'd visited Sydney earlier in the year. Or maybe it was Bruce's parents – Reg and his disapproving wife Dorothy – who warned that Gladys wasn't well.

Apart from her nephew Bruce, I've found only one other person who has memories of Gladys, and that is her niece Geraldine, Gerry's daughter. Like the late Bruce, her impressions of her aunt were those of a child, although she wasn't dazzled by novelty neckties. More than a decade after Bruce gleefully received his aunt's outlandish gifts and heard her extraordinary whistle, Geraldine was more appalled than amused. She learned to scorn a crazed old woman wearing too much make-up, lipstick bleeding, eyebrows roughly drawn. But Geraldine's most disturbing memory is of waiting in a car outside Morisset Psychiatric Hospital, while her father visited his sister.

I've sat in a car outside that hospital myself, barred from entering the grounds of an institution for forensic patients, geriatric patients and those with intellectual disabilities. A new security gate excludes outsiders, not to keep them away from residents but to keep intruders from harming kangaroos that graze the hospital grounds.

From the gateway I glimpsed some institutional red brick buildings, just a few of those constructed on the site since 1906. On the shores of Lake Macquarie, at the end of a wooded road, the hospital is a couple of minutes drive from the township of Morisset, named for a man famed for his brutality when he was Commandant of the notorious Norfolk Island penal settlement. Perhaps it's appropriate then that his name was also given to a place where, 'isolated in a cleared patch of bushland, and walled like a medieval city',[6] stood a Hospital for the Criminally Insane.

Gladys was taken from Bondi to Morisset Hospital in May 1954. She wasn't suffering from the kind of depression that sent her mother, Mary Agnes, to hospital for the final months of her life. Nor was she psychotic or demented, like her grandmother, Mary Gertrude. If inheritance had anything to do with it, Gladys's condition was more likely the legacy of her father. She was suffering from addiction to alcohol. So uncontrolled was her drinking that Gerry obtained a magistrate's order to have his sister confined to hospital under the *Inebriates Act*.

Raised for the stage, Gladys had always been an 'electric spark' who surprised audiences with her whistle and her brazen ways. No longer wanted for her talents and frowned upon in times that again demanded decorous women, Gladys had ceased whistling into the darkness and was drinking herself into it instead.

Records of her twelve months at Morisset Hospital were destroyed by fire some years after Gladys's time there. A perfunctory admission card is all that remains. It shows that she was admitted as Gladys McGrath. By then she might not have cared what she was called. At birth she'd been given the surname Connolly, that of a man who was not her father. She grew up as Gladys Shaw, her family name merely an alias assumed by parents escaping scandal and misadventure. Though Shaw was the name by which she was known at the peak of her stage career, her working days were through. Her marriage to Frank might have been short-lived and also well in the past, but his name was a useful disguise now that she had a shameful illness to hide.

True to form, on admission to Morisset Hospital Gladys lied about her age. She told the hospital she was fifty-two when in fact she was nearly seven years older. She'd always been a girl – a whistling girl, an 'it girl' or a cowgirl – and even in desperate circumstances wasn't about to start admitting, or acting, her age.

Removed from the world's unsympathetic gaze, Gladys was among 450 female and 850 male patients housed at Morisset Hospital in 1954. There she endured an enforced abstinence, more punishment than rehabilitation. I hope that she was at least free to roam the hospital's extensive gardens, work on the farm or in the sewing room, or while away her time under the wisteria on the verandah of the Recreation Hall. Like her grandmother and mother before her, she slept in a dormitory. Unlike them she did not die in hospital.

After a year-long stay Gladys was released from Morisset in 1955, shortly before she turned sixty. Her once very public life was well and truly over, and with it the press coverage that made it possible for me to follow her progress as she roamed the country for so many years.

Letters exchanged between Keith and Gerry show that Gladys returned to Perth some time after leaving Morisset Hospital. In 1960 her brothers made arrangements to retrieve her few possessions from storage in Sydney and ship them to Perth, where it seems their sister was not living alone. In one letter Gerry refers to Gladys and a man named Chilman and to the possibility that the pair would pay the bill for transporting Gladys's boxes, her Punch and Judy marionettes and a puppet theatre to the west.

There was no evidence of Chilman in the zither case. So I looked for traces of him in all the usual places: newspapers and electoral rolls, records of births, deaths and marriages, of war and peacetime. I found a man named William Chilman, a couple of years older than Gladys, who lived in Western Australia for most of his life – except for three years when he served on the Western Front.

In 1915 William Chilman, storeman, left his father in the wheat and mining town of Southern Cross, a town once entertained by Little Gladys and other members of her family. In Perth William enlisted. Like Keith, he was shipped to France from where he returned in 1919, just as Gladys was about to leave the west with the Royal Strollers. In my wishful imagination, I fancied that William was once known as Wilbur, perhaps to distinguish him from a father who was also a William.

Wilbur was the name of the shining, handsome admirer who years before sent photographs and compliments 'to Gladdie'. He was certainly important to her. She'd kept no pictures of her husband Frank, and few images at all of her offstage life, yet the images of Wilbur survived, to be retrieved from a zither case a century after they were taken. In one photograph he was pictured at a mine site. Others show him in a group arranged outside a corrugated iron building. His companions squint or scowl into the light, but Wilbur beams at the camera. The last photograph he sent to Gladys was dated the first of September, 1915. Two days later, William Chilman joined the army.

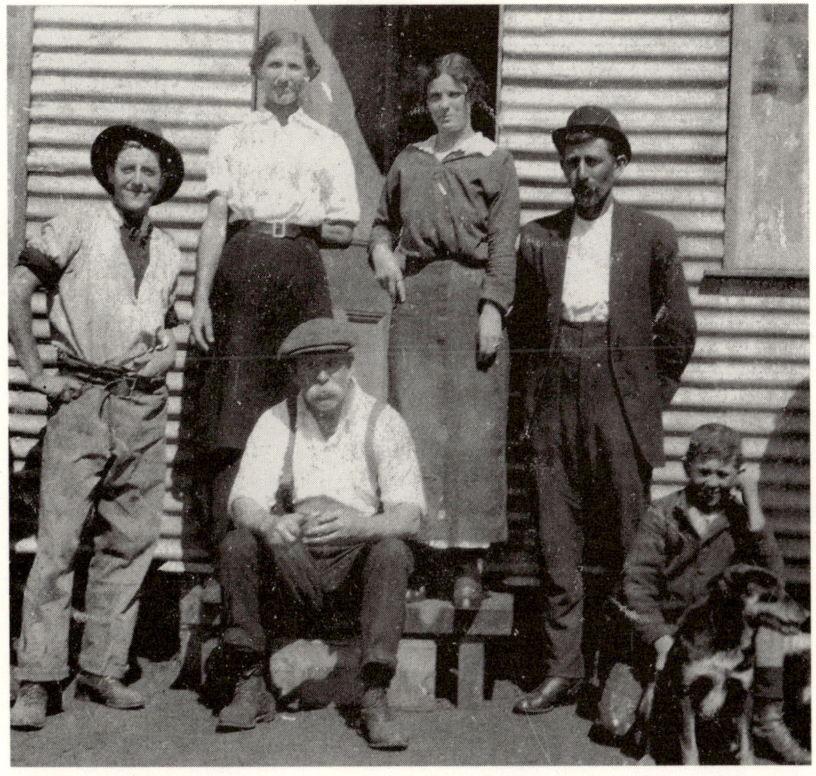

Wilbur, left, 1915

It was plausible, if sentimental, to imagine Gladys reunited with her smiling Wilbur toward the end of her life. It was also consoling. I'd become very fond of the great-aunt I never knew, and the little I learned about her later years seemed so terribly sad. I wished her more lights and laughter. But at the age of sixty-five Gladys suffered a stroke and died, on 15 October 1960.

It was my father's birthday and barely a fortnight since the birth of his third child, my sister Linda. Perhaps Keith and Elsie thought it the wrong time to tell Dad that his aunt was gone. Or maybe they thought that having barely known her in life, he need not be advised. If Dad was told, he didn't share the news. My mother doesn't remember ever hearing anything about Gladys at all, in life or in death.

Her light extinguished, her laughter silenced forever, Gladys was laid to rest in an unmarked grave in Karrakatta Cemetery, her only memorial a handful of photographs that found their way into an old zither case.

18
Finale

I was born in 1956, the year television came to Australia. Like talking pictures, TV took some time to reach beyond Sydney and Melbourne, and Perth's first television station didn't launch until 1959. By then, illness and alcoholism had largely destroyed what remained of the careers of Gladys, Elsie and my grandfather Keith once vaudeville had petered out. The arrival of 'the box' made certain they would never return to popular theatre. Within a few years Australian radio drama would be muted too, along with the voices of countless Australian entertainers.

If Gladys saw television shortly before she died I suspect it thrilled her, just as new entertainment possibilities had always excited her. But Keith, left behind to grieve for his sister and his wife's formerly sunny nature, may have realised that television was the very end of a way of life he'd known since childhood. Less than six months after Gladys died, Keith killed himself.

He's buried not far from his sister, in Perth's Karrakatta Cemetery. Elsie had the words '*Sweet Rest My Darling*' inscribed on his gravestone. They recalled those sung all those years before, at the Luxor, when she was only thirteen and Keith was not long returned from war:

We'll find perfect peace, where joys never cease
Out there beneath a kindly sky
We'll build a sweet little nest somewhere in the west
And let the rest of the world go by...[1]

Of course the rest of the world did not simply pass by. In Australia, the arrival of television intensified the onslaught of imported entertainment. A century of rapid developments in transport, recording, motion picture and broadcasting technologies had already encouraged an invasion of American and English productions and performers. Inadequate protections for local content on television failed to discourage further incursions. Artists, accents and programs from abroad filled early Australian TV schedules, leaving precious few opportunities for Australian entertainers to make the transition to a new medium.

Remarkably, though Elsie never appeared on television, nor on the stage again, she did make a brief return to the airwaves. She was cast in an ABC radio production of *Wait for Me Georgina*. Hers was a minor part in a play ridiculed by one reviewer because its plot revolved around the romantic life of an older woman:

> Supposed to be 'the gay story of a woman who never gave up her pursuit of the man she loved', it actually presents the spectacle of an aged Georgina still capering around after her girlhood flame and still being courted desperately by his rival. The result is a mixture of painful bathos and senile nostalgia.[2]

Ageing single women with romantic and sexual feelings were typically seen as ripe for ridicule. Two of Australia's most popular radio personalities, 'Ada and Elsie' (Dorothy Foster and Rita Pauncefort), built a huge following in the 1940s and 1950s playing middle-aged sisters still looking for Mr Right. Their ribaldry earned them many laughs, but their humour was predicated on the assumption that it was risible for mature women to feel attraction and desire – let alone to be attractive and desirable. When one sister declared her intention to enter a bachelor girl competition, the other reminded her, 'You might be a bachelor, but you're no girl'. Like so many of their gags, the reference to their advancing years won the pair hearty, if derisory, laughter.

My grandma Elsie went on to take a couple more small radio roles. She was 'Mansueta' in *Uncle Martino*, at fifty-five a senior member of a distinguished cast of actors whose work was broadcast around the country on the ABC. The character of Vasilevna the cook, a tiny role in Turgenev's *A Provincial Lady*, was probably her last. There was far less radio drama produced after Australia turned to television, and hardly any made in Elsie's home town of Perth.

On the rare occasions when she came to stay with us in East Malvern, Grandma Elsie would sing softly as she pottered about. I sometimes caught a few words or an odd scrap of melody – whether sung for herself or others I was never quite sure. In my priggish adolescence I found her lack of self-containment a little embarrassing.

With all the conceit of a teenager, I thought her rather childlike, her gaiety decidedly odd for one so ancient. In fact she was only in her sixties. But Grandma Elsie could be tone-deaf to the social atmosphere, her conversational contributions ill-timed and repetitive. Just as Geraldine learned disdain for her badly behaved aunt, Gladys, so I learned to look askance at my grandma Elsie, with her hair nets, Craven A cigarettes and chatter.

Once she took me to see *Finian's Rainbow*, Francis Ford Coppola's film version of a famous stage musical. How it delighted her! She clapped her hands and grinned at me with childlike glee. An ageing Fred Astaire, still a great dancer, played Finian McLonergan, father to Petula Clark's character, who was, like me, named Sharon. She sang of rainbows, just as Elsie had – and of following 'the fellow who follows a dream'.

At only eighteen, Elsie had left the west in pursuit of a man with dreams. Their story didn't end so well, but along the way a few dreams of her own had come true. Elsie Hosking, 'Perth's Little Idol', 'Sunny Day', was an entertainer for more than forty years. Like her sister-in-law Gladys, she had her share of lights and laughter, even if not all her days were like her songs, filled with sunshine and rainbows.

That I heard so little about Elsie's long career, and nothing at all about my great-aunt Gladys and her mother Mary Agnes, was not simply because a vast desert separated Grandma Elsie from my family home. Nor was it because Dad had been raised at a distance from his parents, though physical and emotional remoteness certainly contributed to my ignorance.

At the heart of the silence were deep seams of shame running through my father's entertaining family. Scandal, trauma, addiction and mental illness – Mo's upturned bowl of porridge was a conveniently light-hearted story, told to deflect further inquiries and mask distressing truths.

But the ultimate disgrace may have been disregard. For actresses and comediennes like Gladys, Elsie and their vaudevillian sisters, the invisibility of women in their senior years was a vanishing act that must have felt like failure. They'd enjoyed long and mostly successful performing careers, adapting again and again to new conditions created by the innovations of the twentieth century. Gladys transformed from siffleur to saxophonist, comedienne to cowgirl. Elsie, idolised as a child on the stage, admired as a dainty adult singer of sentimental songs, found fresh satisfactions in acting for radio some forty years later. Yet they could do little to adapt to a culture largely uninterested in mature women. So Gladys and Elsie played girls for as long as they could, lying about their ages and acting youthfully onstage. Then, mortified by middle age, they were redundant. The shame of it not only magnified their frailties but also robbed them of belief in themselves and their achievements. Lacking that confidence, Grandma Elsie couldn't tell her grandchildren proud and satisfied stories about her rainbow days.

There were other kinds of shame involved too. Though my father didn't know much about his parents' careers, and less still about his Aunt Gladys, he failed to tell all that he knew. He'd seen his parents make some of their later appearances at Perth's Tivoli, but I don't recall him ever describing what they did on the stage.

His silence about such matters led me to conclude that he was embarrassed by their work, that he regarded the 'low' comedy and popular theatre in which his parents appeared as less worthy of respect than serious drama. And I suspected that Dad, an advocate for home-grown Australian culture, may have disapproved of his parents' imitations of British and American entertainment fashions.

But Dad's tastes were not parochial. He was an enthusiast for movies made from Hollywood to Ouagadougou, indeed for quality cinema from all around the world. And not all his favourites were serious or profound. Dad was as much a fan of the Marx Brothers and Mel Brooks as he was of Bergman and Rossellini.

I realise now that he was disturbed not by the derivative nature of Australian popular entertainment, nor by its unashamed appeal to popular tastes, but by the racism, anti-Semitism and sexism of so much that was vaudeville. Minstrels, 'coon' singers and Yiddisher comedians, vamps, fat ladies and old maids – all were crass and often cruel stock figures of the variety stage, caricatures that would have appalled my kindly and politically progressive father.

They were the stuff of much popular comedy in the twentieth century, though perhaps not always as simplistically derisory as they seemed at first glance. In acting out the limited range of female archetypes available to them, Gladys, Elsie and their sisterhood of jesters relied upon audiences recognising them as dramatic, even ironic, *reductiones ad absurdum*. It would discredit their intelligence to think they didn't know themselves, and women more generally, to be so much more than the characters they mocked. If anything, their flappers and dreamy girls, naïve maidens and maiden aunts embodied society's ambivalence about the changing place of women in the twentieth century. They provoked laughter because the comediennes who caricatured them knew how to tickle audiences not completely at ease with 'new women' and new ideas about women.

Sadly I have found no recordings of my great-aunt Gladys or my grandma Elsie. I have not heard them whistle and sing. Nor have I seen any film of their dancing, jesting and playing fools and floozies. Many of the theatres of their triumphs have been destroyed to make way for department stores and car parks, though the psychiatric hospitals of their stories have proved more enduring. In a poignant irony, some have even been reborn as places where artists gather. Callan Park is home to a writers' centre, Rydalmere to the Margaret Whitlam Art Galleries, and Heathcote Hospital has become a cultural precinct.

But what my great-aunt and my grandmother did leave behind – in an old zither case and in thousands of newspaper reports – was enough to show that Elsie, Gladys and many of their jester sisters should be larking about beside Stiffy and Mo when we remember Australia's theatrical past.

I like to think that long after her retirement Grandma Elsie took some pleasure in her grandchildren's successes. My musician brother Steve did indeed taste the elation and creative excitement he saw in publicity shots of Keith's Syncopating Jesters. And before Elsie's death I'd already made several documentaries, fortunate to work in times when government support meant Australian filmmakers were not always at the mercy of market forces that advantaged American and British production.

Despite their omission from both the history books and the story of my own family, and though their work was so ephemeral, Elsie, Gladys and her mother Mary Agnes left something more than a case of memorabilia to their descendants.

My inheritance was a powerful idea, handed down through my father to his children, that Australians could create their own art and entertainment. From childhood I knew that art – high or low – did not have to be imported. Early on I also learned that creativity was not the exclusive province of men, and that women's talents were not inferior. It took me longer to learn that women's right to make and be represented in our culture, on equal terms with men, was not universally acknowledged. But in my family it was a kind of birthright.

Outrageous, courageous and funny though they were, in their later years my female forebears – Mary Agnes, Gladys and Elsie – were tragic rather than comic heroines. Applauded if disapproved of as 'different' girls, when they became different women they were isolated, locked away or lobotomised.

But, as things turned out, they were irrepressible. Searching through thousands of footnotes to theatrical history I glimpsed rainbows, lights and sunny days. And when I opened an old zither case I heard the faint but silvery notes of a gifted songstress, the sweet voice of a happy-go-lucky girl, peals of laughter and, out of the darkness, a most surprising whistle.

Notes

Abbreviations:
NAA – National Archives of Australia
NSWSA – New South Wales State Archives
SROWA – State Records Office of Western Australia

Chapter 1: The Wages of Sin

1 'The Sydney Morning Herald', *Sydney Morning Herald*, NSW, 8 February 1892, p. 6
2 When Warrington arrived in the colony of NSW his uncle, John Perry, was a Penrith publican. Transported for seven years as punishment for larceny, Perry arrived in Van Diemens Land in 1820. He gained a certificate of release in 1826 and by the time his nephew arrived had become a well-regarded member of colonial society in New South Wales. Perry owned Orielton, a significant property at Narellan, complete with flour mill. He was a stalwart of St Paul's Anglican church at Cobbitty, where a William Warrington-designed window remembers one of Perry's eight children, Eleanor, who died at the age of eleven. Her mother died the following year. The John Perry who John Warrington met in the 1860s was for the second time a married man, a Freemason and a leading figure in the colony's influential licensed victuallers' association. With such connections, John Warrington had little difficulty finding employment.
3 'Advertising', *Sydney Morning Herald*, NSW, 24 February 1882, p. 10
4 'Advertising', *Sydney Morning Herald*,NSW, 10 April 1882, p. 10
5 NSWSA: Gladesville Medical Case Book, 4/8175, p. 201
6 Ibid
7 NSWSA: Callan Park Medical case Book, 3/4666, p. 163
8 NSWSA: NRS 13495, Divorce No. 3539
9 NSWSA: Callan Park Medical case Book, 3/4666, p. 163
10 NSWSA:NRS 13495, Divorce No. 3539
11 Lawson, L, 'Aimless women', *The Dawn*, Sydney, NSW, 1 May 1896, p. 14
12 Tomalin, C, *The Invisible Woman*, Penguin, London, 1991, p. 13

13 'Bernhardt in Australia', *Pall Mall Gazette*, London, 26 July 1891, p. 15
14 'To Sarah Bernhardt!' *Illustrated Sydney News*, NSW, 6 June 1891, p. 5
15 Loir's uncle, the scientist Louis Pasteur, had sent his nephew to Australia to compete for prize money offered for discovery of a biological cure for the rabbit plague. When Bernhardt arrived in the colonies Loir was experimenting with chicken cholera on Rodd Island, in Sydney's Iron Cove. He offered to quarantine her dogs there and the famous actress went too, spending a whole week on the island shortly before leaving the country.
16 'A Doll's House at the Criterion', *Sydney Morning Herald*, NSW, 14 July 1890, p. 6
17 De Boheme, R, 'Two views of A Doll's House, a woman's view', *Sydney Morning Herald*, NSW, 26 July 1890, p. 4
18 *Newcastle Morning Herald and Miners Advocate*, NSW, 5 January 1892, p. 5
19 Ibid
20 Skinner pursued commercial interests in Australia, most notably in skating rinks that ultimately put many theatres out of business.
21 'Local news', *Maitland Mercury and Hunter River General Advertiser*, NSW, 8 September 1891, p. 5
22 French, CE, *Six Years of Drama at the Castle Square Theatre*, Boston, 1903, p. 66
23 Almost thirty years earlier bushranger Ben Hall held Commissioner Keightley hostage, threatening to kill him if his wife did not return with a substantial ransom. She did, and the story was made legend when Rolf Boldrewood included it in his novel *Robbery Under Arms*.
24 NSWSA: NRS 13495, Divorce No. 3539
25 Ibid
26 Ibid

Chapter 2: The Wrong Man

1 NSWSA: NRS 13495, Divorce No. 3539
2 Ibid
3 'The Lorgnette', *Observer*, Auckland, 4 May 1895, p. 7
4 NSWSA: NRS 13495, Divorce No. 3539
5 Ibid
6 Ibid
7 *Auckland Star*, NZ, 13 July 1895, p. 4
8 NSWSA: NRS 13495, Divorce No. 3539
9 'The wrong man', Harrington, JP & Le Brunn, G, 1890
10 'News and notes', *Hawera & Normanby Star*, NZ, 12 June 1896, p. 2
11 'Musical and dramatic', *New Zealand Herald*, Auckland, 2 July 1899, p. 4

Chapter 3: A Trip to the Moon

1 'The absent minded beggar', Kipling, R,1899
2 'Patriotic fund', *Zeehan and Dundas Herald*, Tasmania, 6 February 1900, p. 2
3 'General news', *Camperdown Chronicle*, Victoria, 5 April 1900, p. 2
4 'Centenary of Mount Gambier', *Border Watch*, Mount Gambier, 2 June 1900, p. 2
5 'Martini Shaw Gaiety Co', *Kerang Times*, Victoria, 4 September 1900, p. 3
6 Ibid
7 'Gaiety Company', *Riverine Herald*, Echuca and Moama, 8 October 1900, p. 2
8 'The Imperial Vaudeville Company', *Bendigo Advertiser*, Vic, 25 May 1901, p. 5
9 'Gaiety Theatre', *Bendigo Advertiser*, Bendigo, 30 May 1901, p. 2
10 'Race Night Larrikinism', *Bendigo Advertiser*, Vic, 6 June 1901, p. 2
11 'The Shaw Gaiety Company', *Riverine Herald*, Echuca and Moama; 19 June, 1901, p. 2
12 'Advertising', *Bairnsdale Advertiser and Tambo and Omeo Chronicle*, Vic, 5 December 1901, p. 3
13 'Concert', *Ovens and Murray Advertiser*, Beechworth, 11 January 1902, p. 2
14 Ibid
15 'Is an Actor a Working Man?', *Barrier Miner*, Broken Hill, 21 February 1902, p. 3
16 *The Newsletter: An Australian Paper for Australian People*, Sydney, 8 March 1902, p. 8
17 'Amusements', *Register*, Adelaide, 14 March 1902, p. 6.
18 'Theatre Royal', *Advertiser*, Adelaide, 8 March 1902, p. 8
19 'Amusements', *Advertiser*, Adelaide, 13 May 1902, p. 6
20 'The Sheeny Coon', Castling, H, 1898
21 'Shilling Pops', *Nepean Times*, Penrith, 13 June, 1903, p. 5
22 'A Fire on a Train', *Maitland Daily Mercury*, NSW, 4 January, 1900, p. 3
23 Ibid
24 'On and off the stage', *Table Talk*, Melbourne, 11 January 1900, p. 16
25 'Shaw's Society Entertainers', *Bathurst Free Press and Mining Journal*, NSW, 30 November 1903, p. 3
26 Ibid

Chapter 4: The Marvellous Shaws

1 'Entertainments', *West Australian*, Perth, 22 October 1904, p. 7
2 'Entertainments', *West Australian*, Perth, 7 November 1904, p.5
3 'Entertainments', *West Australian*, Perth, 29 October 1904, p. 9.

4 'Entertainments', *West Australian*, Perth,15 November 1904, p. 4
5 Famous Australian singer Gladys Moncrieff ('Our Glad') reported that she too was billed as 'Little Gladys the Child Wonder'. Though Moncrieff was slightly older and became significantly more famous than Gladys Shaw, she may not have been the first to be dubbed 'Little Gladys'. It appears that Gerald's promotion of his daughter preceded advertisements in which Moncrieff was similarly described.
6 'Local news', *Albany Advertiser*, WA, 13 January 1906: p. 3.
7 'Local news', *Albany Advertiser*, WA, 3 January 1906, p. 3
8 'The Border Watch, published every Wednesday and Saturday morning', *Border Watch*, Mount Gambier, 18 May 1907, p. 2
9 'Mining And Stocks And Shares', *West Australian, Perth,* 24 December 1907, p. 2
10 'The busker', *Sunday Times,* Perth, 26 January 1908, p. 1 (third section)
11 Ibid
12 'Prospectus of Sunnyside prospecting Company No Liability', *Southern Cross Times,* WA, 4 July 1908, p. 3
13 'Greasepaint patter the busker burnt cork chronicles', *Sunday Times,* Perth, 28 February 1909, p. 1 (third section)
14 The marvellous Shaws', *Riverina Recorder*, Balranald, 13 January 1909, p. 2
15 'Entertainments', *West Australian, Perth,* 13 February 1905, p. 6
16 'The marvellous Shaws', *Riverina Recorder*, Balranald, 13 January 1909, p. 2
17 'Mike voice (at breakfast)' *Sunday Mail*, Brisbane, 21 May 1950, p.9.
18 Unidentified and undated newspaper clipping, Gerry Connolly's scrapbook
19 'Local and general', *Bega Budget*, NSW, 19 March 1910, p. 2.
20 Ibid
21 'A break from the stage', *Mirror*, Perth, 20 August 1921, p. 4 (second section)
22 'The prospectors', *Southern Cross Times*, WA, 31 May 1911, p. 2
23 'Stadium drop curtain', *Southern Cross Times*, WA, 12 July 1911, p. 2
24 'The English Pierrots', the *Southern Cross Times,* 12 July 1911, p. 2
25 'A Break from the Stage', *Mirror*, Perth, 20 August 1921, p. 4 (second section)
26 Ibid
27 'Advertising', *West Australian*, Perth, 10 November 1919, p. 10

Chapter 5: The Tango Girls

1 'Grand entertainment', *Midlands Advertiser*, Moora, 22 May 1914, p. 5
2 'The Tango Girl', *Sydney Sportsman*, NSW, 21 January 1914, p. 2

3 'Beyond the Footlights', *Daily News*, Perth, 16 October 1914, p. 2
4 Rene, R, *Mo's Memoirs*, Reed and Harris, Melbourne, 1945, p. 79
5 'The Vaudeville Live Wire', *Daily News*, Perth, 13 November 1914, p. 1
6 NAA: B2455, Connolly K W
7 'News and Notes', *Daily News*, Perth, 19 September 1916, p. 4
8 Later studies have revealed that *The Battle of the Somme* mixed documentary footage with reconstructed scenes of battle, for propagandistic purposes.
9 'Pavilion Pictures', *Daily News*, Perth, 17 October 1916, p. 2 (3rd edition)
10 'My diary, official war photographer Commonwealth Military Forces', papers of Frank Hurley 1912–1962, National Library of Australia, MS 883, series 1, item 5, p. 39

Chapter 6: Heaven Will Protect a Working Girl

1 *Australian Variety*, 3 May 1916, cited in Pike and Cooper, *Australian Film 1900–1977*, OUP Melbourne, 1980, p. 82
2 Jane King went on to tour Australia and New Zealand with Alan Wilkie's celebrated Shakespearean players, and with Philip Lytton's production of *The Waybacks*, based on a series of Australian bush stories. Jane advocated a theatre born out of Australian stories and characters. In Queensland she co-wrote and managed productions of her own plays; *Billy of the Bluegums*, *Back O Beyond* and *The Girl from the Golden West*. Jane left the stage after she married in 1922. Scenes from *The Joan of Arc of Loos* survive in the National Film and Sound Archive.
3 'Footlight Fancies', *Mirror*, Perth, 10 April 1926, p. 9
4 'The Follies', *Southern Districts Advocate*, Katanning, 26 August 1914, p. 2
5 'Goldfields Shows, Big Doings for the Coming Week', *WA Sportsman*, Perth, 19 July 1918, p. 4
6 'Palace Theatre', *Kalgoorlie Miner*, 24 July 1918, p. 6
7 Djubal, Clay, *'What Oh Tonight': The Methodology Factor and Pre-1930s' Variety Theatre*. Ph D, Uof Qld, 2005, Australian Variety Theatre Archive http://ozvta.com/dissertations
8 'In the city', *Daily News*, Perth, 12 November 1918, p. 6
9 Woodward, OH, *The war story of Oliver Holmes Woodward, Captain 1st Australian Tunnelling Company, Australian Imperial Force*, O.H. Woodward, Adelaide, 1932, pp. 142–143
10 'Gordon's Vaudeville Co', *Goomalling-Dowerin Mail*, WA, 24 January 1919, p. 3
11 'Heaven will protect the working girl (A burlesque ballad)', lyrics, Smith, E, music, Baldwin Sloane, A, 1909

12 'Effie Fellowes talks', *Mirror*, Perth, 26 November 1921, p. 4
13 'Vice and its victims', *Truth*, Perth, 21 December 1918, p. 7
14 'Ladies Gossip', *Express and Telegraph*, Adelaide, 15 December 1894, p. 3
15 'Jottings by the way', Francesca, *Fitzroy City Press*, Victoria, 19 October 1894, p. 3
16 'Track-blazing times', *Sun*, Kalgoorlie, WA, 29 November 1908, p. 6
17 'Advertising', *Windsor and Richmond Gazette*, NSW, 25 September 1897, p. 11
18 'The New Gaiety', *Table Talk*, Melbourne, 6 March 1913, p. 16
19 'The Gordon Vaudeville Co', *Great Southern Herald*, WA, 8 February 1919, p. 3
20 'Vaudeville Entertainment', advertising, *Tambellup Times*, WA, 15 February 1919, p. 3
21 'In quarantine', *Sunday Times*, Perth, 18 May 1919, p. 6
22 'Advertising', *Newcastle Sun*, NSW, 14 July 1919
23 'Amusements', *Newcastle Morning Herald and Miners Advocate*, NSW, 14 July 1919, p. 6
24 'The royal strollers', *Telegraph*, Brisbane, 25 August 1919, p. 5
25 'Comedian Connolly's concoction', *Mirror*, Perth, 18 June 1921, p. 4
26 'The royal strollers', *Brisbane Courier*, 6 September 1919, p. 6
27 'The Blanchard Company', *Tweed Daily*, Murwillumbah, 8 November 1919, p. 6
28 Webber, Frederick C., *Down at Manly Beach [music] / words and music by Frederick C. Webber*, circa 1920, <http://nla.gov.au/nla.obj-176836886>
29 'Majestic theatre', *Mail*, Adelaide, 14 February 1920, p. 2
30 'Films, footlights, plays and players', *Mirror*, Perth, 8 May 1921, p. 4
31 'Last curtain falls on stage folks romance', *Truth*, Sydney, 31 May 1942, p. 14

Chapter 7: Laugh and the World Laughs With You

1 'Evening Post', *Evening Post*, Wellington, 23 March 1920, p. 3
2 'The theatres', *Sun*, Christchurch, 27 April 1920, p. 9
3 'Everybody works but father', Jean Havez, 1905
4 'The lorgnette', *Observer*, Auckland, 22 May 1920, p. 12
5 'The theatres', *Sun*, Christchurch, 20 April 1920 p. 9
6 For a comprehensive account of the revusical's development, see Djubal, Clay, *'What Oh Tonight': The Methodology Factor and Pre-1930s' Variety Theatre*, Ph D, University of Queensland, 2005, Australian Variety Theatre Archive <http://ozvta.com/dissertations>
7 'Entertainments', *Telegraph*, Brisbane, 6 September 1920, p. 8
8 'The follies', *World*, Hobart, 10 January 1921, p. 8

9 'A proprietor's debts', *Examiner*, Launceston, 18 March 1921, p. 4
10 'Mimes, miners and melody-makers', the *Sunday Mirror*, Perth, 27 March 1921, p. 4
11 'Comedian Connolly's concoction', *Mirror*, Perth, 18 June 1921, p. 4 (second section)
12 Ibid
13 'Shaftesbury theatre', the *Daily News*, Perth, 11 June 1921, p. 4 (third edition)
14 Ibid
15 Traditional
16 In a 1921 interview in Perth, Keith said, '...my mother and brother are residents of your city; so I suppose Perth is practically my home town. Unfortunately, in this profession you never stay long enough in the same town to call it your home town'. 'Comedian Connolly's concoction', *Mirror*, Perth, 18 June 1921, p. 4 (second section)
17 'Amusements', *Daily News*, Perth, 21 May 1921, p. 5 (third edition)
18 'Entertainments', *West Australian*, Perth, 21 May 1921, p. 10
19 'Advertising', *Daily News*, Perth, 7 January 1920, p. 1 (third edition)
20 'Entertainments', *West Australian*, Perth, 16 June 1919, p. 5
21 'Shaftesbury theatre', *Daily News*, Perth, 2 October 1920, p. 3
22 'Entertainments', *West Australian*, Perth, 7 May 1921, p. 10
23 'Let the rest of the world go by', Ball, E & Brennan, JK, 1919
24 'Entertainments', *West Australian*, Perth, 14 May 1921, p. 10
25 'Comedian Connolly's concoction', *Mirror*, Perth, 18 June 1921, p. 4 (second section)
26 'Good news', *Mirror*, Perth, 23 July 1921, p. 3 (second section).
27 'Eastern football', *Mirror*, Perth, 27 August 1921, p. 4
28 'Good news', *Mirror*, Perth, 23 July 1921, p. 3 (second section).
29 'Entertainments', *West Australian*, Perth, 10 August 1921, p. 8
30 'Entertainments', *West Australian*, Perth, 3 September 1921, p. 1
31 'Play and pastime', *Westralian Worker*, Perth, 26 August 1921, p. 6
32 'Films, footlights, plays and players', *Mirror*, Perth, 13 August 1921, p. 3
33 'An apology', *Mirror*, Perth, 1921–1956, 27 August 1921, p. 4
34 'Films, footlights, plays and players', *Mirror*, Perth, 10 September 1921, p. 3

Chapter 8: Matrons, Maids and a Murderess

1 'Amusements', *Auckland Star*, NZ, 14 February 1922, p. 7
2 'Stiffy and Mo popular', *Sunday Times*, Sydney, 30 April 1922, p. 6 (social and magazine section)
3 'Stiffy and Mo', *Country Life Stock and Station Journal*, Sydney, 19 September 1924, p. 10

4 James, Dr. Colin G, 'Winners and Losers: The Father Factor in Australian Child Custody Law in the 20th Century', *Legal History* Vol. 10, 207–238, 3 September 2006

5 Lamond, T, *First Half*, Pan MacMillan, Australia, 1990, p. 18

6 Rene, R, p. 101

7 'In The Good Old Vaudeville Days', *Newcastle Morning Herald and Miners' Advocate*, NSW, 16 October 1954, p. 5

8 'Bijou Theatre', *Age*, Melbourne, 27 April 1925, p. 13

9 Phillips, N, 'Yes We Don't' aka 'The Plumbers', 1916, ed. Clay Djubal, *Australian Variety Theatre Archive*, <https://ozvta.com/Texts-unpublished/> accessed 20 July, 2021

10 'Old favorites', *Sunday Times*, Sydney, 30 July 1922, p. 10

11 Ibid

12 'Stiffy and Mo popular', *Sunday Times*, Sydney, 30 April 1922, p. 6 (social and magazine section)

13 Rene, R, p. 65

14 'Advertising', *Sydney Morning Herald*, 7 March 1919, p. 2

15 'World of recreation', *Worker*, Brisbane, 18 May 1922, p. 12

16 'Stray whisperings from the green room', *Sporting Globe*, Melbourne, 30 August 1922, p. 13

17 Ibid

18 'Majestic theatre', *Register*, Adelaide, 30 October 1922, p. 9

19 'Majestic theatre', *Register*, Adelaide, 18 December 1922, p. 9

20 Hunt, G.W, *She was fat, she was, fair, she was forty*, 1890

21 'Entertainments', *New Zealand Herald*, Auckland, 24 March 1923, p.11

22 'Entertainments', *New Zealand Herald*, Auckland, 4 June 1923, p.9

23 'His Majesty's', *Evening Post*, Wellington, 17 July 1923, p.3

24 'Stiffy and Mo', *Country Life Stock and Station Journal*, Sydney, 19 September 1924, p.10

25 'Entertainments', *New Zealand Herald*, Auckland, 13 May 1924

26 'Referee theatreland', *Referee*, Sydney, 3 September 1924, p. 15

27 'Bank clerks at Fullers', *Sun*, Sydney, 16 November 1924, p. 4

28 'Across the Footlights', *News*, Adelaide, 16 January 1925, p. 13

29 Scott, Bennett, Mills, A. J and J. C. Williamson (Firm), *You can't judge a woman by her clothes*, 1903.

30 'Bijou Theatre', *Age*, Melbourne, 18 May 1925, p. 11

31 'Round the shows', *News*, Adelaide, 30 July 1925, p. 2 (home edition)

32 'Film facts and footlight flutters', *Sunday Times*, Perth, 31 May 1925, p. 6

33 'Film facts and footlight flutters', *Sunday Times*, Perth, 21 June 1925, p. 10

34 'Round the Shows', *News*, Adelaide, 30 July 1925, p. 2 (home edition)

35 Shakespeare, W, *Twelfth Night*, act 5, scene 1, lines 372–378 (Feste – a fool, jester, clown)

36 'Six months' season concludes', *Truth*, Perth, 7 November 1925, p. 7

37 'Peeps at people', *Sunday Times*, Perth, 22 November 1925, p. 2 (second section)

38 Edwards, Alfred, *Patients Are People*, Currawong Press, Sydney, 1968, p. 24

39 NSWSA:NRS 5149 [19/114057]

40 University of Western Sydney, *Female Orphan School,* viewed 30 July, 2021, <https://www.westernsydney.edu.au/femaleorphanschool/home/rydalmere_psychiatric_hospital_1888_to_1989>

Chapter 9: Speed and More Speed

1 Johnson, B, *The Inaudible Music*, Currency Press, Sydney, 2000, p. 10, citing *Australian Band News*, 26 July 1926

2 'Tivoli theatre', *Daily Mail*, Brisbane, 12 January 1926, p. 2

3 'Peeps at pictures', *Truth*, Sydney, 31 January 1926, p. 7

4 Stein, H, *A Glance Over an Old Left Shoulder*, Hale and Ironmonger, Sydney, 1994, p. 91–93

5 Johnson, B., p. 11

6 'Amusements', *Daily Standard*, Brisbane, 12 January 1926, p. 2 (second edition – 3 pm)

7 Johnson, B., p. xiv

8 'Theatre Royal', *Newcastle Morning Herald and Miners' Advocate*, NSW, 8 February 1926, p. 6

9 'I remember...I remember', *Teleradio*, *Telegraph*, Brisbane, 16 April, 1938, p. 37

10 'What's on at the shows', *Call*, Perth, 26 February 1926, p. 3

11 'Woman's world', *Daily News*, Perth, 9 March 1926, p. 7

12 'Entertainments', *Telegraph*, Brisbane, 31 May 1926, p. 15 (5 o'clock city edition)

13 'Entertainments', *Brisbane Courier*, Qld, 15 November 1926, p. 19

14 'Cremorne', *Sunday Mail*, Brisbane, 15 May 1927, p. 13

15 'At Cremorne', *Sunday Mail*, Brisbane, 5 June 1927, p. 11

16 'Cremorne theatre', *Brisbane Courier*, Qld, 18 April 1927, p. 15

17 'Bright show', *Sunday Mail*, Brisbane, 17 April 1927, p. 11

18 'Cremorne follies', *Brisbane Courier*, Qld, 23 May 1927, p. 18

19 'Keith's Syncopating Jazz Band', *Morning Bulletin*, Rockhampton, 9 August 1927, p. 11

20 'Keith's jazz band', *Townsville Daily Bulletin*, Qld, 26 August 1927, p. 3

21 'Keith's jazz band', *Dungog Chronicle: Durham and Gloucester Advertiser*, NSW, 30 September 1927, p. 2

22 'Advertising', *Sydney Sportsman*, NSW, 10 January 1928, p. 14

Chapter 10: 1928

1 'Entertainments', *Brisbane Courier*, Qld, 23 January 1928, p. 11
2 'Cremorne follies', *Brisbane Courier*, Qld, 6 February 1928, p. 18
3 'Amusements', *Daily Standard*, Brisbane, 21 January 1928, p. 10
4 'Amusements', *Daily Standard*, Brisbane, 17 February 1928, p. 9 (3 pm edition)
5 *Theatre Magazine*, Sydney, November 1915, p. 47
6 'Advertising', *Kiama Independent, and Shoalhaven Advertiser*, NSW, 24 March 1928, p. 3
7 'Trial Turns – Acts the Regular Audiences Don't See', *Everyones*, Sydney: Everyones Ltd, 1920. p. 9
8 Muriel Pearce quoted in Dreyfus, K, *Sweethearts of Rhythm*, Currency Press, Sydney, 1998, p.59
9 The Royal Commission concluded that rather than a quota to ensure demand for Australian movies, a quota requiring cinemas to exhibit films from the British Empire should be introduced. Then considered British citizens, Australians and their productions would be included in such an arrangement. Australian films, argued filmmaker Raymond Longford, could hold their own in the company of British cinema. Presumably he was concerned that the establishment of an exclusively Australian quota might in turn rule Australian films ineligible under the United Kingdom quota system which deemed Australian productions British. Other arguments against an Australian quota came from exhibitors who claimed it would harm their capital-intensive business of cinema operation. In the end even the recommended British film quota was not introduced.
10 'Top hole', *Sydney Morning Herald*, NSW, 24 May 1928, p. 12
11 Dreyfus, K, p. 60
12 Pearce, M, interviewed by Dreyfus, K, Australian Jazz Museum, 1995, audio
13 'The "League of Notions', *Manawatu Times*, Palmerston North, NZ, 1 August 1928, p. 8
14 NSWSA:NRS 5149 [19/114057]

Chapter 11: Auld Lang Syne

1 'Bijou theatre', *Age*, Melbourne, 24 June 1929, p. 10
2 'Protest meeting in Perth', *West Australian*, Perth, 28 August 1929, p. 17
3 'Reservoirs replenished', *Barrier Miner*, Broken Hill, 18 November 1929, p. 1
4 'Fullers new theatre', *Sydney Morning Herald*, NSW, 10 March 1919, p. 5
5 'Fullers theatre', *Sydney Morning Herald*, NSW, 17 February 1930, p. 6

6 'Fullers theatres', *Sydney Morning Herald*, NSW, 17 February 1930, p. 12

7 'Last curtain', *Sydney Morning Herald*, NSW, 24 February 1930, p. 11

8 Ibid

9 'League of Notions revue', *Brisbane Courier*, Qld, 21 April 1930, p. 20

10 '"Stiffy" looks in', *Mirror*, Perth,10 May 1930, p. 12

11 'Stage & Screen', *Weekly Judge*, Perth, 27 June 1930, p. 1

12 'League of Notions revue company', *Brisbane Courier*, Qld, 19 May 1930, p. 17

13 Inspector General of the Insane, 'Report for the year 1914', in *Parliamentary Papers 1915–16*, Vol. 1, p. 1002, cited at <https://www.records.nsw.gov.au/agency/68#> viewed 3 August 2021

14 NSWSA, Bay View House, NRS-5165 *Medical Case Books*, 1674

15 Ibid

16 Ibid

Chapter 12: Every Day's a Rainbow Day

1 'Bradman's song', *Sydney Morning Herald*, NSW, 7 January 1931, p. 14

2 'Two champions', *Mirror*, Perth, 24 January 1931, p. 7

3 'Bradman's song', *Sydney Morning Herald*, NSW, 7 January 1931, p. 14

4 'Two champions', *Mirror*, Perth, 24 January 1931, p. 7

5 'Grand opera house', *Sydney Morning Herald*, NSW, 19 January 1931, p. 6

6 Ibid

7 'Mr. Scullin', *Sydney Morning Herald*, NSW, 7 January 1931, p. 13

8 Ibid

9 'Picture theatres', *Sydney Morning Herald*, NSW, 7 January 1931, p. 13

10 'Cole's Players', *Nowra Leader*, NSW, 6 February 1931, p. 5

11 Rene, R, p. 121–122

12 'New Haymarket', *Sydney Morning Herald*, NSW, 13 April 1931, p. 4

13 Rene, R, p. 122

Chapter 13: Ladies and Gentlemen, That's Love

1 'The fun of the fair', *Horsham Times*, Vic, 2 October 1931, p. 4

2 'Cole's comedy players', *Horsham Times*, Vic, 25 September 1931, p. 2

3 'Cole's comedy players', *Morning Bulletin*, Rockhampton, 22 June 1931, p. 11

4 'Cole's comedy players', *Morning Bulletin*, Rockhampton, 23 June 1931, p. 8

5 'Theatre Row', *Sun*, Sydney, 24 March 1932, p. 10 (final extra)

6 'Tivoli–Vaudeville', *Age*, Melbourne,18 April 1932, p. 10

7 Stevens, A, 'Skint! Making do in the Great Depression', *Sydney Living Museums*, <https://sydneylivingmuseums.com.au/stories/skint-making-do-great-depression>

8 'The social world & fashions realm', *Truth*, Brisbane, 17 August 1924, p. 14

9 Shand, R, in Lowenstein, W, *Weevils in the Flour*, Hyland House, Melbourne, 1978, p. 272

10 Ib

11 'The Rockhampton diocese', *Catholic Press*, Sydney, 30 June 1932, p. 39

12 'Topics', *Evening News*, Rockhampton, 20 June 1932, p. 8

13 'Cole's comedy players', *Morning Bulletin*, Rockhampton, 20 June 1932, p. 12

14 'Mr. Nat. Phillips Dead', *Brisbane Courier*, Qld, 1864–1933) 22 June 1932, p. 15

15 'Through "Smith's" private projector', *Smith's Weekly*, Sydney, 6 August 1932, p. 8

16 'Endless laugh at Tivoli', *Labor Daily*, Sydney, 17 October 1932, p. 7

17 'Stage Divorce Suit', *Daily Telegraph*, Sydney, 23 November 1918, p. 9

18 ' "Mo" show success', *Daily Telegraph*, Sydney, 26 June 1933, 10

19 'New Tivoli theatre', *Sydney Morning Herald*, NSW, 13 November 1933, p. 6,

20 'Bright show at Tivoli', *Advertiser*, Adelaide, 4 September 1933, p. 10

21 'Cole's varieties', *Daily Mercury*, Mackay, 26 June 1934, p. 10

22 'George Sorlie's Musical Co', *Morning Bulletin*, Rockhampton, 18 June 1934, p. 11

23 'Coles' varieties', *Morning Bulletin*, Rockhampton, 16 June 1934, p. 11

24 'Vaudeville at the Victoria', *Newcastle Sun*, NSW, 15 April 1935, p. 2

25 'Vaudeville at the Victoria', *Newcastle Sun*, NSW, 17 April 1935, p. 6

26 'Film reviews', *Sydney Morning Herald*, NSW, 19 November 1934, p. 6

Chapter 14: Happy Go Lucky Lane

1 'The theatres', *Daily News*, Perth, 11 September 1933, p. 8

2 'Side-splitting "Stud"', *Mirror*, Perth, 2 September 1933, p. 11

3 'Last round up', *Sun*, Sydney, 21 May 1934, p. 10 (final extra)

4 'Advertising', *Sun*, Sydney, 17 May 1934, p. 35 (final extra)

5 'Music, stage & film', *Age*, Melbourne, 4 February 1935, p. 12

6 'Backstage', *Sporting* Globe, Melbourne, 14 September 1935, p. 8 (Edition2)

7 'The serenaders', *Mirror*, Perth, 7 March 1936, p. 8

8 Stella's daughters became even more famous; Toni Lamond as an Australian performer in theatre, film and TV and Helen Reddy as an actor, activist and singer, most notably of her 1970s international hit 'I

am woman'. Toni's son (also Stella's grandson and Helen's nephew) is Tony Sheldon, writer, actor and singer, best known for his role in *Priscilla Queen of the Desert*. In 2018 Sheldon said *As a boy, I thought everybody was in show business. I didn't know people had other jobs, because all my grandparents, parents and aunty did was appear on TV, listen to show records, learn songs and perform in the theatre. ('Tony Sheldon: Why it's been a privilege to work alongside my mum', Sydney Morning Herald*, 28 January 2018)

9 'Serenaders new show', *Sunday Times*, Perth, 10 May 1936, p. 22

10 Ibid

11 'Luxor Theatre', *The West Australian,* August 8, 1936, p. 25

12 'Luxor theatre', *West Australian*, Perth, 26 September 1936, p. 10

13 'Keith Connolly and Stan Foley in Fun at the Rex', *Telegraph*, Brisbane, 24 April 1937, p. 15

14 'The Rex Jesters present their 52nd variety show', *Telegraph*, Brisbane, 1 May 1937, p. 18

15 'The color of her skin often brings a rebuff', *Daily Telegraph*, Sydney, 13 September 1953, p. 46

16 Norman, C, *When Vaudeville Was King*, Spectrum Publications, Melbourne, 1984, p. 249

17 'On the stage', *Sun*, Sydney, 6 November 1938, p. 28

18 'Clever clowning in Frank Neil show at His Majesty's', *Telegraph*, Brisbane, 13 September 1937, p. 9

19 Ibid

20 'New Tivoli show', *Smith's Weekly*, Sydney, 12 November 1938, p. 19

21 'Bright show at Tivoli', *Herald*, Melbourne, 28 March 1939, p. 8

22 'Evening Star', *Evening Star*, Dunedin, 31 July 1939, p. 3

23 'A clever troupe', *Evening Post*, Wellington, 11 September 1939, 4

24 'Chinese revue', *Evening Post*, Wellington, 11 September 1939, p. 12

25 Ibid

26 'All-American revue', *Evening Post*, Wellington, 17 July 1939, p. 4

27 'Funz-a-poppin', *Evening Star*, Dunedin, 31 July 1939, p. 3

28 Pike, A, and Cooper, R, *Australian Film 1900–1977*, OUP Melbourne 1980, p. 254–255

29 'Station 2gn, Goulburn', *Yass Tribune-Courier*, NSW, 1 April 1940, p. 1

30 'About a Quarter to Nine', lyrics by Dubin, A & music by Warren, H, 1935

Chapter 15: The Whistling Cowgirl

1 'At Cremorne', *Truth*, Brisbane, 26 October 1941, p. 35

2 '"Flying colours", new revue at Theatre Royal', *Telegraph*, Brisbane, 21 October 1939, p. 11

3 'Arizona Girls in clever act', *Courier-Mail*, Brisbane, 21 October 1939, p. 2

4 'Stage, filmland, and vaudeville', *Journal*, Adelaide, 12 May 1923, p. 3
5 'Radio concert', *Lithgow Mercury*, NSW, 18 June 1940, p. 3
6 'Theatre has "face-lift"', *Courier-Mail*, Brisbane, 29 November 1945, p. 5
7 'Midnight frolics', *Canberra Times*, ACT, 25 January 1945
8 'Display advertising', *Canberra Times*, ACT, 9 January 1945, p. 3.
9 Ibid

Chapter 16: Sunny Day

1 'Molly's people and parties', *Mirror*, Perth, 17 December 1949, p. 21
2 Royal Perth Hospital, patient records, 1954–55
3 Ibid
4 Scoville, WB, 'Late results of orbital undercutting', the *American Journal of Psychiatry*, Vol. 117, Issue 6, December 1960, pp. 525–532
5 Dept of Health, 'Follow up report on leucotomy cases arranged through Heathcote', Treatment of Patients – Leucotomy and Psychosurgery 1947–1973, File 1962/336, Cons 3614, SROWA
6 Frame, J, *An Angel at My Table* (chapter 15), first published 1984, reprinted in *An Autobiography*, Random House, NZ, 1989, p .222
7 Smith, S, 1977, as cited in Showalter, E, *The Female Malady: Women, Madness, and English Culture, 1830–1980*, New York: Pantheon Books, 1985, p. 210
8 'A matter for conjecture, leucotomy in Western Australia', 1947–70, Martyr, P & Janca, A, *History of Psychiatry*, 2018, Vol. 29 (2) 199–215
9 Sargant, W & Slater, E, 1972 as cited in Clare, A, *Psychiatry in Dissent*, 1976, 2nd edn, Tavistock Publications, London, 1980, p. 313–314
10 Ibid

Chapter 17: Nylons and Nonsense

1 'People: Human stories of the week', *Sun*, Sydney, 10 October 1948, p. 7
2 'For women...vaudeville "more appreciated now"', *Newcastle Morning Herald and Miners' Advocate*, NSW, 25 January 1950, p. 5
3 'Advertising', *Morning Bulletin*, Rockhampton, 2 June 1950, p. 2
4 'Sorlie's revue is high order entertainment', *Illawarra Daily Mercury*, Wollongong, 31 October 1950, p. 5
5 'Truth calls the tune-in', *Truth*, Brisbane, 27 December 1953, p. 25
6 *Morisset Hospital Precinct*, New South Wales State Heritage Register, https://apps.environment.nsw.gov.au/dpcheritageapp/ViewHeritageItemDetails.aspx?ID=5000867, accessed 17 September, 2021

Chapter 18: Finale

1 'Let the rest of the world go by', Ball, E & Brennan, JK, 1919
2 'Radioh!', *Farmer and Settler*, Sydney, 21 January 1955, p. 16

Select Bibliography

Books and Theses

Bishop, Catherine, *Minding Her Own Business: Colonial Businesswomen in Sydney*, NewSouth, Sydney, 2015

Brisbane, Katharine (ed), *Entertaining Australia, an Illustrated History*, Currency Press, Sydney, 1991

Clare, Anthony, *Psychiatry in Dissent*, 1976, 2nd edn, Tavistock Publications, London, 1980

Catharine Coleborne, *Madness in the Family, Insanity and Institutions in the Australasian Colonial World 1860-1914*, Palgrave Macmillan, London 2010

Colligan, Mimi, *Canvas Documentaries, Panoramic Entertainments in Nineteenth Century Australia and New Zealand*, Melbourne University Press, Melbourne, 2002

Davies, A and Stanbury, P, *The Mechanical Eye in Australia, Photography 1841-1900*, Oxford University Press, Melbourne, 1985

Davies, Will, *Beneath Hill 60*, Random House Australia, 2010

Dreyfus, Kay, *Sweethearts of Rhythm*, Currency Press, Sydney, 1998

Djubal, Clay, *'What Oh Tonight': The Methodology Factor and Pre-1930s' Variety Theatre*. Ph D thesis, University of Qld, 2005, Australian Variety Theatre Archive http://ozvta.com/dissertations/

Djubal, Clay, *Harry Clay and Clay's Vaudeville Company – 1865-1930: An Historical and Critical Survey*, MA Thesis, 1998, Australian Variety Theatre Archive, https://ozvta.com/dissertations/

Finlayson, Damien, *Crumps and Camouflets, Australian Tunnelling Companies on the Western Front*, Big Sky Publishing, NSW, 2010

Frame, Janet, *An Autobiography*, Random House, NZ, 1989

Garton, Stephen, *Medicine and Madness: A Social History of Insanity in New South Wales, 1880-1940*, UNSW Press, 1988

Griffen-Foley, Bridget, *Changing Stations, The Story of Australian Commercial Radio*, UNSW Press, 2009

Johnson, Bruce, *The Inaudible Music*, Currency Press, Sydney, 2000

Laird, Ross, *Sound Beginnings, the Early Record Industry in Australia*, Currency press, Sydney, 1999

Lamond, Toni, *First Half*, Pan MacMillan, Australia, 1990

Love, Harold (ed), *The Australian Stage, a Documentary History*, New South Wales University Press, Sydney, 1984

Lowenstein, Wendy, *Weevils in the Flour*, Hyland House, Melbourne, 1978

Matthews, Brian, *Louisa*, McPhee Gribble, Melbourne, 1987

Matthews, Jill Julius, *Dance Hall & Picture Palace, Sydney's Romance with Modernity*, Currency Press, Sydney, 2005

Norman, Charles, *When Vaudeville Was King*, Spectrum Publications, Melbourne, 1984

Pike, Andrew and Cooper, Ross, *Australian Film 1900–1977*, OUP Melbourne, 1980

Rene, Roy, *Mo's Memoirs*, Reed and Harris, Melbourne, 1945

Showalter, Elaine, *The Female Malady: Women, Madness, and English Culture, 1830–1980*, New York: Pantheon Books, 1985

Simon, Linda, *Lost Girls, The Invention of the Flapper*, Reaktion Books, London, 2017

Speed, Lesley, *Australian Comedy Films of the 1930s*, Australian Teachers of Media, Melbourne, 2015

Stein, Harry, *A Glance Over an Old Left Shoulder*, Hale and Ironmonger, Sydney, 1994

Tomalin, Claire, *The Invisible Woman*, Penguin 1991

Van Straten, Frank, *Tivoli*, Lothian, Melbourne, 2003

Waterhouse, Richard, *From Minstrel Show to Vaudeville: The Australian Popular Stage, 1788-1914*, NSW University Press, Sydney, 1990

West, John, *Theatre in Australia*, Cassell Australia, Sydney, 1978

Wright, Andrée, *Brilliant Careers, Women in Australian Cinema*, Pan Books, Sydney, 1986

Wright, Clare, *You Daughters of Freedom*, Text Publishing, Melbourne, 2018

Articles and Essays

James, Dr. Colin G, 'Winners and Losers: The Father Factor in Australian Child Custody Law in the 20th Century', *Legal History* Vol. 10, 207–238, 3 September 2006

Martyr, Philippa & Janca, Aleksander, 'A matter for conjecture, leucotomy in Western Australia', 1947–70', *History of Psychiatry*, 2018, Vol. 29 (2) 199–215

Scoville, William B, 'Late results of orbital undercutting', the *American Journal of Psychiatry*, Vol. 117, Issue 6, December 1960, pp. 525–532

Website

Djubal, Clay, *Australian Variety Theatre Archive*, https://ozvta.com/

List of Illustrations

Principal Cast

The family

GLADYS SHAW	Whistler, comedian, actor, saxophonist and whip- cracker. A performer for more than 50 years.
ELSIE HOSKING	Singer of sentimental songs, actor, dancer and comedian. Also known as Sunny Day and Elsie Connolly.
MARY AGNES CONNOLLY	Burlesque actress, mezzo soprano and music teacher. Also known as Claire Delmar, Madam Marie and Mrs Shaw.
MARY GERTRUDE WARRINGTON	Mother of Mary Agnes Connolly
KEITH CONNOLLY	Comedian, dancer, actor – the 'Beau Brummel of vaudeville'.
GERALD SHAW	Basso, theatrical manager and miner. Dubbed the 'musical mineralogist,' his real name was Harry Morewood Thomson.
GERRY CONNOLLY	Radio announcer, musician and actor.
HILDA WARING	Dancer and ballet mistress, also known as Hilda Wong Hing and Hilda Connolly.
KEITH CONNOLLY (JNR)	Journalist, film critic, son of Elsie Hosking and Keith Connolly.

Some colleagues and friends

FREDDIE WEBBER	Instrumentalist, dancer, comedian, composer. Sometimes known as the 'College Boy.'
DAISY MERRITT	Whistler, dancer and character comedienne. Celebrated for her work with husband Nat Phillips, and Roy Rene ('Mo').
NAT PHILLIPS	Better known as 'Stiffy (the Rabbitoh)'. Producer, writer, actor, and celebrated comedian.
ROY RENE	Comedian, actor and singer. The 'Mo' in 'Stiffy and Mo', and later the star of radio's 'McCackie Mansion.'
DAISY JEROME	Comedienne and singer. American born Jerome was a star of the English music hall popular in Australia. Also known as 'the electric spark.'
EFFIE FELLOWS	Male impersonator who sometimes appeared as 'Master Freddie Manners' and 'Bobby Folson'. After appearing on American and English stages, Effie returned to Australia where she was known for her signature tune, 'I've Never Seen a Straight Banana.'
JEANNE CRACKNELL	The 'Bulls Eye Girl,' sharp shooter, whip-cracker and rope-twirler.
NELLIE SMALL	Male impersonator and singer. Of West Indian ancestry, she was sometimes incorrectly described as an 'American negress'.
NELLIE KOLLE	Male impersonator, singer, mimic, pianist and pantomime principal boy.
STUD FOLEY	Comedian, writer and songwriter. Also known as Stan Foley. One time stage partner of Stiffy (Nat Phillips)

Family Tree

John Warrington
Mary Gertrude Boyd (b. 1839)
Edward Connolly
Mary Agnes Warrington (b. 1864)
Harry M. Thomson (aka Gerald Shaw) (b. 1873)
Maud Warrington
John Connolly
Reginald Connolly (b. 1888)
Dorothy Carlyle
Leslie Connolly (b. 1890)
Frank McGrath
Gladys Connolly (aka Gladys Shaw) (b. 1895)
Keith Connolly (b. 1897)
* Elsie Hosking (b. 1907)
Gerry Connolly (b. 1908)
Hilda Wong Hing
Bruce Connolly
Barry Connolly
Keith Connolly (b. 1928)
Joan Broomhall
Geraldine Connolly
Andy Hosking
Ethel Owens
* Elsie Hosking (b. 1907)
Lydia Hosking
Sharon Connolly
Stephen Connolly
Linda Connolly
Rohan Connolly

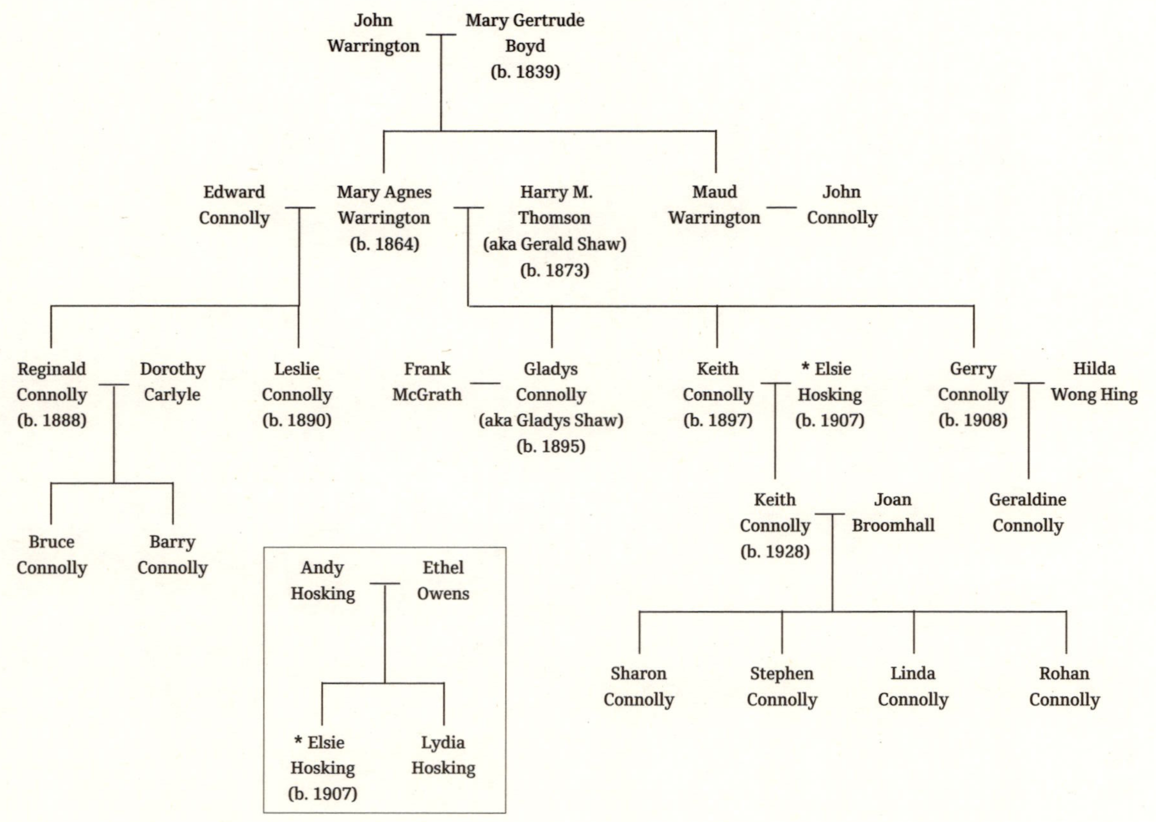

Acknowledgements

The miraculous National Library of Australia database, *Trove*, and the National Library of New Zealand's *Papers Past* made it possible for me to find my lost great aunt, and many others who people this book. I am so grateful to those important institutions and their staff, and to those at National Archives of Australia, the National Film and Sound Archive, the State Library of NSW, the State Library of Western Australia, NSW State Records and Archives and the Fryer Library at the University of Queensland. They are national treasures all.

Less well known but no less treasured is Dr Clay Djubal's Australian Variety Theatre Archive, (https://ozvta.com/), a labour of love which documents people, places and works of Australia's popular stage in the formative era of the late nineteenth and early twentieth centuries. Dr Djubal's work fills a gap in our cultural history, which has sometimes struggled to include ephemeral artforms such as minstrelsy and vaudeville.

Geoffrey Bradshaw, my partner and comrade, supported the research and writing of this book in every possible way. I thank him for caring, and for his generosity, advice and confidence in the project.

My mother, Jo Connolly, patiently endured years of my questions about members of Dad's family, most of whom she never knew. I thank her too for keeping Dad's family photographs and documents safe after his death.

In the course of my research I met Geraldine Connolly, my father's cousin. Her memories and family records greatly helped my research, and the time I spent with her was an unexpected pleasure.

For their encouragement and advice over the years taken to complete this work I thank Gail Cork, Rhonda Pryor, Jeannine Baker, Anna Grieve, Franco di Chiera and Molly Reynolds. I am grateful to Kaz Cooke and Virginia Lloyd for their belief in the book, and for helping me toward publication. And to Terri-ann White of Upswell Publishing for expertly ushering *My Giddy Aunt* into being. For their patience and attention to detail thanks to editor Jocelyn Hungerford and typesetter Keith Feltham.

Ann Curthoys is an historian I have always admired. Her generous introduction to *My Giddy Aunt* is especially appreciated.

Thanks also to Currency Press for permission to quote from *The Inaudible Music* and *Sweethearts of Rhythm*, to the Janet Frame Literary Trust for permission to quote from *An Angel at My Table*. All efforts have been made to seek permissions for use of quoted materials from other books. The Publisher invites correspondence regarding permissions not formalised here.

About Upswell

Upswell Publishing was established in 2021 by Terri-ann White as a not-for-profit press. A perceived gap in the market for distinctive literary works in fiction, poetry and narrative non-fiction was the motivation. In her years as a bookseller, writer and then publisher, Terri-ann has maintained a watch on literary books and the way they insinuate themselves into a cultural space and are then located within our literary and cultural inheritance. She is interested in making books to last: books with the potential to still be noticed, and noted, after decades and thus be ripe to influence new literary histories.

About this typeface

Book designer Becky Chilcott chose Foundry Origin not only as a strong, carefully considered, and dependable typeface, but also to honour her late friend and mentor, type designer Freda Sack, who oversaw the project. Designed by Freda's long-standing colleague, Stuart de Rozario, much like Upswell Publishing, Foundry Origin was created out of the desire to say something new.